Collaborative Thinking

How to Build and Sustain College Consortia

SARAH K.A. PFATTEICHER

JOHNS HOPKINS UNIVERSITY PRESS | *Baltimore*

Printed in the United States of America on acid-free paper

2 4 6 8 9 7 5 3 1

Johns Hopkins University Press
2715 North Charles Street
Baltimore, Maryland 21218
www.press.jhu.edu

Library of Congress Cataloging-in-Publication Data

Names: Pfatteicher, Sarah K. A., 1968– author
Title: Collaborative thinking : how to build and sustain college consortia / Sarah K.A. Pfatteicher.
Description: Baltimore : Johns Hopkins University Press, 2025. | Includes bibliographical references and index.
Identifiers: LCCN 2025002663 (print) | LCCN 2025002664 (ebook) | ISBN 9781421453323 paperback | ISBN 9781421453330 ebook
Subjects: LCSH: Consortia | University cooperation
Classification: LCC LB2331.5 .P48 2025 (print) | LCC LB2331.5 (ebook) | DDC 378.1/04—dc23/eng/20250410
LC record available at https://lccn.loc.gov/2025002663
LC ebook record available at https://lccn.loc.gov/2025002664

Special discounts are available for bulk purchases of this book. For more information, please contact Special Sales at specialsales@jh.edu.

EU GPSR Authorized Representative
LOGOS EUROPE, 9 rue Nicolas Poussin, 17000, La Rochelle, France
E-mail: Contact@logoseurope.eu

COLLABORATIVE THINKING

CONTENTS

For Lorna M. Peterson (1940–2024),

who led FCI as she lived her life:

with fierce and joyful humanity.

INTRODUCTION

Better Than We Are: Consortial Thinking in a Competitive Landscape

If the goal is to be better, the mindset must be new.

SEVERAL YEARS AGO, before the pandemic forcefully reminded us of the.communally interconnected nature of our lives, I was talking with a college president about possible new collaborative ventures in the higher education consortium I'd been tasked to lead. I noted that campuses face a number of grand challenges, from racism to climate change—issues that touch all of our institutions and the communities in which we sit. I suggested that consortial work could be especially powerful in addressing such issues. What hadn't been created alone could hardly be fixed alone. After a brief conversation, the president paused and said slowly, "Oh. I see. You want us to be better than we are."

The conversation turned, the meeting ended, and the day moved on. But those words have stuck with me: "Better than we are." I've puzzled over what that president meant. Was it simply an acknowledgment of the consortium's purpose? "Your role is to help us improve." Was it a suggestion that my aspirations were naively optimistic? "You want this, but that's not who we are." Or was it, perhaps, a realization of new possibilities? "Oh, we could do more than we've considered!"

Whatever the president's intent may have been, I've taken my own meaning from that conversation: There is a collaborative way of thinking that differs from the daily work of most campus-based administrators, and adopting a consortial mindset can shift our assumptions about how higher education can function and what we can achieve, whether we work in a consortium or not. In short, if the goal is to be better, the mindset must be new. It is a potent approach to the important work of educating the next generation of leaders and building knowledge that will shape the work our graduates do and the world they will inhabit.

I lead one of the oldest and largest consortia in the United States. As executive director of this nonprofit organization, I report to a board of directors composed of the leaders of our member campuses—four presidents and a chancellor, if we count the voting members. My job, on most days, is indeed to help the campuses be better than they are and on some days to help them be better than they want to be. As stated in our founding Agreement of Association, "The primary purpose of the corporation is to promote the broad educational and cultural objectives of [the member campuses] by encouraging and fostering closer cooperation and understanding among the faculty, staff, and students of the [member] institutions, and by promoting and developing opportunities for joint lectures, concerts, plays, games and other activities, for sharing the use of the educational and cultural facilities of the [member] institutions and for a better understanding of the peoples, cultures and institutions of other nations."

It is a broad charge: We are simultaneously engaged in the logistical minutiae of promoting extracurriculars and the higher calling of striving for a better understanding of our global community. The job of the consortium is, in short, to serve as a counterweight to all the forces encouraging campuses to act alone. Competition for students, funding, faculty, rankings, resources, and attention—these are the drivers of so much activity on campus. The consortium calls on the campuses to consider how they might be better *with* one another, instead of better *than* one another. It's not always easy work, but I've become convinced that this consortial way of thinking is powerful and can also elevate the work of individual campuses that are not members of a consortium.

Collaborative work is timely and important; calls for more partnerships and collaboration appear frequently in higher education conversations. *The Chronicle of Higher Education*, for instance, has a research brief on "Stronger Together Than Alone? Assessing College Leaders' Attitudes Toward Mergers and Other Partnerships." EY Parthenon issued (and updated) a report called *Strength in Numbers: Strategies for Collaborating in a New Era for Higher Education*. And the *Inside Higher Ed* podcast *The Key* aired (and re-aired) an episode on "Mergers and Major Cross-College Collaboration."[1] Entire books are dedicated to the subject of campus partnerships, including *The Synthetic University* (Shulman, 2023), *Collaboration in Higher Education* (Abegglen et al., 2023), *Strategic Mergers in Higher Education* (Azziz et al., 2019), and *Consolidating Colleges and Merging Universities: New Strategies for Higher Education Leaders* (Martin and Samels, 2017), to name a few.[2] Dissertations have analyzed and documented consortial work, including "Trust Within Higher Education Consortia" (Yankech, 2015), "Strength in Numbers" (Dinicola, 2023), and "Going Beyond Traditional Consortia" (Affolter-Caine, 2008).[3] Many of these works encourage campuses to dive into collaboration, and some advocate cooperation as a panacea for whatever ails a campus. An *Inside Higher Ed* column went so far as to call consortia an "easy button" for higher education.[4] While I welcome more campuses to engage in such partnerships—and this book is intended to help those who are interested in pursuing both new and existing collaborations—it is not work that should be undertaken lightly. As we'll see in the pages ahead, cross-campus collaboration requires commitment and resources to do well. But for those willing to invest, the community-mindedness that characterizes consortial work can expand and extend the work that campuses do and can strengthen stand-alone campuses too.

Higher education as it exists today is in many ways built on competition; the desire to do more and be better than other institutions shapes how faculty are hired and promoted, determines which academic programs are offered, and affects what facilities are built.[5] For some (though not all) American colleges, competition also affects which students are admitted. Competition is deeply embedded in Western culture far beyond the "groves of academe," and we are living in an age defined by divisiveness and individualism. The pandemic and the widespread advocacy to "flatten the curve" by collectively taking fewer risks ironically highlighted and exacerbated this divisiveness and individualism. Faced with the most serious threat to global health in a century, many of us—as individuals, as organizations, and as communities—found it difficult to agree on how to respond, a reaction not uncommon in the face of a crisis. The isolation many of us undertook, either voluntarily or reluctantly, closed us in, away from the normal and numerous daily interactions of prepandemic days. We established bubbles, limited contact, narrowed our focus. Anyone who has flown in an airplane knows the phrase "Put on your own mask before assisting others." It's an important lesson in emergency management. If you become incapacitated, you can't help anyone else, so take care of yourself first so you can help others. But what became harder in the pandemic was to remember the second half of that phrase: so you can help others. Certainly, many frontline, essential, and health care workers leaned heavily into helping others, often at great personal cost. But powerful motivations propelled many of us to focus on self-protection (of our health, our freedom . . .), even at the expense of others.

A heartbreaking anecdote from early in the pandemic illustrates the dangers of combining this narrowed focus with a competitive spirit. In early March 2020, it became clear that many campuses would close and send students home midsemester, but for an uncertain duration. Campus leaders were eager to assure their communities that they were doing everything possible to support and protect their students. One campus leader proudly announced that they had managed to acquire (buy up) every available moving box in the region so that students could quickly store their belongings on campus or ship them home. Meanwhile, across town, another campus leader sent an email pleading with everyone in the community to provide any containers they could offer to help students pack their belongings. They reported that no moving or shipping boxes could be found anywhere and would the community please drop off any available containers; used boxes or old suitcases would be ideal, but *even garbage bags would be welcome*. The juxtaposition of one community gloating over their acquisition of a precious resource while their neighbors pleaded for garbage bags for students to use as luggage broke my spirit. These campuses had been close partners for more than half a century. The worst of the pandemic had not yet come anywhere near us, and we had already descended to this.

As discouraged as I was about the boxes, I knew we could do better. I had seen it before and grasped for the optimism that such cooperation would come again. In the meantime I pulled the campus leaders aside and did what I could to call them back to the communal spirit they and their predecessors had built. This pattern would repeat itself in the years ahead, as we grappled with bubbles and containment, testing and isolation, and teaching in tents and online. Campus leaders' decisions were driven by a desire and a need to keep the community safe. The challenge came in defining the scope of that community. Faced with unprecedented conditions and complex decisions at every turn, campus leaders had little energy or time to broaden their thinking and consider how we might do this better together. On too many days, it was as much as could be hoped when a single campus leadership team reached a consensus on how often to test or where to isolate students or what it meant to turn a residential campus into an online school with remote employees. And still, in the moments when cross-campus conversation was possible, good things resulted, and campus leaders, when asked, remained committed to the idea of collaboration, even as its application became difficult.

Coming back together is necessary and healthy, particularly in the face of an expanding mental health "crisis."[6] Many campuses struggled to address the growing demand for mental health care even before the pandemic, and the need today is strong. But as much as we need more trained counselors and readier access to treatment, we can and should supplement these efforts to expand training and access with complementary efforts to support and strengthen healthy habits and communities. Human connection is key. Even tiny efforts at community help. In mid-2022, as we hoped the pandemic might be waning, journalist Catherine Pearson described it as "a challenging time for friendship and connection in the United States, which is in the throes of a loneliness crisis that has grown more complicated—and more acute—during the pandemic." As an antidote to this crisis, she offered research on "the power of a casual check-in text," noting that "new research suggests that casually reaching out to people in our social circles means more than we realize." Pearson asserted not only that human connection would help us heal but also that research was "emphasiz[ing] the power of small moments of connection."[7] Another 2022 publication reported that half of all employees were suffering from burnout and loneliness and noted that the most recommended responses, "relieving stress, teaching mindfulness, and/or reducing workload [all] treat burnout as an individual condition." This report suggested instead that community response and engagement would be more effective: "Greater human connection may . . . be key to solving the problem."[8]

Research also tells us that community building and collaboration can support the core mission of higher education: learning. See, for instance, *Learning with Others: Collaboration as a Pathway to College Student Success*, in which Clifton Conrad and Todd Lundberg argue for defining student success in terms of "collaborative learning over individual achievement." The form of collaboration Conrad and Lundberg describe entails not merely doing the same work but as a team; it involves working in a fundamentally different way, beginning with defining the task collectively. They argue that a less individualized and more collaborative approach to education would better "educate students to become shared problem-solvers who are equipped to take up challenges facing our communities, nation, and rapidly changing world, including food shortages, childhood poverty, inequality, political polarization, and our deteriorating environment."[9]

If they are correct that individual students will be better equipped by preparing together, a parallel claim may well be true for institutions—that approaching their work with a collaborative mindset also leads to better results. Evidence of the power of collaboration exists in an array of settings. The Stakeholder Alignment Collaborative provides examples of consortia in industries ranging from biomedicine to research computing, ascribing their success to this "distinctive institutional arrangement that tends to be nonbureaucratic, adaptable, and able to work at local or global scales as needed." Indeed, these authors argue that "decades from now, historians will celebrate consortia as a defining feature of the 21st century."[10] Elsewhere, an article on what sociologists call "collective impact" argues that "large-scale social change comes from better cross-sector coordination rather than from the isolated intervention of individual organizations."[11] In the blunt words of one consortium director, "We can hardly tell our students to prepare for a global stage when their colleges are unwilling to operate across boundaries."[12]

As my conversation with the president about being "better than we are" suggested, in spite of such research findings collaboration is not embedded in daily expectations on most campuses. It may occur in parallel with campus work or may come as an afterthought, but it is rarely the initial driver, or a core objective, or even a means to an end. Furthermore, the governance structures on a campus can work against collaboration, as they typically prioritize the well-being of that individual campus (and at times even of factions within that institution). This volume is intended to help address and overcome these hurdles by exploring why collaboration can be valuable, describing the range of models and scales in which it can function, and offering concrete steps for initiating and nurturing such work. Although my own recent experience is rooted in a formal (and substantial) consortial structure, I draw here on a full range of collaborations, from modest informal partnerships to full operational mergers. No one collaborative model will suit every set of institutions, but a collaborative mindset can help even a stand-alone campus to approach its work in productive and creative ways.

I still believe, as I advocated to that president, that if we are going to address the headline issues of the day with any hope of meaningful change, we can do more together than separately. To do so we need to build the conditions, skills, and motivation to foster teamwork and collaboration. The conditions that support collaboration—a sense of shared purpose, deep trust, a commitment to communication—are needed whether our aim is to improve higher education or to secure a functioning democracy.[13] We also need to develop and practice the skills that enable us to see the world from a vantage point other than our own: the ability to pause, listen, and question not only others' claims but also our own assumptions. Motivation is needed as well because, as a former leader in this work was fond of saying, collaboration is an unnatural act.[14] It takes intention and effort, a willingness to delay satisfaction, and the patience to trust in the long game. As a result, in order to establish the right conditions and build the necessary skills, we also need to nurture the desire to undertake collective work, to build and sustain the motivation needed to see the payoff.

In the chapters that follow, we'll describe what consortial partnerships look like—how they're structured, funded, and governed—and the benefits they can bring, including efficiencies and cost savings as well as grander visions, expanded opportunities, and broader impact. In addition to these tangible logistical features, we'll also consider the conditions, skills, and motivation needed for collaboration to be successful. Consortia represent just one model of collaboration, and others are valuable too. But consortia, among the most structured and studied forms of cross-institutional collaboration, can offer lessons in how to play well together in a variety of higher education settings.

Although the concept of cross-campus collaboration, particularly via a consortial structure, is timely, it is far from new. A handful of consortia formed in the 1920s, driven in part by the language of efficiency then in vogue in industrial settings. In response to growing demand for higher education following the GI Bill and the coming baby-boom generation, federal funding and foundation investments in the mid-twentieth century spurred what is often (mis)cited as the initial wave of consortia of the 1960s. In the 1990s the rapidly increasing role of computers and information technology in campus operations and concern over rising costs led to another round of new consortial collaborations.

Within these broad trends and generalizations are surprising and inspiring stories. In the post–World War II years, for instance, leaders from four institutions in New England began one notable conversation. They understood that their campuses would need to respond to the growing and changing population of college seekers, and they looked to one another for support and inspiration in setting a course forward. These four campuses had been working together for nearly half a century already, sharing library resources and offering correspondence courses together, so this new conversation was a natural extension of existing relationships. After a long stretch of exploratory work, the task force realized their institutions could not adapt quickly or dramatically enough to address the coming influx. Instead, they presented the four presidents with a startling recommendation: found a fifth college. Instead of expanding the existing campuses' facilities, build new capacity to meet the demand and shape this new institution to experiment with new approaches to education. Instead of tenure, provide "ten-year" contracts. Instead of grades, give students narrative assessments. Instead of offering an established set of majors, allow (indeed, expect) students to design their own curricula. Instead of a hierarchical administrative structure, engage the whole campus community in governance. Instead of setting all this in stone, build the entire institution to continually adapt. Construct the equivalent of a laboratory school a place to try out new ideas, to test assumptions, and to gather evidence about unconventional methods. And do all this surrounded and supported by more established structures. Enable the new institution to draw support, advice, and even courses from the existing institutions. It would be preferable, they argued, to build this experimental venture as a stand-alone institution rather than use the Meiklejohn model of an experimental college within an existing university, as had been done a generation earlier. In 1965 the four campuses—Amherst, Mount Holyoke, and Smith Colleges, and the University of Massachusetts—created a legal structure to facilitate this new venture. They called it Four Colleges, Incorporated. A year later, after Hampshire College had been formally established, the consortium filed paperwork to change its name to Five Colleges, Incorporated.[15] The history of consortia is filled with bold, visionary stories like this one.[16]

A century has now passed since the founding of the Claremont Consortium (1925) and the Atlanta University Center Consortium (1929). It is more than a half century since the Big Ten Academic Alliance (1958), the Great Lakes Colleges Association (1962), Five Colleges, Incorporated, and several of their sister consortia became formalized nonprofit entities, followed by a flurry of publications about the model. And more than a quarter century has come and gone since the most recent wave of consortia came online in the 1990s, including the Council of Public Liberal Arts Colleges (1992), The Boston Consortium (1995), Five Colleges of Ohio (1995), and the Colleges of the Fenway (1996). Histories of individual consortia abound, and some of the most instructive examples are included in the bibliography and notes, including those by Peterson (on Five Colleges, Incorporated), Salwak (on the Big Ten), Affolter-Caine (Claremont and others), Anderson (Associated Colleges of the South), Duke (Claremont), and Elkin (Great Lakes).[17] Among the most notable and timeless books on consortia more generally are Patterson's *Colleges in Consort* (1974), Neal's *Consortia and Interinstitutional Cooperation* (1988), and several edited volumes by Dotolo and colleagues, especially *Best Practices in Higher Education Consortia* (1999).[18]

What is new? What can and should we consider that we cannot find in the existing literature? The world has, of course, changed since the middle of the last century. Far from booming growth in enrollments, colleges now face looming generational decline (the demographic cliff, as it has been called). State support for public higher education has been decreasing for more than a generation, placing increasing financial pressures on campuses. New regulations and a broadening expectation of accommodation increase the administrative obligations (and thus costs) of campuses. Growing public concern about the cost of attendance and the burden of student loans that are outpacing earning potential for many graduates add pressure to campus budgets. Increasing curricular, fiscal, programmatic, and personnel oversight by politicians, trustees, and donors constrain higher education leaders. Globalization and our planetary interconnectedness have become even more evident in recent years. Climate change and the pandemic are two of the most pressing examples, and it is perhaps no coincidence that these global challenges have been accompanied by a growth in nationalism and other forms of extremism around the world.

This book is not about these trends, but the work and potential of consortia exist within this context. Although collaboration has been a frequent topic in the news and opinion columns of late, little detailed guidance (particularly from those with experience in this work) is available on how to succeed in cross-campus collaboration in this environment.[19] For those interested in the current landscape of higher education, there is no shortage of literature to consult. I recommend *What Universities Owe Democracy* (2021) by Ronald Daniels; Arthur Levine and Scott Van Pelt's *The Great Upheaval: Higher Education's Past, Present, and Uncertain Future* (2021); Cathy Davidson's *The New Education: How to Revolutionize the University to Prepare Students for a World in Flux* (2017); and recent works by Nathan Grawe, including *The Agile College* (2021).[20]

When the presidents of four of my consortium's institutions met in the 1950s to kick off the work that would lead to the founding of Hampshire College and the formalization of Five Colleges, Incorporated, they had the luxury of long-standing relationships and the expectation that many of them would have sufficiently long tenure to see the payoffs of work even a decade away. For collaborative work, the most notable feature of the current decade is that as the reasons to engage in partnerships are growing, the conditions that support collaboration are receding. The trust, the institutional knowledge, and the relationships forged through difficult times with an expectation of longevity are all harder to come by today. The average tenure of a college president is less than six years; for provosts it is less than four.[21] Given the complexity of the job, it hardly seems enough time to develop the skills and experience to manage a single, small campus. Consortial work requires sufficient comfort in the daily duties of leadership to enable presidents, provosts, and others to envision new possibilities and enough time to make them a reality.[22]

This volume is meant to help new campus leaders get quickly up to speed on this portion of what could be. Much of what is here was known to the presidents who had the vision to sustain and formalize the Five College Consortium and similar consortia, but it took them time to learn—a luxury most current leaders don't have. Certainly, this book cannot build trust among strangers or create relationships where they don't exist. But it strives to make transparent and accessible some opportunities and cautions that might otherwise take years to come into focus. And for those leaders who are not entering an existing consortium but who possess an interest in exploring what new partnerships might have to offer, the pages that follow provide some guidance about what to expect and when to look elsewhere for solutions.[23]

The intended audience also includes a new generation of consortial employees and leaders. I am the first executive director of Five Colleges to have been born after it was founded. It is part of why I so often tell its creation story—to keep me connected to the spirit and vision that made this organization possible and to remind me and my campus colleagues that what seems impossible, or audacious, or downright crazy can in fact happen if the will is there. It is also important to note that a great deal of consortial work throughout the twentieth century was conducted informally, based on handshakes and memory. It is true in my own consortium. As a new generation comes into leadership, institutional memory fades. And an increasingly regulated and litigious context means that many of those informal arrangements are no longer adequate (or even legal, in some cases). As we have learned in recent years, even long-standing protocols and practices can be quickly upended by a single leader who fails to see their value or who questions every possible boundary. This book is not a legal guide, but it does provide some guidance on how to capture and formalize agreements that we want to sustain through increasingly rapid changes in leadership, even as it reminds us that compliance is less compelling than collaboration and that regulations are a poor substitute for relationships.

The goal in the pages that follow is to offer equal parts information, caution, and inspiration. Drawing on research, experience, and case studies of both successful and unsuccessful consortia, the volume is organized around five components of successful collaboration:

1. The shared *motivation* to be "better than we are" and the ability to articulate that motivation as well as the goals desired from collaboration
2. The shared *optimism* that things can be done and will be worth the effort required
3. The shared *generosity* to consider the good of the whole and the long view over the short term
4. The shared *commitment* of time, people, and resources to do the work well
5. The consistent shared *attention* to the evolving needs and possibilities of the collaboration

Together these five elements—motivation, optimism, generosity, commitment, and attention—characterize the consortial mindset. Each chapter focuses on one aspect of the consortial mindset, highlighting elements that successful collaborations share and ending with questions and exercises to continue the exploration and to support those who are either entering an existing consortium or interested in building a new one.

To set the stage, chapter 1 describes the range and scope of collaborative models that already exist across US higher education, noting that this approach to academic administration is not new but emphasizing the current landscape. Consortia can be large or small, broad or focused, extensive or limited. Whatever their shape, cross-campus partnerships are not new or even unfamiliar. The focus here is on organizations calling themselves consortia, but other forms of collaboration exist as well and can provide models, alternatives, and counterpoints. The forms follow their consortial functions, with the range of structures reflecting the diversity of motivating factors that drive these collaborative efforts.

Chapter 2 narrows in on the level of specific consortial efforts, ranging from academic partnerships (sharing faculty, courses, cocurricular activities, or even entire credentials) to administrative partnerships (back-office functions from human resources and insurance to procurement and information technology) to community partnerships (with K–12 schools, chambers of commerce, transit authorities, museums, and other cultural institutions). Campuses can coordinate on anything—professional development, emergency management, library acquisitions, and far, far more. This chapter provides examples of the creative array of possible partnerships, noting that the key feature of the most successful collaborations is a set of clearly articulated and agreed-upon goals and the optimism that they can be achieved.

Chapter 3 acknowledges that collaborative initiatives require leadership and explores the decision-making structures that can support collaboration. Who gets to choose which collaborations to pursue? Who should manage their creation and curation (and cessation, when appropriate)? And how do existing governance structures, from faculty senates to senior teams to boards of trustees help (or hinder) the work of collaboration? Authority, mindset, and policies all play a role in the success or failure of collaborative ventures and are explored here. Clear lines of authority and well-defined roles are critical features to build into collaborative efforts, and at their best they reflect a spirit of generosity driving the effort.

Chapter 4 turns to the resources needed to make collaborative initiatives happen—the staffing, funding, and management structures required to initiate and sustain not only specific initiatives but the exploratory and relationship-building work that paves the way for future partnerships. The nature of the work to be done, along with the governing and management structures to do it, should determine the staffing levels and model required, which in turn should drive funding decisions and structures. This chapter provides principles and guidance for recognizing and making these crucial resource decisions. Above all, aspiring and existing consortial leaders should commit to and invest in the relationships that will support the work.

Chapter 5 provides cautionary tales to remind us that collaborations, once established, cannot function on autopilot. This chapter emphasizes the importance of ongoing attention to the foundational work of collaboration, regardless of the specific goals and initiatives in one's real or desired portfolio. These pages return to the themes of building relationships, trust, and a shared sense of purpose that are critical to long-term success and offer practical guidance on how to build these essentials while offering stories of collaborations gone awry. Continuing care and attention are needed to build and sustain successful collaborations, and leaders should regularly revisit and assess not only the collaboration's individual initiatives but also its overarching motivations, goals, commitments, and relationships.

Templates, sample documents, and tools are included throughout, and each chapter ends with a worksheet to guide further exploration. The conclusion draws the five elements of consortial thinking back together and encourages those doing, joining, or considering collaborative work to ask themselves five questions that mirror the five elements of the consortial mindset:

1. Motivation: Do you know why you're doing this and what you hope to achieve?
2. Optimism: Do you believe it can work and that obstacles can be navigated?
3. Generosity: Are you willing to share both responsibility and credit?
4. Commitment: Are you able to devote the necessary time and resources to be successful?
5. Attention: Will you stay invested and attentive as the collaboration matures and evolves?

Some readers will have already been persuaded to join in this work. Others will find themselves in a position that engages them in existing collaborations. Some may want to get involved in work that is already underway or get back to collaborative work that has fallen into disrepair or renew a commitment to this powerful and challenging world of collaboration in higher education. Wherever you are and whatever your motivation, welcome to the work. Let's get started.

CHAPTER ONE

Why and How We Collaborate (Motivation)

The right consortium is the one that serves.

IN HIGHER EDUCATION consortial work, we often say that if you've seen one consortium, you've seen one consortium.[1] It's a helpful reminder that there are as many ways to structure collaborative work as there are collaborators to envision such partnerships. The Big Ten Academic Alliance (BTAA or Big Ten), Claremont Colleges Services (known as the Claremont Consortium), and Five Colleges, Incorporated (FCI; also called the Five College Consortium, or simply Five Colleges) are among the best-known examples, and even these three differ vastly in scale, structure, and function.

The range of structures is no accident. The Big Ten, Claremont, and Five Colleges were each founded in a particular place, by particular people, for a particular purpose. The environmental drivers of the moment motivated individual campus leaders to establish specific goals for their collaborations. Progressivism, a booming (if fragile) postwar economy, and the efficiency movement of the 1920s, combined with a desire to compete with but not duplicate Stanford, all shaped the vision for building what would become the Claremont Colleges (most of which did not actually exist when the "consortium" was established).

BTAA and the Five College Consortium both came about in the post–World War II era as the baby boom generation came of age, yet the two consortia look quite different. One has well over a dozen large public universities serving hundreds of thousands of students from coast to coast; the other consists of one public and four private campuses within a few miles of each other that collectively serve fewer students than many of the individual campuses in the Big Ten.

To understand an existing consortium or to build a new one requires, first and foremost, gaining an understanding of the drivers, motivations, and goals. Why does (or should) this collaboration exist? To what end? Through what mechanisms? The answers to these questions don't dictate a single formulaic answer to what a consortium will look like, but they do provide a critical foundation for all that comes afterward. A failure to articulate and build consensus around a clear motivation for collaborating is the most frequently cited reason for the collapse of consortia. In other words, each consortium is unique, yet all feature a defining motivation.

The Association for Collaborative Leadership, the professional association for higher education consortia, lists some 50 organizations in its directory. Wikipedia lists 75 organizations in its "College and university associations and consortia in the United States" category. Neither of these lists claims to be comprehensive. Indeed, consortia themselves represent just one form of cross-campus work. State systems of higher education, athletic leagues, mutual aid partners, twinning (a.k.a. sister) campuses, and other structures exist alongside organizations calling themselves "consortia."

Attempts to count consortia beg the question of what we mean by a "consortium." As Donn Neal, former executive director of the Pittsburgh Council on Higher Education, once put it, "There is no typical consortium." Having noted that caveat, in his classic and still remarkably relevant 1988 volume *Consortia and Institutional Cooperation*, Neal defined a consortium as "a semi-permanent organization, typically supported largely by financial contributions from its members, that employs a professional staff whose sole responsibility is to encourage and to facilitate cooperative activities between and among its members, and between them collectively and others."[2] As a working definition, Neal's remains a useful construct.[3] In practice, the details vary. The organization can be registered as a 501(c)(3) or not. The budget can be as low as a few thousand dollars or approach $50 million. Staff can be less than a single full-time equivalent (FTE) or amount to several hundred employees. Member institutions can number as few as 2 or 3 or more than 700.[4] It's worth noting that Neal's characteristics—structured, funded, and staffed—have also been cited as critical elements of successful collaborations in a variety of settings, a point we'll return to throughout this volume.[5]

The "structured" piece of the definition is an important place to begin and is, as Deb Mashek argues in her accessible and informative book *Collabor(h)ate*, captured in the three features of any true collaboration, regardless of the field: It must be intentional, the participants must be known to one another, and these participants must be working toward something concrete.[6] Collaboration, in short, does not happen by accident.

If structure is so critical to collaboration, why is there so much variety and inconsistency in the structure of American consortia? Given such a long history, why have consortia yet to coalesce around more common features? The answer, in short, is that form follows function. Or, as Simon Sinek titled his best-selling motivational guide: *Start with Why*. Sinek argued for the importance of beginning with purpose in any business or organizational venture, and similarly, the most successful consortia—the strongest, longest-lived collaborations—each began with a clear why, with leaders who found or crafted a shared motivation and used that drive to shape the organization they built to suit the purpose.[7] In other words, the fact that structure is so critical itself explains the variety because the structure of a consortium reflects the very purpose of the organization. Let's step back and get a clearer sense of the range of models.

Throughout this volume we'll talk about many of the most established and best-known, and more than a few less-recognized, consortia. Each

Table 1.1 Consortial Quadrants

Diverse missions Geographically close	Diverse missions Geographically spread
Shared mission Geographically close	Shared mission Geographically spread

has unique features, and most share some common lessons. The landscape can be dizzying. That said, a few basic categories of collaboration can help provide a framework for understanding the available options.

Two characteristics are important to start with: geography and mission. Envision a box with four quadrants, as shown in Table 1.1. Along one axis is "Geography," ranging from colocated to widely spread. Along the other axis is "Mission," ranging from mission-similar to highly distinctive. These quadrants provide some convenient, if imprecise, buckets to use as we begin to think about collaboration. Most formal consortia fall into the upper-left and lower-right quadrants, in which the member schools share either a geographic location or a common institutional mission, though we can find examples in all four corners.

In the upper-left category of "diverse missions, geographically close" are some of the oldest and best-known consortia: the Claremont Colleges (Southern California), the Colleges of the Fenway (CoF; Boston), the Five College Consortium (western Massachusetts), and others. Collaboration frequently began in these groups *because* of their proximity. The seven Claremont campuses were intentionally built close enough to share key services and facilities. The campuses of CoF (currently five in number) are contiguously located in the heart of Boston next to the Longwood Medical Area, a lively academic neighborhood that also houses at least eight hospitals and research institutes. The members of the Five College Consortium are all within a six-mile radius on the opposite side of the state from Boston (far closer than many consortia's campuses but markedly different than the colocated campuses of Claremont and Fenway). Leaders of the Claremont, Fenway, and Five College institutions were able to communicate frequently (even in the pre-Internet era) and shared similar educational, political, and social landscapes, enabling them to explore partnerships even when the missions of their campuses felt disconnected. Indeed, the varied missions often meant that these campuses could offer one another access and opportunities that would otherwise have been unavailable and reduced the hurdle that direct competition for students might have presented. These consortia with diverse institutional missions but shared geography often share library materials, personnel, courses, and cocurricular activities—assets that are easily transported or can be readily accessed from nearby locations.[8] Other consortia in this category include the Atlanta University Center Consortium in Georgia, the Lehigh Valley Association of Independent Colleges in eastern Pennsylvania, and the Associated Colleges of the St. Lawrence Valley in far upstate New York.

In the lower-right category of "shared mission, geographically spread" are some of the largest consortia in terms of participants: the Big Ten Academic Alliance, with 14 members and growing; the Council of Public Liberal Arts Colleges, with 30 members; the American Indian Higher Education Consortium (AIHEC), with 37 members; and the NELLCO Law Library Consortium, with over 140 members, are a few examples. These consortia often resemble professional associations in which the members gather out of shared or overlapping interests, enabling them to collaborate despite the geographic challenges. The Colleges of the Sisters of St. Joseph and the Adventist Colleges and Universities consortia, for instance, bring together campuses that share a religious affiliation; the campuses of The New American Colleges and Universities are "grounded in the legacy of Ernest L. Boyer." The Annapolis Group; historically Black colleges and universities (HBCUs); the Seven Sisters; and even the American Association of Colleges and Universities, the Council of Independent Colleges, and the like are other examples of this sort of professional association or interinstitutional relationship, even though they would probably not call themselves "consortia" per se. Many of these "shared mission, geographically spread" consortia collaborate on professional development programming, communities of practice, and advocacy work, which benefit from the similarities across the institutions but do not require daily contact or physical proximity to be effective.

In the lower-left category of "shared mission, geographically close(r)" are consortia that can look similar to the "shared mission, geographically spread" category in terms of portfolios, with a common institutional mission and a focus on sharing non–geographically dependent programs such as professional development and advocacy, but that are regional rather than national or international. The Professional Arts Consortium (often called ProArts) in the greater Boston area, the Green Mountain Higher Education Consortium in Vermont, the New York Six in upstate New York, and Five Colleges of Ohio (not to be confused with the Five College Consortium in western Massachusetts) are just a few examples. The campuses in these consortia are not colocated but tend to be within a few hours' drive of one another, allowing for relative ease of interaction compared to, say, the campuses of the Big Ten Academic Alliance, which now spread from California to New Jersey, or the Associated Colleges of the South, distributed across 12 states. Shared purchasing and contracting and local or state-level advocacy work can be part of these portfolios, as full colocation is not necessary for such collaborations. These consortia typically came into being later than either of the previous categories: ProArts was founded in 1984, Five Colleges of Ohio in 1995, New York Six in 2010, and Green Mountain in 2013. We will talk more about the waves of development of consortia shortly.

Examples of consortia in the upper-left category of "diverse missions, geographically spread" are harder to find, largely because it is important that a group of campuses has some commonality around which to form a collaboration. State systems of higher education that include flagship, regional, and community campuses spread across a state, such as the Connecticut State Colleges and Universities system and the State University of New York (SUNY) system, arguably fit this description, though such systems are not usually referred to as "consortia."[9] At least one state has developed Regional Higher Education Centers that serve as academic-program-sharing consortia within an existing state campus system, expanding the reach of the system's institutions to new geographical locations in the state.[10] An unusual partnership that fits this "diverse missions, geographically spread" category is that of St. Andrews University, a small, mostly undergraduate liberal arts institution in North Carolina, and Webber International University, a primarily business-oriented school 500 miles away in Florida. This duo operates in many ways like a consortium, though for the purposes of accreditation St. Andrews is now known as a "branch" of Webber International. Two international examples fit in the "diverse missions, geographically spread" category. The AMICAL Consortium is a group of 29 American-modeled institutions (AMIs) across 20 countries, including its host campus, the American University of Paris. With funding from the member institutions and the Mellon Foundation, the consortium focuses on administrative sharing (particularly in library and technology resources) and pedagogical enhancements (especially in digital literacy and scholarship).[11]

Another example of a consortium with diverse institutions and widely spread geography is operated by the Qatar Foundation, whose Education City campus in Doha houses branch campuses of universities from across the United States and Europe.[12] Each institution's Qatar campus offers a focused curriculum. For example, Northwestern University in Qatar offers journalism and communication, Virginia Commonwealth University–Qatar offers arts programs, and HEC Paris offers executive education. The Qatar campus deans work with staff from the Qatar Foundation to manage the collaborations. Education City, as the Qatar Foundation explains, "is a pretty unique place. During just one short walk—or tram ride—around campus, you could be visiting an Ivy League university, cross the street to browse one of the region's largest libraries, and then attend an open-mic at the neighboring university behind it."[13] Although their Qatar satellites are all situated within a shared campus of about five square miles, the participating institutions are widely spread and have come together in Education City for reasons that look quite different than, say, the colocated schools of Claremont or Fenway. The goal in Doha is to "make Education City a unique model of academic and research excellence, pioneering a new approach to multidisciplinary, global education and enabling breakthroughs that benefit Qatar and the rest of the world."[14] These geographically dispersed institutions share the Qatar campus to enrich Qatar's ability to provide a world-class set of educational offerings with minimal start-up time, and they in turn receive financial benefits that can support their home campuses.

Another example of a collaboration of diverse institutions across a broad geographical area comes from the International Association of Emergency Managers University and Colleges Caucus. The IAEM-UCC manages the National Intercollegiate Mutual Aid Agreement (NIMAA), which supports campuses in providing and receiving aid among one another in moments of crisis. IAEM-UCC encourages campuses to participate in other mutual aid agreements as well, but NIMAA signatories recognize NIMAA as a key commitment.[15] Note that, as with Education City in Qatar, for NIMAA the diversity of the institutions and their geographic locations is offset by a specific, shared interest. The focus on emergency management is clearly articulated and defines the scope of the NIMAA collaboration.

These four quadrants provide a simplified picture of the estimated 70-odd higher education consortia operating in the United States. Let's add a third dimension to capture the breadth of the collaboration. Combining the scope of the portfolio with the characteristics of closeness of geography and mission described in the quadrants above might give us a cube—the axes for "Geography" and "Mission" but with an additional axis added for "Scope," to capture targeted versus broad collaboration. This three-dimensional mapping allows us to describe consortial types with a bit more nuance than the quadrant picture. The Boston Consortium for Higher Education, with its varied group of 24 members, all in or near the Boston area and with a focus on enterprise functions, is an example of a consortium in the "diverse missions, geographically close, targeted scope" category. The Quaker Consortium, with 3 liberal arts colleges and a large private research university in the Philadelphia area managing a limited portfolio of activity, is another example of this diverse, close, targeted form of collaboration (note that the 3 colleges also partner without the university as the Tri-College

Consortium). The Boston Library Consortium, NELLCO Law Library Consortium, and HBCU-MSI Course-Sharing Consortium of the Southern Regional Education Board fall in the "shared mission, geographically spread, targeted scope" category. The Massachusetts Higher Education Consortium (MHEC)—a purchasing collective that despite its name serves colleges and universities across New England—is an example of a consortium in the "diverse missions, geographically spread, targeted scope" category.[16]

So we can map existing (or potential) collaborations in these three dimensions, characterizing them by the range of institutional missions they represent, the breadth of the geographical region they cover, and the extent of their portfolio of activity. It is worth noting here that this third dimension—the scope of collaboration—often changes over time. Institutions can evolve from completely distinct entities that operate with no connections or coordination to fully overlapping circles in which one institution becomes subsumed within another (or merges with another of similar size). Or new institutions can break off from existing ones, or collaborations can expand and contract over the years while the institutions remain independent entities. In 1969, graduate student Richard Lancaster proposed a five-stage model of consortium development "progressing from ad hoc cooperation through more complex cooperation to true interdependency."[17] The (now defunct) National Institute for Technology in Liberal Education described consortia as operating on a "collaboration continuum," which it defined as "the pyramidal movement from networking to coordination to cooperation to collaboration to integration."[18] Lawrence Howard discussed the "semantics of cooperation," noting that "interinstitutional cooperation . . . roughly covers a continuum: at one end are those groups which are tightly knit with an administrative emphasis, and at the other are those with looser, more occasional ties in which faculty members and students are the prominent participants."[19] In whatever way we describe the extent or maturity of a collaboration, the key for our purposes here is to note that the overlap may (and likely will) change over time—beginning as standalone campuses (circles in a Venn diagram), touching occasionally and then moving back away, or gradually becoming closer—and that the progression is unlikely to be linear.

At one extreme, cross-campus collaboration can result in a merger of two or more campuses, or in one campus acquiring another, in whole or in part. Recent examples include Wheelock College becoming part of Boston University, or Marlboro College becoming part of Emerson College, or multiple state universities in Pennsylvania and Vermont and Wisconsin consolidating into tightly knit networks of interlocking campuses in each of those states, perhaps with a single administration, even as the physical campuses remain geographically separate.[20] Some of these mergers arose out of long-standing partnerships that evolved into a more integrated whole, and others were new relationships, often driven by changing demographics, financial exigencies, and legislative mandates.

Although recent examples such as these may come more readily to mind, the landscape of higher education in the United States has always been shifting and evolving in this way, for reasons emerging from the time. The University of Pennsylvania came into existence when the state drew up a new constitution and issued a new charter uniting the College of Philadelphia and the University of the State of Pennsylvania in 1791; Radcliffe College, founded as Harvard Annex to serve women students when Harvard University itself did not, officially merged with Harvard in 1999. Lest we think that such mergers are straightforward, it is worth noting that even in the case of Radcliffe and Harvard, which were designed to function together, the official merger raised challenges, including determining responsibility for alumnae relations and fundraising, managing the end of Title IX exemptions granted to single-sex institutions, and adapting an array of contractual obligations, from donor agreements to building leases.[21]

Hobart and William Smith Colleges provide an unusual example of a tightly bound collaboration that is deeper than a consortium, but short of a full merger, and that has evolved over time. Hobart College for men was founded in 1822, and William Smith College for women was established in 1908 after founder William Smith "befriended a number of suffragettes and activists" and saw the need for educational opportunities for women. William Smith College, though it was considered a separate institution from the beginning, was operated as a department within Hobart College until 1943. Today, as their website explains, "Hobart and William Smith Colleges preserve their own identities while benefitting from a shared campus, faculty, administration and curriculum."[22] Saint John's University and the College of Saint Benedict in Minnesota provide another example of nearby single-sex institutions that had long operated as siblings eventually coming together under a single administrative umbrella, in this case in what the trustees called not a merger but a "strong integration."[23]

Cross-campus collaboration has also been known to create new campuses, as happened with Hampshire College. There is evidence, too, that a precursor to Five Colleges, Incorporated called the Committee on University Extension of the Connecticut Valley Colleges, which included Amherst, Mount Holyoke, Smith, and the campuses now known as the University of Massachusetts Amherst and Springfield College, was founded in 1914. This group "helped to organize Holyoke Junior College" (now Holyoke Community College) in the 1940s.[24] Several of the Claremont campuses, too, were developed by their consortial predecessors.

Some collaborations run their course, as when Indiana University–Purdue University Indianapolis (IUPUI) dissolved its partnership of more than half a century and separated into two independent institutions, or when Wheelock College stepped out of the Colleges of the Fenway as it merged into Boston University. Indiana University and Purdue University had each existed since the nineteenth century, and both operated extension programs in Indianapolis, though neither university was housed in the city. In 1968, campus leaders, with encouragement from the mayor of Indianapolis, sought to collaborate to build "a great state university in Indianapolis" and merged their programs to form IUPUI. Over more than 50 years, the joint campus grew from a modest commuter campus to the third-largest undergraduate institution in the state, and "Indiana University owned and operated the IUPUI campus, while Purdue granted degrees for some of the academic programs." In 2024, IUPUI split into Indiana University Indianapolis and Purdue University in Indianapolis, with the two parent campuses stating a desire "to promote economic growth and to create new jobs" as the reason for the break.[25] The story of Wheelock's departure from the Colleges of the Fenway and merger into Boston University is described in detail in *When Colleges Close*. The shift from being an independent institution participating in a consortium to being subsumed within a large university was driven by financial pressures resulting, in large part, from declining enrollments and demographic changes in New England. As this case highlights, participating in a consortium is not a path to assured financial success.

The three dimensions of the consortial cube are hardly perfect and not always straightforward. Consider the Tulsa Higher Ed Consortium, established in 2021, which includes not only higher education campuses but also nonprofits, the chamber of commerce, and others. This collaboration is clearly geographically close, and the participating partners share a commitment to higher education, but their individual organizational missions are far broader than we would find in a set of campuses. Or consider the collaboration among Bates, Bowdoin, and Colby Colleges in Maine and four tribal governments from the Wabanaki tribes in Maine: "The goals of this union were to link both cohorts by encouraging more Native American youth to consider higher education at the premier liberal arts colleges in the state, and for the campus communities to become more aware of the long history and rich tradition of the Wabanaki people."[26] Bates, Bowdoin, and Colby share similar institutional missions, but their collaboration in this case is not with other residential, undergraduate liberal arts institutions but with tribal governments. Do we map this collaboration as having shared missions or diverse missions? Do we consider these campuses and governments geographically close or distant? Is the scope of their collaboration targeted or comprehensive? There is no objectively "right" answer here.

Campuses can also join multiple consortia. Five of the colleges in the Great Lakes Colleges Association (GLCA) also belong to Five Colleges of Ohio, and Amherst and Smith Colleges are members of the New

England Humanities Consortium as well as the Five College Consortium of western Massachusetts. Some consortia are explicitly designed as nonexclusive collaborations, such as the Higher Education Recruitment Consortium, which supports its more than 500 member organizations in "recruiting and retaining outstanding and diverse employees," and the MHEC purchasing consortium, which provides "ready-to-use contracts" with regional vendors to hundreds of campuses across the region.[27]

In all these characterizations, it is important to note that "diverse," "close," and "targeted" and their opposites are loose terms. Do the campuses in FCI share a mission because they are all residential campuses with a strength in liberal arts education, or are their missions diverse because they include a state flagship, two women's colleges, and an experimenting campus? Is MHEC, with its focus on New England–based institutions, geographically close because it is not national or geographically spread because it covers more than a single metropolitan area? Is the scope of collaboration among the Colleges of the Fenway "targeted" because it focuses on a relatively small number of initiatives compared to Claremont, or is it "broad" because it offers far more collaboration than the Tri-Co consortium in Philadelphia? The consortial cube rubric provides one way of thinking about the distinctions in geography, mission, and scope. (For ease of printing, the "cube" is rendered in Table 1.2 in a two-dimensional grid.) The consortial cube model is advantageous because it allows us to articulate the features of a given consortium and to mentally map consortia relative to one another, not because it recommends any specific location within the cube. The precise mix of characteristics is less the point than the fact that there is a mix. As Franklin Patterson stated in 1974, "A consortium of colleges or universities by nature has to be unique, a vehicle specified by the needs, interests, and opportunities peculiar to the institutions that become associated."[28]

Thus, no judgment is intended here: The right collaboration is the one that can exist in its context. In the national association of consortia, the Association for Collaborative Leadership (ACL), there is no grand classification scheme and no established tracks or subgroups

Table 1.2 **Consortial Cube Rubric**

	Close	Mid-range	Widespread
Geography	Walkable or easily traversed in under an hour	Focused in one state or region—can get between campuses with relative ease	Widely dispersed—could not visit more than one or two campuses in a day
Mission	Significant overlap in campus mission, student populations, and perhaps in size and curricular array	Overlap in at least one or two key areas (commitment to the liberal arts, residential campuses, MSIs) but with differences in several key areas (public/private, single-sex/coeducational, small/large enrollment)	Significant differences in campus missions, with a mix of public/private, small/large, residential/ commuter, liberal arts/ professional training, etc.
Scope	Collaboration focused on one program or type of initiative	A few areas of shared activity but not a comprehensive set of shared offerings	A widely varied portfolio of shared programming, with the ability to readily add new programming

(though each consortium's dues are tied to its size). The world of formal higher education consortia is too small to overemphasize fine distinctions, and the main criterion for membership is self-identification as an organization or individual interested in advancing higher education collaboration. It is also fair to say that the individuals who choose to lead and work in consortia tend to be more interested in collaboration than in distinction, so ACL meetings naturally tend to focus on what is shared and to work across any differences. As former senior staff member Jackie Pritzen at Five Colleges put it in 1991, it is sufficient that a consortium's members are "enough alike to share, and different enough to use each other well."[29]

The cube's axes of "Mission," "Geography," and "Scope" are intended to describe the array of existing models in a simplified way and to spark the imagination of those not yet in this work by laying out some possibilities. What would it look like if we partnered with campuses that share an interest in a common topic, rather than assuming we must collaborate with our nearest neighbors? How could we collaborate with our nearest neighbors even though our missions may not overlap? The answers can likely be mapped in these three dimensions of mission, geography, and scope but need not look like any other existing collaboration to be effective. These axes of "Mission," "Geography," and "Scope" are also useful in helping collaborators to articulate what they share and where they diverge. Each piece of this triad is an opportunity for concurrence if addressed well, or conflict if addressed poorly or not at all.

Chapters 3 and 4 explore administrative structures in more detail, but for the moment we will simply note that some collaborations are highly informal, while others operate under binding legal and contractual arrangements. In general, the consortia with the broadest portfolios tend to operate as 501(c)(3) nonprofit organizations alongside the collaborating campuses, typically with their own staff of anywhere from one person to dozens, including an executive director (sometimes called the president or CEO). Younger and more limited partnerships can be successful with just a memorandum of understanding or a contract or even a handshake, with staff time contributed in-kind. As mentioned above, the right structure is the one appropriate to the need and goals of the partners. Funding models vary as well, as we will discuss in Chapter 4. Some consortia are dues based; others assess campuses for expenses based on the portfolio of activity; and other partnerships fund specific initiatives as one-off agreements. Although grant funding can seed new projects and even new organizations, relying on external support as the core funding for long-term collaborative efforts is ill-advised, as we will see in studies of failed consortia.

Donn Neal's definition of a consortium as a structured, funded, and staffed collaboration remains relevant after four decades because it speaks to intention and commitment—such partnerships are not accidental; they are designed. Campuses come together, as one scholar of consortia described it, to "achieve more, do something better, or reduce the cost of an activity."[30] But the specifics of why and how they do so vary widely and importantly. In the consortial cube, we have seen a variety of types of consortia—small to large, close-knit to far-flung, focused to comprehensive. This range exists because the underlying motivations vary. "Academic consortia form," as two longtime consortial leaders put it, "for one simple reason: to serve their member institutions."[31] That simplification is true, but because those institutions, their leaders, and their priorities, needs, and resources all vary, the way that each consortium serves its campuses will differ as well.

In his classic work *Colleges in Consort*, Franklin Patterson provides another simplified description of the "ideological impulses that inform the consortial movement," arguing that campuses partner for only two reasons: to enhance their academic programs or to improve their bottom lines.[32] Allowing for the fact that campuses can also enhance nonacademic programs, we might reformulate Patterson's typology to say that campuses collaborate either to improve quality or to save money. At FCI, we expand this dyad to a triad to describe the core purposes to our work: to become more effective, efficient, or experimental.

These generalizations are true across the variety of consortia and throughout their history. But a closer look at three distinct eras of consortial development reminds us that the societal context shapes when and how consortia come to be and helps determine how their founders enact their visions. The evolution and expansion of higher education in the 1920s, 1960s, and 1990s prompted new efforts at collaboration.[33] A look at these three eras and the origin stories of several collaborations illustrates how motivation drives details.

Higher education in the early twentieth century was being shaped by the Progressive Era, the post–World War I baby boom (smaller than the one to come after World War II but still significant), and high immigration. Social activism and political reform encouraged responsibility and democratic ideals, targeting corruption and inefficiency. Frederick Winslow Taylor's groundbreaking book *The Principles of Scientific Management* (1911) advocated for time management studies and a division of labor that increased factory efficiency and simultaneously helped spur unionization efforts.[34] By 1920 women's suffrage had been won, but disenfranchisement of African Americans was also taking hold, and the United Daughters of the Confederacy was peppering the South with monuments intended to celebrate and spread white supremacy.[35] Progressivism found expression in prohibition, and a backlash emerged in support for eugenics and immigration restrictions. The tug and pull of these sometimes conflicting economic and social changes took place during an era of evolution in higher education as well. Enrollments tripled at some state institutions, and state and federal investments in higher education grew dramatically.[36] Research universities had been expanding for several decades.[37] The expansion of public K–12 education supported growth in higher education enrollments. Between 1910 and 1930, the number of undergraduate degrees conferred grew from about 37,000 to more than 120,000 per year.[38]

The economic boom of the early twentieth century helped families fund these higher enrollments and spurred businesses and foundations to invest more. This growth in enrollment and investment, steeped in an era of efficiency studies, encouraged experimentation as well as expansion in higher education, and these changes fostered conversation and collaboration. The Association of American Colleges (later the American Association of Colleges and Universities; AAC&U) was founded in 1915 with "inclusiveness and interhelpfulness as twin themes." As the history of AAC&U notes, "Interhelpfulness was the key, as these institutions struggled to define their purpose and reassert their importance in the changing landscape, and set standards for effective practice."[39] The same year, the American Association of University Professors came into being, undertaking investigations and defenses of academic freedom, in keeping with the founding document of the organization: *Declaration of Principles on Academic Freedom and Academic Tenure*.

Alexander Meiklejohn's work provides an example of the experimentation happening on college and university campuses in the 1920s. Meiklejohn had been president of Amherst College from 1912 to 1923, where he developed a reputation for pushing reforms that also pushed the college faculty, alumni, and trustees, ultimately ending in his forced retirement. He moved to the University of Wisconsin in Madison, where in 1928, with the support of the university's president, he founded the Experimental College: It "had no formal classes and the curriculum stressed an in-depth study of a single topic at a time, devoting the first year to the civilization of Greece and the second to the civilization of England."[40]

Meiklejohn saw campuses wrestling with how to meet "the commercial demand for highly trained college graduates" while continuing to accommodate "the classical demand for scholars" and sought to address this tension by creating a more integrated curriculum that would serve as a foundation for whatever explorations graduates might later take up. President Frank at the University of Wisconsin similarly envisioned "educating people by teaching them to understand life situations."[41] Together, these two men, with the support of the findings of a commission on educational policy, realized their vision required a dramatic change: "It was evident that an attempt to tinker with the existing system would invite chaos, and, instead of accomplishing anything, would defeat its own purpose."[42]

Meiklejohn hoped that his "college of tomorrow" would "stimulate students to take responsibility for their own learning," preparing them to participate in democracy itself.[43] It was a visionary approach to an unsettled time. Although the "college" closed in the 1930s, elements of it remain a century later, in the form of the Integrated Liberal Studies Program, which still provides an interdisciplinary approach to the study of the liberal arts.[44]

The particulars of Meiklejohn's plan may have been unusual, but as his biographer Adam Nelson wrote, the era was replete with experimentation in higher education:

> Dozens of experiments had already begun, and dozens more were on the drawing board. Bennington College in Vermont and Sarah Lawrence in New York were pioneering new forms of artistic education for women, while Deep Springs College in California started a rugged new work-study program for a small community of men. Reed in Oregon and Swarthmore in Pennsylvania introduced honors programs with more rigorous and unified courses of study for undergraduates. Rollins College in Florida initiated a striking new "conference plan" of individualized instruction, while Black Mountain in North Carolina sponsored innovative arts and humanities programs for adults.[45]

As Nelson also noted, this era of growth, adaptation, and experimentation produced two higher education collaborations that still exist a century later.

The Claremont Colleges established their consortial structure in 1925, based on the Oxbridge model of a set of colleges, each with its own faculty and disciplinary focus organized around a central administrative entity providing core services. Indeed, when Pomona College President James Blaisdell envisioned this innovation, Pomona was the only college in the Claremont area. Population growth and economic prosperity suggested that additional capacity would be needed in the near future, and Blaisdell wanted to compete with Stanford by means other than simply growing Pomona to match its northern counterpart's scale. As Blaisdell wrote in 1923: "My own very deep hope is that instead of one great, undifferentiated university, we might have a group of institutions divided into small colleges—somewhat on the Oxford type—around a library and other utilities which they would use in common. In this way I should hope to preserve the inestimable personal values of the small college while securing the facilities of the great university. Such a development would be a new and wonderful contribution to American education."[46] It would be a stretch to suggest that Blaisdell's vision led inexorably to the Claremont Colleges as we know them today—detractors existed and financial challenges arose, as they are wont to do—but his vision of a group of small institutions sharing a core set of services and facilities in order to function with the advantages of a larger institution bears close resemblance to the structure today, with seven institutions all located on a multicollege campus.

As one education historian has noted, in the late nineteenth and early twentieth centuries, "emulating the residential colleges of Oxford and Cambridge" was seen as "a way to reinvigorate American undergraduate education."[47] In addition to the efforts at Claremont, at least half a dozen US campuses attempted such a model, including Harvard, Yale, Princeton, the University of Chicago, and (later) the University of California, Santa Cruz. More than 40 institutions would eventually explore at least the residential elements of the Oxbridge model. For the most part, these efforts were inspired by an idealized (and thus less than accurate) understanding of the English model that did not translate well to early twentieth-century American settings. Claremont became the exception in this set of experiments, successful in part because it took the Oxbridge model loosely, adopting it selectively and adapting it over time, and in part because it was not a large university attempting to emulate smaller-scale colleges but a small college looking to grow without losing the intimacy of its character.

By 1926 the Claremont University Consortium consisted of three campuses: Pomona College, "a college of the New England type" focused on undergraduate liberal arts, established in 1887; Claremont Graduate University, offering masters and doctoral degrees, begun in 1925; and Scripps College for women, founded in 1926. To a greater extent than in other consortial settings, the Claremont schools did not need to adapt to one another because, as educational historian John Duke noted, "Each new college was founded to help complement the existing curricular offerings of the group." Early collaborative initiatives included a shared library, business functions, a joint student health service, a central heating plant, and a shared auditorium. The other four campuses that now form the full consortium were not created until after World War II ended: Claremont McKenna College (1946, with a focus on business and public affairs), Harvey Mudd College (1955, offering engineering, science, and math programs with a liberal arts context), Pitzer College (1963, emphasizing social and behavioral sciences), and Keck Graduate Institute (1997, offering professionally oriented master's degrees).[48]

Whereas Blaisdell envisioned the Claremont consortium before the campuses that would join it were established, the campuses in Atlanta, Georgia, that came together in 1929 to form the Atlanta University Center Consortium (AUCC) had existed for several decades. They were all HBCUs founded in the aftermath of the American Civil War to provide a world-class education to Black Americans still barred from study on most other campuses, even after the end of slavery.[49]

The vision for the AUCC came in part from a campus leader uniquely situated to see the benefits of cross-campus collaboration. John Hope was in 1929 the president of both Morehouse College (founded 1867) and Atlanta University (1865) and "saw the potential gains" of working across campus lines. To be fair, the campuses, located in a single neighborhood near downtown Atlanta, had been collaborating for many years in less formal ways, including sharing faculty (and Hope as president), before beginning in earnest to explore "cooperative measures that could result in savings of expenditures for all three institutions." President Hope recruited Spelman College (1881) to join with Morehouse and Atlanta University to form the Atlanta University Center. The trustees and presidents "began to assess ways in which they could utilize their services and resources more effectively and efficiently." They created the formal structure "to coordinate and manage the cooperative efforts of various programs and services offered by the colleges." Today the four member campuses share a library, cross-registration, career services, some academic programs, and campus master-planning activities.[50]

It seems to be no accident that these HBCUs joined forces during the early years of an era known as the Great Migration, which by the 1970s would result in some 6 million African Americans leaving the post-Reconstruction South for the hope of better opportunities farther north. The AUCC campuses' long history of partnership prior to the formal agreement of 1929 likely helped the collaboration survive the disruptions of the stock market crash that would come just months later, though the membership has shifted in the century since then. In 1988 Atlanta University and Clark College merged to form Clark Atlanta University (still a member). Morris Brown College (1881) and the Interdenominational Theological Center (1958) became members for a time but are no longer in the AUCC. Morehouse School of Medicine was founded in 1974 and remains a member of the AUCC. In 1938 a parallel organization called the University Center in Georgia brought Agnes Scott College, the Atlanta College of Art, Columbia Theological Center, Emory University, the Georgia Institute of Technology, and the University of Georgia together in a consortial structure that still exists today as the Atlanta Regional Council for Higher Education. It now includes the four member campuses of the Atlanta University Center along with 14 other area schools.

As with the Claremont Colleges, the member campuses of the AUCC—currently Clark Atlanta, Morehouse, Spelman, and Morehouse School of Medicine—span a range of missions, with two single-sex liberal arts colleges, a graduate university, and a professional school, but share an identity as HBCUs as well as a geographic location. Both Claremont and the AUCC continue to share key services and facilities as well as courses, enabling the member campuses to focus on their distinct missions and audiences while benefiting from the breadth and scale made possible through collaboration. Claremont was purpose-built, the member institutions expressly founded to add to the consortium and benefit from its existing resources. In other words, the consortium shaped the types of institutions to be founded, rather than the other way around. The AUCC campuses were not created to form a consortium, but they were built for the common purpose of providing access to Black students. In this way the AUCC campuses' collectively shared mission also shaped the construction of the institutions long before the consortium was envisioned. In short, the individual campuses of these two pioneering consortia, even before their formal collaborative structures were established, never existed as fully isolated institutions. The unusual circumstances in Southern California and metro Atlanta may explain why these two consortia did not represent or inspire a broader trend of formal cross-campus collaboration in the 1920s.

The mid-twentieth century saw a burst of growth in consortia of such magnitude that even though Claremont and the AUCC laid important groundwork, the history of consortia in US higher education is often traced to the 1960s rather than the 1920s. One retrospective reported that "hundreds of colleges and universities in the United States became involved in consortial arrangements" between 1950 and 1970. A 1967 study found that more than 1,000 higher education consortia existed in 1965–1966. Another study from the era reported that "one in four colleges or universities currently participate in consortia."[51] It is worth noting that the definitions used to reach these numbers (from hundreds to over a thousand) were inconsistent. It is also worth noting that by the late 1980s, many of these early consortia had ceased operations. But by any measure, these decades saw tremendous interest in cross-institutional collaboration, and by 1987, even allowing for the failed experiments, more than 135 formal consortia could be listed.[52]

As with the collaborations formed in the 1920s, this new generation of consortia was shaped by factors across and beyond higher education. Conversations began in the 1950s as campuses grappled with the growth brought on by the GI Bill and the looming baby boom generation due to reach college age in the mid-1960s. Student activism and unrest also encouraged campus leaders to partner in new ways. Significantly, these broad cultural changes were accompanied by a burst of federal and philanthropic interest and support that inspired and funded many of the new experiments in "interinstitutional cooperation," as it was often called in these years, and encouraged formalizing collaborations that had long existed without legal recognition. According to one description of the 1960s, the interest in consortia by philanthropic foundations and the federal government "stemmed partly from an intellectual commitment to the notion that collaboration is a good idea, but it also reflected the realization that if colleges and universities were to meet the new demands being placed upon them they needed to find ways of sharing their energies and resources."[53] Three national developments had particularly significant impact in these years: interstate compacts, Title III legislation, and foundation funding.

An interstate compact is "a legally binding agreement between two or more states [that] establishes a formal, legal relationship among states to address common problems or promote a common agenda." The National Center for Interstate Compacts lists 268 such compacts in its database, including 4 regional higher education compacts that among them include 47 states (all but New York, New Jersey, and Pennsylvania). The Center for the Study of Federalism describes these 4 collaborations as "vehicles for interstate and interinstitutional cooperation to help solve problems related to higher education, to facilitate data and information exchanges, and to increase cost savings through collective purchasing power."[54]

The Southern Regional Education Board began in 1948 "to foster development and joint use of higher education facilities throughout the region, to generally advance elementary, secondary, and higher education and improve the social and economic life of the South" and now includes 16 states. It is the only compact of the 4 to include K–12 education in its mission. The Western Interstate Commission for Higher Education was established in 1953 "to help Western states increase educational opportunities for their citizens, improve colleges and universities, expand the supply of specialized manpower, and inform the public as to needs of higher education" and now includes 15 members. The New England Board of Higher Education, formed in 1955, aims "to foster development and joint use of higher education resources among the six New England states." The Midwestern Higher Education Compact was established in 1991 and "provides greater higher education opportunities and services in the midwestern region, with the aim of furthering regional access to, research in and choice of higher education for [our] citizens."[55] It currently has 12 members.

As one regional compact partner explains, the scope of collaboration is dictated primarily by the participants' interest: "The compacts have worked together where their partners—states or the institutions within states—deem collaboration to make sense." For the New England Board of Higher Education (NEBHE), for instance, the motivation to collaborate came "when six visionary New England governors—realizing that the future prosperity of New England rested on higher education—committed their states to the shared pursuit of academic excellence."[56] NEBHE's portfolio includes regional conferences, a journal, and a program that enables out-of-state students within the region to pay reduced tuition at partnering public campuses if they enroll in an academic program not available in their home state. The compacts' specific functions vary but can include fact-finding, data analysis, policy advocacy, student exchanges, liability insurance, health plans, procurement, and more.[57]

The portfolios of these regional compacts share some similarities with consortia in these same regions, with the distinction that the compacts are legal agreements among state governments rather than among higher education institutions. It's worth noting here that a system of advocacy organizations representing private institutions emerged in this same era, beginning with the Independent Colleges of Indiana in 1948 and followed by many others, including the Association of Independent California Colleges and Universities in 1955, the

Wisconsin Association of Independent Colleges and Universities in 1961, the Independent Colleges and Universities of Texas in 1969, and the National Association of Independent Colleges and Universities in 1976, to name just a few. Although advocacy is the common and primary function of these independent colleges and universities organizations, some also engage in joint purchasing and other collaborations.

The creation of these governmental compacts spurred the development of consortia in three ways: by demonstrating the power of collaboration to a broad audience, by encouraging campuses to collaborate directly before being required to do so by law, and by motivating noncompact campuses to collaborate in order to compete with those in compacts. Other variations on regional compacts and independent institution advocacy groups would emerge over time. Six public campuses in southeastern Massachusetts collaborate through the CONNECT consortium (connectsemass.org), and nearly two dozen institutions collaborate through the New Hampshire College and University Council (nhcuc.org). A later variation on the regional compact model is the Lowcountry Graduate Center, a state-funded collaboration established in 2001 among three institutions in the Charleston, South Carolina, area to align academic credentialing with workforce needs in the region.

Federal action also promoted cross-campus collaborative efforts in this era. Title III is part of the Higher Education Act of 1965, which authorizes federal aid programs that support college students as well as the higher education institutions they attend. It is this legislation that enables financial aid loans, federal work study, and student assistance programs like TRIO, and Congress has revised and reauthorized the act periodically in the last half century. Each section (or "title") of the act covers a specific set of programs and funding, and Title III covers Institutional Aid (sometimes referred to by its subsection Strengthening Institutions), with a focus on minority-serving institutions (MSIs), including tribal colleges, HBCUs, and Hispanic-serving institutions. The structure of Title III represented a significant shift in the focus of federal funding for higher education, from support for specific programming to "general assistance which looks to upgrade the institution as a whole" by "strengthen[ing] the institutions which are weak but which bear the major brunt of the teaching task."[58]

Title III funding in the 1960s encouraged MSIs to collaborate to achieve improvements in facilities, faculty, curriculum, and services.[59] By one count, in just the first year after the passage of the Higher Education Act, some 84 interinstitutional collaborations had been funded; by year two the number of funded collaborations had grown to 249.[60]

One of these Title III–funded collaborations was the Appalachian Consortium Special Development Project, known more commonly as the Appalachian Developing Institutions Consortium, a group of eight open-admissions two-year institutions in North Carolina, whose leaders had advocated for the consortium's founding because "only through a cooperative arrangement could the institutions overcome limitations arising from an entire region being depressed and having low taxable resources" as well as a dearth of funding and expertise to effectively execute their shared mission of accessibility.[61] (This consortium differs from the current Appalachian College Association, a consortium of 35 private liberal arts colleges across the central Appalachian Mountains.) The Small College Consortium is another example from this era: a group of 54 campuses that received Title III funding and reported in 1977 that this funding had inspired them to increase their own contributions to the work of the consortium.[62]

Title VI funding from the Civil Rights Act of 1964 also fostered such collaborations by providing funding for new partnerships and joint programming. One example is the elaborately named Centers for International Business Education and Research Minority-Serving Institution and Community College Consortium.[63]

For similar reasons and in consort with the federal government, philanthropic foundations provided funding to initiate and support new collaborations in the mid-twentieth century. The Phelps-Stokes Fund, for instance, sponsored the Cooperative College Development Program beginning in 1965 to provide training to development officers at MSIs receiving endowment support via Title III, helping campuses build the skills to manage and sustain their new endowments. Phelps-Stokes was a nonprofit established "to overcome inequities in education," particularly for women, African Americans, and Native Americans. The fund appears to have ceased operations sometime after 2011, but while it existed it claimed credit for helping to create "landmark institutions [including] the United Negro College Fund, American Indian Higher Education Consortium (AIHEC), and numerous Historically Black Colleges and Universities."[64] The power of such investments is further illustrated by AIHEC's description of itself as the vehicle through which "Tribal Colleges nurtured a common vision and learned to see themselves as a national movement" after centuries of displacement, regulation, removal, and worse, when the shape and status of higher education for Native Americans was dictated and often destroyed by non-Native actors.[65]

The Robert R. Moton Memorial Institute undertook a similar effort with funding provided by the Alfred P. Sloan Foundation. Sloan funded matching grants to build endowments at HBCUs, while the Moton Institute ran training programs for presidents, trustees, chief financial officers, and development officers in endowment management. Sloan's efforts and funding in this space led to the creation of other collaborations, including the Council for Opportunity in Graduate Management Education in 1970, a group of 10 graduate management schools to share recruiting efforts and fund fellowships, and the Consortium for Graduate Study in Management in 1971, which comprised 6 campuses with similar recruiting and fellowship goals.[66]

The Mellon Foundation, Ford Foundation, and others joined in these development efforts as well, offering seed funding to incentivize cross-institutional collaborations. These efforts to enhance the agency of underresourced institutions at times had unintended consequences, as in the creation of the Council for Advancement of Small Colleges, "a coalition of colleges passed over by the Ford Foundation in its distribution of $260 million to 630 institutions in 1955."[67] Shut out of funding from Ford, they simply formed their own collaborative.

The Work Colleges Consortium, although not formally established until 1995, has its origins in this era. The distinguishing characteristic of Work Colleges is their intent to "engage students in the purposeful integration of work, learning, and service." Beginning in the early 1970s with a grant from the Educational Foundation of America, four-year colleges with this focus began to share best practices, and additional funding from the Charles Stewart Mott Foundation in 1982, the Ford Foundation in 1987, and a provision in the 1992 reauthorization of the Higher Education Act led to increasing collaboration and the formal establishment of the Work College Consortium in 1995, with eight current members across seven states, from Texas to New Hampshire.[68]

The combination of interstate compacts, federal legislation, and foundation funding drove the creation of consortia in this post–World War II era. The Big Ten Academic Alliance (BTAA), founded in 1958 as the Committee on Institutional Cooperation, represents these intersecting trends. One history of the BTAA reports that it was formed "as a countermove to prevent a compulsory regional compact for the midwestern states." One of the founding presidents tells a more interpersonal story of its creation, noting that the presidents of the Big Ten athletic conference had been meeting twice a year for some two decades "to discuss their mutual problems," including "the Midwest Universities Research Association; the Midwest Library Center; future trends of faculty salaries; an exchange of information regarding policies governing service of retired professors; the encroachment of the state upon university management and the responsibilities of governing boards; the implications of a proposed interstate compact concerning medical, dental and veterinary education; educational television; preservation of academic freedom policies and practices; accrediting practices of the North Central Association; and policies regarding student fees."[69] Herman B. Wells, the Indiana University president from 1938 to 1962, described a conversation with James Perkins, then–vice president of the Carnegie Corporation. Perkins asked Wells about the semiannual meetings of the presidents of the Big Ten institutions and whether they really talked only about football at these gatherings, declaring it "a pity" that the public primarily associated the Big Ten with athletics rather than academics. "We do talk about other things," Wells responded. "In fact, we spend most of our time discussing educational problems." Wells went on to explain that "we have a budget and staff to prepare the background material for our athletic decisions. To have effective discussions leading to decisions, we need also a joint secretariat for educational matters." In an exchange that seems the epitome of a gentlemen's agreement of the 1950s, the conversation quickly reached its conclusion:

PERKINS: "How much would it cost?"
WELLS: "Oh, I don't know—as a good guess, $50,000 per year."
PERKINS: "Go back to the Council [of Big Ten presidents] and see if they'll do it, and I will recommend the project to our trustees."[70]

The resulting $294,000 grant from the Carnegie Foundation, followed by a second grant of $100,000, helped the group to begin formalizing its work in academic collaboration. As Wells summed up, "The working philosophy of the CIC has always been to help each member institution develop in depth and to exploit its own areas of strength, and then to make the combined strength available to all."[71]

Like the Big Ten, the Associated Colleges of the Midwest (ACM), incorporated in 1958, also grew out of an athletic conference with 10 original members, all small liberal arts colleges in Illinois, Iowa, Minnesota, and Wisconsin. The founding members cited three purposes for their new organization:

- To advance the interests and to contribute to the educational effectiveness of the member colleges of the organization;
- To develop and assist the member colleges in improving the efficiency of their operations both administrative and cultural;
- To assist the member colleges in developing additional sources of revenue.[72]

Other athletic conferences would later follow this trend of creating a parallel organization to coordinate academic initiatives. The CAA Academic Alliance formed in 2002 as the academic arm of the Colonial Athletic Conference, with 14 members across 9 states facilitating cross-campus faculty research, student mentoring, and communities of practice. The America East Academic Consortium formed in 2014 with a focus on "elevating the academic profile" of the 10 member campuses and expanding opportunities for students, faculty, and staff.[73]

GLCA, incorporated in 1962, provides another example of how mid-century social trends and funding streams spurred collaboration. The original 12 campuses have now become 13: Albion College, Allegheny College, Antioch College, Denison University, DePauw University, Earlham College, Hope College, Kalamazoo College, Kenyon College, Oberlin College, Ohio Wesleyan University, Wabash College, and the College of Wooster. All are liberal arts campuses "rooted in the Protestant religious tradition and its concern for moral and academic education," and all are "academic islands situated in small midwestern towns." These institutions were founded between 1824 and 1866 in Michigan, Ohio, and Indiana. In 1958 the campus presidents (already aware of the recently established ACM) attended a conference hosted by the Ford Foundation on undergraduate programs in international education that highlighted "the increasing importance of institutional cooperation to the future of higher education in America." Two of the campuses received follow-on funding for a joint international program, and three years later Ford provided $500,000 to expand the effort to the dozen schools that would create GLCA. Although the ACM model and the Ford funding were important, the GLCA presidents stated that "economic and social conditions that were beyond the control of any individual college" helped them see collaboration as "an increasingly necessary strategy for coping, continuing to survive, and continuing to excel."[74]

In 1969 the presidents of Clark University, the College of the Holy Cross, and Worcester Polytechnic Institute invited their colleagues at seven other area campuses to join them in establishing the Colleges of Worcester Consortium in central Massachusetts "during a stressful period of student unrest and . . . economic pressures." As the executive director reported three decades later, "It quickly became apparent to those presidents that a formal arrangement to support cooperation could provide advantages and enable a self-sustaining enterprise to emerge. Among the early efforts at cooperation were joint faculty development programs, joint community relations, and eventually the adoption of a preexisting, regional library cooperative."[75] The Colleges of Worcester Consortium continues today as the Higher Education Consortium of Central Massachusetts, with a similar set of members, but a dramatically changed leadership structure, financial model, and staff size.[76]

The disruptions of mid-century America, along with stimulation from legislation and funding, encouraged these and other campus leaders to formalize and extend some long-standing partnerships and to explore working across campus boundaries in ways that most of their predecessors had not considered. As one of them noted in 1964, "Today, more than ever before in history, the world is bringing its needs to the doors of these institutions." Many of these consortia would not survive to the equivalent of adulthood, and some that survived underwent significant change. Two consortial trends dominated this era—geographically dispersed collections of campuses with similar missions (ACM, GLCA, and the like) and the formalization of collaboration among institutions with long records of cooperation (Five Colleges, Big Ten, and others).[77] A 1999 study found that of all the consortia in existence in that year, 64% had been founded between 1961 and 1980.[78] By the early 1980s, however, the mid-century boom had come to an end, and the total number of consortia would continue to decrease until the end of the century, leading to questions about how to manage the remaining collaborations, as one author mused, "in a period of decline."[79] The Nashville University Center, for instance, was founded in about 1969 on the model of the Atlanta University Center a quarter century earlier, and the Higher Education Center for Urban Studies was established in 1968 in Bridgeport, Connecticut, with funding from the US Department of Health, Education, and Welfare, but by 1984 both had closed.[80]

A new set of pressures late in the 1900s spurred another round of collaborative efforts. The increasing role of computers and concern over the rising cost of higher education were the most significant trends in this era. Desktop computers and information technology more broadly brought changes to modes of work and communication; added new costs to campus budgets; and raised unfamiliar questions about training, staffing, and funding in this newly interconnected landscape.[81] Higher education costs accelerated not only because of these novel technologies but also due to increasingly expensive research technology and staffing, as well as growing specialization in the higher education workforce (with academic staff taking over a number of roles formerly held by faculty, from registrar and admission functions, to advising and student affairs, to compliance and community relations). The spate of new consortia in this era led boards of trustees to realize that "strategic institutional management frequently entails partnerships" and thus an expectation that "institutions will work together rather than compete unnecessarily and inefficiently."[82]

Philanthropic funding would again prompt experiments and growth in consortia. The Mellon Foundation under the presidency of William G. Bowen played a key role. In her biography of Bowen, Nancy Weiss Malkiel describes the "enduring value" of many of Bowen's initiatives during his 1988–2006 tenure, including "the establishment for varied purposes of consortia of small liberal arts colleges to provide the requisite scale for certain activities and to encourage shared information and problem solving [and] institutional collaborations among liberal arts colleges in areas including faculty career enhancement and staffing, health care for emeriti, study abroad programs, uses of information technology, and administrative support."[83] Given this set of drivers, it is no surprise that the consortia formed in this era emphasized cost savings and other efficiencies like joint faculty appointments.[84]

The Associated Colleges of the South (ACS) incorporated in 1991 to "create and build programs not possible on an individual basis [and to] increase the efficiency of their [members'] operations." Like many of the consortia formed mid-century, ACS campuses are spread across a wide region—16 liberal arts colleges and universities across 12 states. The founding purposes noted the value of "creating enduring networks" for faculty, staff, and students while also acknowledging the financial benefits of ACS serving as "a laboratory in which new ideas can be tested and programs incubated without excessive fear of failure, and where joint projects can attract significant financial support from funders looking for the biggest 'bang for their buck.'"[85]

The Colleges of the Fenway formed in 1995 as a collaboration of five campuses located along the Fenway thoroughfare in Boston: Emmanuel College, Massachusetts College of Pharmacy and Allied Health Sciences, Simmons College, Wentworth Institute of Technology, and Wheelock College (Wheelock recently left the consortium and was absorbed into Boston University.) The presidents set three goals for their nascent partnership: "to enhance the academic environment and academic opportunities for students and faculty, to slow escalating costs through joint purchasing and the sharing of resources, and to retain their identities as small private colleges while offering the resource advantages of a much larger academic institution."[86] Cross-registration, shared recruitment activities, and collective procurement all became part of the CoF portfolio and remain so three decades later.

The variety of consortia is enormous. Whatever model you have or choose, it's important to understand what it is meant to be and why. No version is inherently good or bad, but some models have done well and many efforts have failed. (Well, there may be one bad variation; as a guide to school-community partnerships warned, "When people start a partnership to get good publicity, it usually doesn't work."[87]) It is possible to have great diversity in institutional missions and yet find shared purpose; it is possible to have similar missions and yet find complementary features in one another. It is possible to be geographically dispersed and yet find reasons to come together physically or virtually; it is possible to be geographically close and yet not be in competition. It is possible to do a few things or many. These characteristics alone do not make for success or failure. But they are important to identify and understand at the outset, as they are the foundation on which the rest is built.

Most of the consortia described here have been successful in their efforts and have continued to exist for decades. That sort of longevity requires ongoing care and feeding and the ability to adapt to shifting circumstances, as suggested by Peter Senge's work on learning organizations.[88] Claremont's newest campuses were founded during two subsequent booms in consortia—three new campuses in the post–World War II decades and another in the 1990s—and helped respond to the demands of each era. The Five College Consortium campuses began collaborating during the years in which Claremont and the Atlanta University Center came into being but formally established Five Colleges, Incorporated (FCI) in the 1960s as demographic pressures and funding streams made the 501(c)(3) structure more appropriate, providing the campuses a vehicle through which to found Hampshire College and to accept multi-institutional grants. And in the 1990s, FCI, like CoF, built a fiber-optic network to help the member campuses meet the new demand for online access.

Throughout all these changes, these successful consortia have been able to return to or revise a shared understanding of their purpose as a touchstone. By contrast, many consortia that did not survive their initial efforts struggled in this area. The short-lived Higher Education Center for Urban Studies (Bridgeport, Connecticut), for instance, "was created more as a reaction to a set of evolving circumstances than as either a commitment to meet a need or the consequence of a carefully laid long-range plan."[89] It is little surprise, then, that this collaboration lasted barely more than a decade. Indeed, that it came about at all is unexpected and perhaps best explained by the power of the leadership of H. Parker Lansdale who, as a colleague recalled, was the "heart and soul" of the collaboration and "when he left it dissolved."[90] One study of three failed consortia found a common theme across them: "Mission definition and articulation was a problem for each of the consortia and [led to] the member institutions perceiv[ing] the consortia as ineffective."[91] If the underlying mission is unclear, it becomes difficult to gauge what success looks like, with disagreement and disappointment the likely outcomes. But if the mission is clear, success can be possible, whether driven by, as one guidebook advises, "a shared sense of crisis or of hope" and even when that driver is "accompanied by a shared sense of confusion about what should be done to move forward."[92] Mary Churchill and David Chard describe the difference between the boards of Hampshire College and Wheelock College as each sought a strategic partner in the late 2010s: "At Hampshire, the trustees became sharply divided on the best course of action. . . . Wheelock's trustees were not immune to this challenge but had taken the time to work through their disagreements [so that] when they reached a consensus, they were also motivated to be successful."[93] The motivation and goal should be clear at the outset (or negotiated early on), even if the path ahead remains uncertain. The Wheelock board's consensus helped it find its strategic partner in Boston University. Ironically, Hampshire's struggle to find a partner with whom to merge helped open the door to its continuation as a stand-alone campus within the Five College Consortium.

To be clear, mission clarity does not require lockstep alignment. A history of the Great Lakes Colleges Association says, "Like the elephant of the fable, the association exhibits different characteristics to different observers."[94] The Five College Consortium campuses, for instance, broadly agree that the goal is to be better together than the schools would be separately. But on my listening tour in my early days as executive director, I heard each campus leader express a notion of what "better" looked like for that institution. Hampshire is better able to serve its students in creating their individualized majors because students have access to a set of courses, research materials, equipment, and faculty that no other institution its size can claim. Mount Holyoke's commitment to international engagement benefits from a World Language Center that offers all Five College students access to roughly 50 lesser-taught languages in addition to the dozen or so more commonly taught ones available directly through the campuses, a feat no other residential liberal arts campus in the country can boast. Amherst's ability to recruit faculty is enhanced by the spousal and partner hire program that sets the consortium apart from many other small private colleges. The University of Massachusetts can recruit students to the state flagship campus where they will benefit from access to the resources and opportunities of a major research institution while also being able to enroll in small classes across the valley. And Smith College can operate an engineering major whose small group of faculty can find professional camaraderie with a college of engineering just a few miles away. Though the first example each campus leader offered differed from that of their peers, in truth all five campuses benefit from the expanded course catalog available through cross-registration, the wide array of language instruction, the partner hire program, the shared recruitment activities, the communities of practice, and other pieces of the portfolio too numerous to mention. But the campuses all agree that engagement in the consortium helps them be "better than we are."

Throughout the last century, the motivation to form higher education consortia has come from a combination of external factors—financial, social, demographic, legislative, and technological—and from specific leaders willing and able to take advantage of the moment. In each era, funding might be available . . . or shrinking. Student pipelines might be burgeoning . . . or headed for a cliff. Technology and legislation might be demonstrating the power of connection . . . or sparking the fear of external control. The particulars may vary, but consortia tend to form in moments of disruption. It is worth noting, though, that crisis doesn't always prompt a communal spirit. The current moment in higher education feels disrupted in its own way by the demographic cliff, lack of public confidence in institutions, social unrest after a global pandemic, significant turnover in campus leadership, and the increasingly obvious (and challenging) effects of climate change. We can respond to these disruptions in one of two ways: by holding more tightly onto our individual identities, accomplishments, and resources in hopes the competition will find us on top or by joining together in hopes of lifting all our boats to a better future.

FOR FURTHER EXPLORATION

Step 1. Clarifying Motivation

Perhaps you've joined a campus in an existing consortium or you've been a faculty member in a campus that is part of a consortium, but your work has so far focused on your home campus. Or perhaps you're considering a job on a campus that is part of a consortium. Or you're thinking about starting a collaborative venture. How might you begin to wrap your hands around what this partnership is or could be?

The three axes of the consortial cube—"Geography," "Mission," and "Scope"—provide a starting point. Where do/might we sit in the consortial cube? Are our partners geographically close or distant? Are our missions closely aligned or varied? Is the work we want to do together limited or comprehensive? What do we have in common with our current/potential partner institutions? What unique features or resources do we bring to the table? How does our positioning on this grid affect the shape of our organization: its mission, governance, staffing, and so forth?

There is no best position on this grid. The right position is the one that suits the partners' interests, needs, and resources. In general, at least one of these areas ought to be narrow, and at least one ought to be broad. That is to say, the institutions need to have something in common—either geography or mission or a specific shared need on which to build the collaboration. And the institutions should also differ in some key way in order to complement one another and make the collaboration worthwhile: either the campuses operate in different communities, or the missions don't significantly overlap, or the scope of potential shared projects is broad because each institution is bringing a different strength or resource to the table.

Beyond those basics, some additional questions can help us to get oriented or to begin exploring or expanding a partnership. The focus here is on ensuring a clear motivation. Each partner may contribute different resources and receive different benefits from participation, but as a group we should be able to articulate a shared vision and set of expectations.

- What is our motivation and what are we trying to accomplish? Why does/should this collaboration exist? To what end? Is our primary goal to improve quality, save money, enhance experimentation, try some combination of the above, or is it something else entirely? The strategic planning tools and worksheets designed by David LaPiana and his team can provide extra support in articulating shared interests: www.lapiana.org/insight/the-nonprofit-strategy-revolution-2/ (more on this in Chapter 3).

- Who is the "we" in this collaboration? Is the motivation driven by the presidents? Provosts? Directors of libraries or information technology or another unit of the campuses? Do we expect or need engagement across many layers of our institutions, or is this a targeted collaboration in one specific area of our campuses? We'll look later at who does the daily work of collaboration, but for the moment, who are the leaders of these efforts?
- What is happening around us that is shaping our interest in collaboration in this moment? Are we responding to a particular disruption? Are new leaders on the campuses? Is new legislation expected? Is a shift in enrollment underway or anticipated?
- Who else is doing this kind of work? Are there existing consortia we should be aware of and might learn from? Have similar activities been documented (e.g., in a report to a funder or as a consortial history)? The Association for Collaborative Leadership website (www.national-acl.org/) is a helpful resource here.
- Wherever we are today (from imagining a new consortium to managing a long-standing one), what will it look like in a year if we make good progress on our goals? What could we be celebrating in 12 months' time if we're successful? Do we collectively share the motivation required to get us there?

The answers to these questions might already exist in founding documents, by-laws, and job descriptions, or you might be sketching them on a cocktail napkin in between sessions at a conference. The form and particulars matter less than the fact that a shared motivation and explicit expectations can be articulated as you undertake the work ahead.

CHAPTER TWO

"Things Can Be Done" (Optimism)

Hurdles will exist and can be overcome.

TWO THINGS ARE true in consortia. The possibilities for collaboration are endless. And all of them are hard. Undertaking collaboration requires both an openness to the range of opportunities and an awareness of the effort each will demand. The allure and the caution find their balance in optimism—the confidence that things can be done, that hurdles will exist but can be managed, that the effort will be worthwhile in the end. It requires, as one scholar called it, an "enthusiasm for the possible."[1] One place to find and feed that optimism is in examples of what others have accomplished, in stories of successful projects that seem impossible but for the fact that they exist. And lest that optimism become too wide-eyed, we can temper our enthusiasm with cautionary tales of seemingly simple projects that failed to take root.

As noted in Chapter 1, there is no inherently good or bad combination of campuses for the purpose of collaboration; it's a question of how the leaders of those campuses approach the possibility of partnership. Similarly, no shared projects are inherently good or bad. When the will exists to try something together, it is possible to do almost anything well, providing the participants have the vision needed to see—or to build—the right circumstances. As one author put it in an essay tellingly titled "The Limits of Cooperation": "The chief executive officer of a consortium must be an eternal optimist. Anyone who has 'been there' knows the advantages that accrue from having such a mindset. It means that you face challenges with confidence. It means that you bring a work ethic that says 'Things can be done.' It means that success is expected. Molding educational and institutional diversity into an organization with common goals requires a positive, confident attitude. Constraints and roadblocks are everywhere."[2] Lest one doubt the severity of the roadblocks, consider this tale from the Five College Consortium (FCI), told by Stuart Stoke (Four College Coordinator, 1961–1964) to a successor, E. Jefferson Murphy (1975–1987): "The early days often encountered opposition. I recall a senior faculty member who, when hearing that I was to be the coordinator, said vigorously to me 'Kill it.' Expending some of your own college's money on four colleges seemed to be seriously close to treason."[3]

Murder and treason may be extreme (and, one hopes, hyperbolic) reactions to the prospect of collaboration, but one should be prepared to meet with reluctance in the early going. (One scholar of collaborative leadership notes that the word "collaborate," which we are using here as a near-synonym for cooperate, has a second meaning more akin to collusion, as in "collaborating with the enemy."[4]) Indeed, the naysayers and challenges don't ever fully disappear, but each success brings with it a dose of confidence for the next effort. One consortial leader described such successes as "a magic time" in a collaboration, when participants shift from an individual to a group mindset and begin "thinking that they are we instead of I," noting that this magic tends to happen "when they have solved a problem together and done it well. Once they do that it's an amazing thing." Another leader talked about this mental shift as "the aha moment," when suddenly potential collaborators "see the connections of how addressing a particular issue not only helps their small liberal arts school but a community college or a four year [*sic*] public research institution with over 25,000 students compared to a campus with under 1,000."[5] The first president of the Great Lakes Colleges Association called this "the contagion of shared experimentation."[6]

Consortial work is a balancing act. The participating campuses are—and typically want to remain—independent institutions. And they want to gain something through collaborating with other institutions—generally either an expansion of opportunities or a reduction in expenses. Consortial portfolios represent the select range of activities in the overlap of a Venn diagram of possibilities: initiatives that allow institutions to maintain their autonomy and distinctiveness while simultaneously bringing a benefit worth whatever time and energy will be required to build it. It may be something they want but don't need or something they need but can't afford. It may be something so large they would be unable to build it alone or so mundane they have no need to stake their reputation on how it is accomplished. And as we'll discuss further in Chapters 3 and 4, even the best ideas require having the right folks at the table at the right time along with sufficient funding if they are to take hold. As one scholar put it, campus change begins with "an untidy cocktail of quests for power, competing views, rational calculation and manipulation."[7] Transforming that cocktail into a successful collaborative brew requires persistence, imagination, optimism, and often luck. There is a Goldilocks quality to the work of building a consortial portfolio. The synchronicity, when it happens, feels magical and helps spur the optimism needed to try again. The range of ideas and possibilities for collaboration is endless, but the number of successful initiatives is relatively small. Given this imbalance between potential and payoff, it can be all too easy to become discouraged and walk away. In the face of so many hurdles, optimism is essential.

What do consortia do? Anywhere there is need, capacity, or interest can be the focus of collaboration. Library acquisitions, study abroad, faculty development, risk management, software subscriptions . . . If it's a noun it can be shared. Any person, place, thing, or idea can be the starting point.

A faculty member's appointment can be split across several campuses. A staff member can be shared when each campus needs less than one full-time equivalent (FTE) of effort in an area, such as a theater production worker, insurance claims processor, information technology accessibility coordinator, Title IX investigator, or emergency manager. These arrangements come about for one of several reasons. Maybe a campus wants to hire in a new area but can't afford (or doesn't need) a full-time position, or the expertise is so specialized that it can't simply be added to another employee's portfolio. A frequent solution is to contract out for such work, often at rates far above what would be necessary for a staff salary and without the benefits of being embedded in the campus culture. A shared hire can bring stability and alignment. The arrangement may be temporary, until funds can be found for each campus to make a full-time hire or until the position can be proven essential. These arrangements can also be long-term solutions, particularly for small campuses, and each successful partnership can build the model and the trust for additional collaborations.

An off-site storage facility can be co-owned. An office building or performance venue or residence hall can be shared. A meeting space can be available to multiple campuses. Again, these can be temporary solutions or more permanent. In one recent example, a residence hall fire on one campus just before the start of term prompted that campus to partner with another institution in an existing consortium for temporary residential space. The second institution happened to be underenrolled and benefited from the revenue of filled beds. Insurance covered many of the costs, including the supplemental shuttle bus service to transport students back and forth. In the category of more long-standing partnerships, FCI has for decades owned a field station on behalf of the member campuses, providing research and teaching access to a unique ecological site, and FCI in turn partners with The Nature Conservancy (TNC) to manage the property, leveraging TNC's conservation and land-management expertise and personnel.

A piece of expensive laboratory equipment can be shared. Heavy landscaping machinery might not be needed daily on each campus and can transported. Cots for an emergency shelter are stored in a trailer, co-owned by the campuses and available for deployment as needed. Software, subscriptions, and insurance can be negotiated on behalf of a group, providing broader access or better coverage at lower rates.

Library acquisitions and deaccessioning can be coordinated so that nearby libraries need not duplicate infrequently used but important items.

Academic work can be discussed, produced, and presented in multicampus events. Grant proposals can be submitted collaboratively. Courses can be made available across campuses. Professional development workshops can be offered to consortium members. Speakers can be co-invited for public lectures or brought in to meet with classes on several campuses, enabling campuses to share speaker fees and travel expenses.

Libraries, procurement, and courses are perhaps the most common shared activities. But professional development, transportation, and advocacy are also popular, and the full list is difficult to catalog. A 2010 study by the Association for Collaborative Leadership—the national association of consortia—made an attempt and produced a list of programming activity in its member consortia that included professional and faculty development; cross-registration; academic, library, and international programs; purchasing and information technology; emergency preparedness and planning; economic development and sustainability programs; legislative and public advocacy; faculty appointments and faculty exchanges; and programs to enhance access to higher education.[8]

These examples can all work. Indeed, each of them has worked in at least one consortium. But the concept for a new collaboration is only the starting point. Sharing can be possible in the abstract and yet fail to be realized for any number of reasons. Key personnel can be distracted by crises or simply by a daily workload that leaves no room for envisioning new possibilities. Timing can be not quite right, with leadership turnover or a pending strategic plan placing one campus in a holding pattern and unable to make new commitments. A new leader might still be learning their community and their trustees and be unwilling to make a bold decision until they have built some social capital. Often, though, the obstacles are mundane. Campus A needs to renew a vendor contract in the next month, while Campus B just signed with a different vendor, and Campus C workflows feel set in stone and would need to be altered to agree to a joint contract. Or it just isn't possible to find enough meeting times with the right people in the room to do the work of alignment. Or Manager X had a falling out with Manager Y years ago, and the two are uninterested in working together. For so many reasons, it is often simply easier to go it alone.

Consider the case of one consortium's efforts to share a seemingly straightforward purchasing contract. At the start of the project, the group thought "standard 8.5 × 11 white paper seemed simple enough." What they quickly uncovered was a tangle of issues that was anything but simple.

> In fact, antitrust regulations limit access to pricing information across multiple institutions. Consortium management spent a fair amount of time with our attorney ensuring that we would not stumble into an illegality. To add to the complication, there was no consistent standard for paper among the member schools: some needed white paper, others needed recycled paper, still others expected desktop delivery by their vendor, some insisted their logo be on the packaging, and so on. Pricing? No one could disclose, except through a blind survey submitted to the consortium with an agreement about confidentiality. . . . Worse, we believed few of the eleven members would switch vendors based on the price of a single category of item, nor should they.

This organization eventually found ways around, over, and through such hurdles, noting that "the inquiry began to peel back the layers," but clearly it was not straightforward: "Simply identifying inefficiencies or redundancies is not solution implementation."[9] Another consortium reported taking eight years to develop a joint purchasing program: "Until the very end of the process, the institutions simply were not ready to make a commitment—a commitment that, once made, produced major benefits and a basis for expanded cooperation."[10]

These conversations take time in part because there are so many details, overlaps, and conflicts to uncover and negotiate. But as an American Council on Education (ACE) report on curricular collaborations reminded readers, "Working through mechanics is not the only objective of such working groups." These groups, committees, and task forces are also about building relationships, trust, and optimism. One faculty member explained how engaging in extended conversation with peers "changed people's minds from 'We have never done it that way' to 'Well, maybe we could try this' to 'We could change our rules.'"[11]

Another organization—this one a partnership between campuses and local businesses intended to support school-to-work transitions—found that a lack of communication about specifics could derail seemingly solid plans. Early in the project, the school personnel asked the business partners if they were "willing to have students come to your business to learn about what you do," and all said yes. Once the program was underway, schools contacted the businesses "to arrange for students to spend about a week at the job site, 'shadowing' employees" and found the businesses surprisingly reluctant, with just 15% agreeing to accept students. The rest said, "I thought you meant, 'Could students come for an afternoon tour of the facility?' Having kids here for a week would disrupt our business." That simple miscommunication had repercussions for the rest of the partnership because "school personnel felt the businesses led them astray, and the businesses ended up thinking school people were pushy and didn't understand the 'real world.'"[12]

"Institutional collaboration and its management," said one scholar, "is often fragile and irrational."[13] And it is also, that same scholar noted, "increasingly important" in our educational landscape, which means we must find ways to navigate the fragility and irrationality. Cost savings can result from some consortial efforts, to be sure. But, frequently, an up-front investment of time and human resources is required to see the payoff. Consider, for example, the creation of FCI's Risk Management office, which manages insurance procurement, among other things. Grant funding encouraged the campus chief financial officers and their teams to meet and determine that procuring insurance together could be beneficial. From the time of the first discussions to the first documented cost savings (jointly negotiated coverage for a specific policy, at a rate below that of individual institutions) was about three years. And each year after that a new policy or two got negotiated, adding to the savings. But a cross-campus group of people needed to sit in a room long enough to decide they were willing to collaborate and then agree on the particulars of what that would look like. How much coverage do we each want or need? What deductible are we willing to accept? How much can we each afford to pay for our portion? All the work of going to market individually still needs to happen, along with the added complexity of considering everyone's needs, priorities, and budgets. Once that ground has been paved, it becomes easier to move along the next time, but it takes intention and effort. It may be possible to elide some of this work, such as by presidential mandate, but there's peril in that approach, as the power of collaboration comes in large part from the process of coconstructing it. As important as it is, this investment of effort is becoming harder to countenance in an era when the average tenure of a college president is less than six years. A new president would have to initiate a consortial effort immediately on arrival to have any hope of seeing a reasonable payoff before their term is up.

If the entirety of a collaboration focused on 8 ½ × 11 paper, the work entailed would hardly be worth the effort. But leaders on these campuses were convinced that engaging in a broad portfolio of sharing would be well worth it. Paper was just the beginning, but an important one, uncovering challenges and offering a model for future negotiations. As one consortium leader said, "We probably all have one—some small pilot project between a couple of campuses [that] suddenly revealed that we *can* create a model for sharing and communicating and getting things done."[14] The long view is essential in this work, which itself is hard in an era when campus leaders are rotating quickly in what one study participant called the "constant churn of leadership." In one 6-year period at FCI, for instance, 14 of the 15 core campus leaders turned over at least once, and one campus saw 4 different presidents in 15 months. Consensus and commitment don't often thrive amid such turnover, which can send even long-standing agreements into chaos. As another study participant noted, "If we're not investing in taking the time to educate people on what this is and why it's valuable and why it's important and get people engaged, then when . . . the president leaves or a leader leaves, they could just decide, I don't want to be a part of this. And it could all fall apart."[15]

As two seasoned consortium leaders note, "To say simply that consortia are about consensus building is to understate the vulnerability of every decision to factors too numerous to estimate."[16] In the face of the potential challenges, a key aspect of the consortial mindset is optimism, the belief that obstacles can be overcome, that good things are possible, that effort and commitment will pay off. The campuses that shared housing after the fire, for instance, benefited from "failed" conversations during the pandemic about potentially sharing summer housing. The COVID-19–era discussions didn't result in sharing at that time but helped the campuses surface the array of issues that needed to be considered, from staffing to dining and from transportation to insurance. In one moment those issues felt insurmountable, but a year later they became manageable. Maybe we can't get the joint vendor contract this time, but can we at least schedule another discussion before the next renewal? Is there preparatory work we can do while we wait for the new president to be installed? Can we gather data or sketch out a plan or locate pilot funding so the new provost might be primed to get an early win when they arrive? Can we schedule some time together to help smooth over disagreements and repair relationships? Or is there a different cross-campus team without these animosities that might be able to move the conversation forward?

As we'll discuss further in Chapters 3 and 4, consortia that have dedicated staff whose daily work is to envision, grow, and sustain collaboration, who can locate and navigate around the obstacles, have an advantage. It's not that campus leaders and staff can't do the same collaboration-building work, but campus personnel have a primary obligation that is not partnership. A campus president, dean, department chair, or facilities director is tasked with caring for their campus or unit first, with collaboration usually seen as a nice add-on . . . when it's possible, relatively easy and straightforward, and clearly benefits either finances or reputation. It makes sense that campus-based folks focus on what they are paid to do: I work on behalf of my campus first, and if that oxygen mask is securely on, *then* I reach out to help others or partner outside. In this mindset, collaboration is an extra, a supplement, something to be thought of *after* attending to all in-house concerns and tasks. It's a bonus but separate from and secondary to the care and feeding of one's home institution.

But what if campus leaders approached their work with a different mindset? If the North Star of a campus leader is not the health of their institution for its own sake but its ability to provide students with the most robust educational opportunities and comprehensive support it can afford, then collaboration becomes not an add-on but a key part of the tool kit. If the goal is not only to secure an individually healthy institution but also to support the overall health of the community or even of higher education broadly, the daily work is not "me first, then maybe us." Instead, it involves thinking about the impact of each campus's work on a larger whole. If the job is to model for students what a healthy democracy looks like, what better example than cross-institutional collaboration? This consortial mindset doesn't ask any campus to give up its distinctiveness or its autonomy or its institutional success, but it does ask leaders to respect and attend to the effects of their distinctiveness and autonomy and success on others. It asks campus leaders to take pride not in amassing all the moving boxes but in distributing those boxes equitably and in supporting those who find themselves without any.

There is great power in approaching the work of higher education leadership from the mindset that working together could make us better than we are. A call to optimism and collaboration is of course far easier said than done. As one consortial leader noted more than 40 years ago, "The first and most pervasive reason why the consortium will not solve every problem in higher education is the fact that in our society—from child-rearing practices to Olympic competition, and from bake-offs to presidential races—competition is not only condoned, but rewarded and encouraged."[17] In this essay on "The Limits of Cooperation," Donald Johnson goes on to detail the structures, attitudes, and misunderstandings that can appear as barriers to what he calls "consorting" but still observes that "one can survive—even actually flourish—amid all the limits on interinstitutional cooperation" if we bear in mind the benefits "so that the limitations and barriers do not paralyze us." Collaboration may not be our default setting, may not be rewarded in the structures that surround us, and may not come easily, but when done well, as one scholar of consortia advocated, it "makes the impossible possible" by "unlocking potential and driving progress."[18]

This optimism can come in part from confidence in a particular type of initiative—for example, that joint procurement will save campuses money or that sharing courses will expand student opportunities. Optimism can also be fed by intangible, elusive, ineffable confidence that collaboration will be valuable even if the specifics aren't yet visible or can't be calculated in advance.

In the creation of the Claremont Colleges, detractors existed. "It is obvious that such a plan bristles with difficulties," Pomona graduate E. H. Kennard conceded in the campus magazine. Even so, he called upon his fellow alumni and campus leaders to forge ahead with bold optimism, arguing that the vision of a collection of small, interconnected campuses

> can be made to succeed only by a group of men and women who believe in its possibilities and will patiently seek the goal through decades of effort. These devoted spirits will have to resist continually the common American passion for seeking the easiest course and the utmost simplicity. . . . The start must be made in such a way as to commit Pomona definitely to the broad outlines of the plan. The only way to accomplish this would seem to be *to walk boldly out into the sagebrush and stake out college number two*.[19]

Claremont had the advantage of building from scratch, it is true. In most cases such altruism and faith are unlikely to be present or viable in the early days. Most consortia begin with more concrete, measurable, and limited goals.

In choosing a potential project, it's important that each campus maintain its distinct identity and autonomy, but that leaves room for two broad types of collaborative efforts. The easier and perhaps more obvious space is in what are loosely called "back-office functions," the things you would not tout on the cover of your alumni magazine or include in your prospective student tour—they are necessary but not unique. Procurement is a frequent example, as are human resources, facilities management, custodial services, risk management, and emergency preparedness. Even professional development might fit this category, since training in areas like cybersecurity and supervisory skills are unlikely to be institutional differentiators. Typically, the driver here is a desire for cost savings, but the benefits may be found in quality as well. Sharing professional development offerings across campuses, for instance, can allow for a broader array of training. Partnering on providing counseling services can enable campuses to have access to expertise in diverse areas of practice. Sharing these administrative functions is also appealing because, often, fewer stakeholders are involved. Few folks care who owns the off-site library storage facility, as long as they can have books delivered from it quickly and easily.

Less obvious than these administrative functions are the big-ticket opportunities—those offerings that (far from being behind the scenes and invisible) are highly public "value-adds" that would be difficult or impossible for a single campus to do alone. The Five College Center for World Languages, for instance, offers dozens of less commonly taught languages, which supplement the 15 or so languages that a single campus can offer through a more traditional, campus-based department. Collectively hiring a special visiting professor can make it possible for a campus with fewer resources to share in inviting a big-name scholar, as FCI has done with James Baldwin and Joseph Brodsky, or explore a new academic field collectively, as FCI has done in areas from film and media studies to queer, trans, and sexuality studies. FCI has also partnered to provide internships, field trips, and research opportunities in areas such as geology, astronomy, and coastal and marine sciences, to name just a few. A single campus might struggle to support undergraduate access to a world-class telescope, but a jointly funded partnership with a major observatory can make it possible. Intercampus transportation is one example of a less "exciting" but still significant shared function that can facilitate many other collaborations. Two volumes of essays by established leaders in consortial work describe additional collaborative project examples in detail: *Pushing the Boundaries of Collaboration: What Consortia Can Accomplish* (2016) and *Leveraging Resources Through Partnerships* (2002).[20]

And yet . . . no matter how compelling the idea, there are so many reasons not to do this work, so many ways it can go wrong. In the words of one consortial leader, "Think of it as juggling a ball. Keeping one ball in the air is relatively easy. As additional balls are added, the task becomes increasingly difficult. The same can be said for creating and managing successful collaborations. The powerful impact of these factors is revealed when they are considered together and the effects of their interactions are recognized."[21]

How do we skillfully juggle all these balls? How do we balance optimism and caution? Acknowledging the difficulties but temporarily setting them aside can be an important starting point. In 2008, the English professor Peter Elbow described what he called the "believing game" as a counterpoint to the "doubting game" that describes how so many of us in academia respond to new ideas. In the doubting game, we question, poke, criticize, and attempt to disassemble new ideas, all with an eye toward ensuring the ideas that succeed are the strongest, most reliable, most defensible. In the academic search for truth, the doubting game serves a critical purpose, and it is a skill for which many of us have been trained and rewarded. "The doubting game represents the kind of thinking most widely honored and taught in our culture. It's sometimes called 'critical thinking.' It's the disciplined practice of trying to be as skeptical and analytic as possible with every idea we encounter. By trying hard to doubt ideas, we can discover hidden contradictions, bad reasoning, or other weaknesses in them—especially in the case of ideas that seem true or attractive. We are using doubting as a tool in order to scrutinize and test."[22] In scholarly academic work, this doubting and critical thinking are essential to the process and help produce quality research. But in administrative work (whether collaborative or not), relying on doubt can bring everything into question, often in ways that impede progress. If one's goal is not to find the truth but to nurture and pursue and achieve a vision, this skepticism and critique can be deadly if engaged in too early in the process. Building and sustaining a consortium (or a single campus) is a different venture than building and transmitting knowledge. New ideas can easily be destroyed by such skepticism. And so Elbow asks that we develop an additional skill, "the disciplined practice of trying to be as welcoming or accepting as possible to every idea we encounter," not to replace doubting but to deploy from time to time, thoughtfully. Elbow calls this the "believing game," in which the goal is

> not just listening to views different from our own and holding back from arguing with them; not just trying to restate them without bias; but actually trying to believe them. We are using believing as a tool to scrutinize and test. But instead of scrutinizing fashionable or widely accepted ideas for hidden flaws, the believing game asks us to scrutinize unfashionable or even repellent ideas for hidden virtues. Often we cannot see what's good in someone else's idea (or in our own!) till we work at believing it. When an idea goes against current assumptions and beliefs—or if it seems alien, dangerous, or poorly formulated—we often cannot see any merit in it.[23]

Once "believing" has nurtured an idea into something of substance that can withstand some examination, the doubting game can and should return. But doubting should be used to strengthen worthwhile initiatives, rather than destroy them all before they've had a chance.

Peter Elbow is not alone in noting the power of actively looking for possibility.[24] The *99% Invisible* podcast by Roman Mars is based, as the show notes explain, on the premise that "design is everywhere in our lives, perhaps most importantly in the places where we've just stopped noticing."[25] In well over 500 episodes, Mars has explored the origins, purposes, and meanings of everything from mile markers to monuments, garbage disposals to quinine, album covers to soccer jerseys. He tells a story, for instance, of the old Montgomery Ward building in Chicago, which has a concrete column at each of its four corners. Mars had noticed the columns and recognized them as unusual but understood them in a new way when an architectural tour guide explained that their purpose was to support not the building but an egalitarian business structure by ensuring no one could have a corner office. His show revels in these details that are right in front of us but invisible unless we take the time to look and to ask.

President Bill Clinton interviewed Roman Mars in 2022 on his own podcast *Why Am I Telling You This?* They discussed the power of viewing the landscape with an informed eye, aware that it came to be with intention . . . and can be changed (again). Mars noted, for example, that the pandemic helped demonstrate that even seemingly static structures such as streets and sidewalks can be adapted and multipurpose: shared and used to provide space to gather (think sidewalk dining) as opposed to simply being paths to traverse the city. The disruption of lockdown and the necessity of finding new ways to go about our daily lives, Mars explained, "kind of dislodges us to think about the possibilities that these built structures that seem so permanent, so fixed, are really malleable reflections of our values, and they can always be reexamined and . . . they really can change."[26]

I'm reminded of Carol Dweck's concept of the growth mindset, the power of believing that our talents are not established at birth but are shaped and changeable throughout our lives.[27] Mars's idea might be a malleability mindset, the power of believing that our physical and institutional surroundings, too, are capable of being reshaped throughout their lives. Mars was thinking of cities, roads, and urban landscapes and Dweck of children and students, but this concept of malleability—and belief in that malleability—might apply, too, to higher education and to consortial efforts. What do we see daily without seeing its potential? Dweck's point in part is that mindset can help or hinder growth, regardless of biological underpinnings. Mars similarly suggested that if we cede power and potential by believing in the fixedness of our surroundings, the established status quo *does* tend to remain. What might we change if we believed we could?

Mars is well acquainted, as am I, with the legacy of urban planner Robert Moses and depictions of him by Robert Caro in *The Power Broker* and by Langdon Winner in *The Whale and the Reactor*.[28] Winner's assertion that "artifacts have politics" is canon in the history of technology, thanks largely to his and Caro's memorable depiction of Robert Moses's structures as having fixed and limited functions that constrain who can use them and how—from highways that bisect and destroy neighborhoods to bridges too low for buses to pass under, thus limiting who can access the beach beyond. These constraints surely exist in our institutions and our infrastructure, but capitulating to their power is not in the consortial mindset.

How can we nurture the malleability mindset and encourage playing the believing game? Campus leaders and consortial staff can help. One study of 50 collaborative initiatives cited "strong leadership in the process" as key to success. The kinds of skills called upon in this process included "keeping stakeholders at the table through periods of frustration and scepticism [*sic*], acknowledging small successes along the way, helping stakeholders negotiate difficult points and enforcing group norms and ground rules."[29]

In addition to guiding specific initiatives and programs, consortial boards, advisory groups, and other cross-campus gatherings should be (and should provide for others) spaces to explore what the campuses *could* do together. There must be space for possibility, for dreaming. For those possibilities to have the chance to grow requires transparency, even vulnerability. Share ideas, possibilities, priorities (and resources). Experiment with believing together. Ask, "What if?" Be open to sharing credit for an idea, program, or initiative and encourage the players to keep at it as the doubting game enters the fray. The pandemic forced every campus to enter the believing game because there was no room for an alternative. Campus leaders had to think creatively and on a short timeline, had to move ahead with the hope that all would turn out well. Can we retain that open-minded flexibility without the fear of death spurring us on? Can we be driven instead by the optimism that collaboration can make us better than we are, and by the curiosity to explore how we might go about it?

When we speak of consortia, we often think of the formal, structured arrangements that drive reputations and cost savings. But behind these concrete and clearly identifiable accomplishments lies a deep network of informal activity and relationships that help support the whole. Informal and loose partnerships exist alongside established and systematized governance structures (and can often form the basis for deeper engagement over time). Many campus employees first encounter the work of the consortium in a community of practice: an interdisciplinary faculty seminar where pre-tenure professors share their work in progress, their daily challenges on the tenure track, and their lives outside of work; a leadership development program where mid-career faculty explore ways to contribute to their campus in the next phase of their work lives; an occasional lunch or videoconference for staff in facilities or procurement to discuss upcoming projects and vendor experiences; a writing accountability group or a cross-campus disciplinary conversation in which peer faculty share thoughts on curriculum planning or emerging issues in their field. These semistructured opportunities for engagement can lead to jointly sponsored speakers, cross-campus miniconferences, and shared events such as a poetry prize, a film festival, or an entrepreneurship competition. While none of these collaborations require a consortial structure, even a small amount of support—staff to help schedule meetings, space in which to gather, funding to incentivize and seed new experiments (and food, always food)—can move a collaboration from being the topic of a brief impromptu conversation ("Wouldn't it be nice if . . .") to a fully formed idea taking root.

FCI and many of our sister consortia depend on these gatherings to set the stage for everything else in the portfolio. Phillip DiChiara, formerly head of The Boston Consortium, describes the importance of such conversations in setting the stage for optimism: "Dialogue leads to relationships, relationships lead to trust, and out of trust comes opportunity."[30] These interactions may seem insignificant, but the pandemic highlighted their importance, as some groups met more regularly thanks to videoconference platforms and the urgent issues of the moment, and other groups paused to make room for the extra work of adapting to the crisis or had been meeting in person and did not or could not shift to virtual meetings. In my experience—and in that of many of my consortial colleagues, if annual conference conversations are any indication—groups that began or continued to meet during the pandemic have emerged stronger, and groups that took a pause have struggled to come back to prepandemic levels of collaboration.

As important as optimism is, it's also crucial to know when to walk away, when an initiative is not viable or has been successful but is no longer needed. As participants in one study noted, failure need not always be something to avoid: "If you really want to increase the success rate at the consortium, by definition the failure rate is going to increase. You need to experiment closer and closer to the edge. If everything we do is successful, we're not trying hard enough, we're not pushing the envelope."[31] Consortial programs often have a life cycle. Shared initiatives may make sense at a particular moment in time but can either mature to the point that sharing is no longer necessary or respond to needs that no longer exist. For example, an emerging interest in electronic music in the 1960s led to the creation of the Five College Electronic Music Studio, located at Hampshire College. After a few years, three other campuses established their own independent versions of that studio and its equipment. As the Five College Coordinator noted, "A pessimist might call it a set-back—cooperation was cumbersome and difficult. . . . An optimist would say that this was a resounding success. We cooperated on an expensive experiment but found that demand for the facilities was so great that each institution, to be viable, should now offer this new tool for study on its own campus."[32]

Similarly, in 2005 the campuses of FCI developed a Five College Film Studies major. At the time no campus had the array of faculty and courses needed to support an entire credential, but the five together could offer a respectable program. Over time, as the discipline matured and student interest grew, each campus added faculty and coursework in film and media studies. By the early 2020s, the campuses began to establish stand-alone film majors at each institution, and the shared program is now winding down. Students on any campus can and do continue to benefit from coursework on the others, but cross-registration is no longer required to enable a student to complete a major in film; faculty can and do continue to benefit from engagement with the larger Five College film community but now have colleagues on their home campus as well.

Sometimes shared activity helps seed development of individual programs on the campuses and becomes duplicative; other times the collaboration makes sense in one moment and ceases to be viable as the marketplace changes. Early in its existence, the Associated Colleges of the Midwest (ACM) developed a set of shared off-campus study programs with external grant funding. For over half a century, ACM provided valuable support to the consortium's member campuses wanting to offer international and domestic off-campus study programming. The scale of the collective made these programs affordable and logistically feasible. But by the early 2000s, third-party providers had entered the market and were able to offer the benefits of operating at an even greater scale. After 20 years of declining enrollments and internal efforts to address concerns, the board appointed a review committee and accepted its recommendation to sunset all ACM international off-campus study programs in 2019. By 2023 the consortium had closed all its domestic study-away programs but continued to offer such opportunities to students through two third-party providers.[33] ACM's experience illustrates the importance of continual review of the consortium's portfolio and awareness of the evolving landscape in which it functions, along with a willingness to reconsider the shape of a program that has long been a signature offering.

Making programming decisions about which initiatives to undertake, which to revise, and which to sunset is at least as challenging in a consortial setting as on an individual campus, and a structured process for review and action can be helpful. David LaPiana developed a useful strategic planning framework for nonprofit organizations, which we'll discuss in more detail later. A key tool in LaPiana's workbook is the strategy screen, a rubric based on the organization's mission and priorities that can be used to assess potential initiatives. At FCI we adapted LaPiana's model into a version that suits our particular needs. We identified costs and benefits against which we can measure any initiative, and for each of those criteria, we assign one of four scores, based on the extent to which the initiative would be a strong contributor to the overall FCI portfolio.

For FCI, a successful (or promising) shared initiative should have at least some of these characteristics:

- It should either save financial and human resources or at least be cost-neutral.

- It should build on a strength the campuses either have or want to achieve.
- It should serve a community significant enough to be worth the investment.
- It should align with campus missions and strategic plans.
- It should be at least as viable if done together as individually.
- It should support a culture of collaboration.
- It should improve equity and access.

Other organizations may identify a different set of criteria for their purposes or rate them differently. In FCI's case the list is not in priority order, not all initiatives in our portfolio share all these characteristics, and most initiatives accomplish more in some of these areas than in others. In addition, we always have room for an initiative that doesn't meet these criteria, provided leadership has determined there is interest and need. The list is meant to help focus conversation and prioritize activity, not to prematurely reject an idea that might be beneficial in ways not considered here or that might respond to an emerging and unanticipated need.

At FCI we've taken this list a step further, creating a rubric to assess initiatives, as shown in Table 2.1. Note that the rubric doesn't gauge the *quality* of the initiative or how well it's being carried out; it helps analyze whether the initiative is one that could benefit from collaboration.

A few things are important to note about this screening tool. First, it was developed by FCI staff in close consultation with our provosts, chief financial officers (CFOs), and board of directors and was approved by each of those groups. That buy-in has been critical, and the tool reflects consensus about the criteria that mattered to the campuses when it was adopted. It is also fair and honest to say that on many occasions the tool isn't directly used, but its existence (and annual renewal) helps to keep decision-makers aligned in how we think about opportunities.

Second, it has changed over time. We developed a temporary version for use during the pandemic to explore which programs needed continuing funding and support while the campuses were closed or in

Table 2.1 Sample Project Screening Tool

		Strong contributor *Score 5 points*	**Moderate contributor** *Score 3 points*	**Weak contributor** *Score 1 point*	***Noncontributor*** *Subtract 5 points*
COSTS	Financial	____ Saves campuses money or is cost-neutral (e.g., one-time expense covered by grant/gift)	____ Requires minimal to modest expense	____ Requires substantial new or additional campus investment	*____ Requires substantial new investment and/or has no identified source of funding*
COSTS	Human	____ Reduces necessary staffing compared to alternatives (or predecessors)	____ Relies on existing staff (i.e., no changes needed)	____ Requires new/additional staff hiring or substantial (re)training or is redundant with campus staffing	*____ Requires extensive skills not found in or desired by FCI or member campuses*
BENEFITS	Strength	____ Adds to an existing strength or establishes a new strength area	____ Enables maintenance of an existing strength or prevents loss of existing strength	____ Supports a noncore project; not tied to an existing or desired strength	*____ Would be detrimental to existing strengths*
BENEFITS	Audience	____ Serves a large or critical community across all five campuses	____ Serves a significant or important community at three or more campuses	____ Serves a primarily external or supplemental audience	*____ Does not have an identified audience with interest in this area*
BENEFITS	Mission	____ Mission critical to campuses (they would find a way to do this even if FCI didn't exist)	____ Aligns with campus missions/priorities	____ Supplemental to campus missions/priorities	*____ Orthogonal to campus missions/priorities*
BENEFITS	Viability	____ Campuses could not do this alone (e.g., funder requires submission via a consortium)	____ Campuses would struggle to do this alone, or FCI can do it more efficiently or better	____ Campuses could do this without FCI support/involvement	*____ Campuses already do this without FCI assistance*
BENEFITS	Collaboration	____ Actively nurtures or furthers collaboration across the campuses	____ Maintains existing collaboration across the campuses	____ Allows collaboration	*____ Works against collaboration*
BENEFITS	Equity	____ Actively nurtures or furthers equity	____ Enables improvements in equity	____ Maintains existing levels of equity	*____ Works against equity*
		Total strong score: ____	Total moderate score: ____	Total weak score: ____	Total negative score: ____

TOTAL SCORE (for Discussion, Not Determinative, Purposes): ______
Highest possible score: 40
Lowest possible score: –40
Ideal cutoff for inclusion: 30

lockdown and which should be paused until we returned to more normal functions. Because it has been tailored to local interests and priorities and to fit a particular moment, it should not simply be adopted elsewhere in its current state. A worksheet is provided at the end of this chapter to help craft a similar tool in other settings.

Third, although the tool asks users to assign scores, it is intended and used as a conversation tool rather than a quantitative or formulaic instrument. For example, when the Five College Provosts Council and FCI staff used the tool to review a slate of existing academic programs, each member independently completed the screen for each program and then compared notes during meetings. If everyone's scores agreed the program was a strong contributor overall, little discussion was needed. If scores were mixed, the tool helped us see where the disagreements arose—sometimes enrollment in a program was strong on one campus but consistently low on another, for instance—and guided conversation toward a consensus based on the overall costs and benefits. Low scores did not necessarily result in a program closing or losing funding, but did provide an opportunity to consider carefully the reasons for the low scores. One program served a largely off-campus population, for instance, and therefore did not initially seem to align well with campus missions, but one provost advocated that its existence helped persuade faculty to relocate here due to the vibrant community offerings, making it a selling point for that campus. Another program had mediocre scores but was in an area that would have been politically difficult for the provosts to cancel in that moment, so they chose instead to invest in strengthening the program, which effectively improved its scores.

Two further lessons should be mentioned here related to assessing a consortial portfolio. One is that not every campus needs to participate in every joint venture. It is better that only those who can fully commit be in the mix on a given project. The other is that in the early days of a consortium (and often in the early days of new campus leaders in a consortium), there is a tendency to count pennies, to track whether each initiative has an appropriate return on investment, and to assess each initiative as a "tub on its own bottom" (in an old phrase used more recently to describe the Harvard budgeting process).[34] As Phillip DiChiara of The Boston Consortium once noted: "Not every school will be interested in every initiative, but once a portfolio of successes has accumulated, it will show a distribution representative of the whole, and with this more sophisticated understanding—and appreciation—of teamwork in place, remaining quid pro quo attitudes typically soften."[35]

As a consortium matures, as leaders become more familiar with and comfortable in their partnerships, and as the portfolio broadens, it becomes easier to assess the success of the consortium not simply as the sum of individual parts but to ask, as is often done by Five College CFOs: "Does the bottom line amount I pay into the consortium each year feel like the right amount given what my campus gets out of it?" This is not to say that individual programs don't get reviewed or that costs should not be thoughtfully set and carefully managed. But it's best not to get lost in the details, counting leaves and missing the benefits of the forest. Fairly often a provost will say something like "This particular project isn't a huge benefit to my campus, and I probably wouldn't pay this much on my own, but I also know that I get a lot from that other project that far exceeds what I put in, so on balance I'm happy." This sangfroid is more likely, too, because in a large consortium with a deep portfolio, some benefits come without a fee. For FCI, as we've noted, cross-registration is a powerful tool for broadening the curriculum, recruiting new students, and meeting the evolving interests of current students and yet no funds change hands: No tuition dollars are exchanged, no dues are required of campuses to participate, and there is no budget line to cover the administrative time spent managing the process. Less measurable, perhaps, but equally important, the camaraderie of working in a community of peers where you can seek support, advice, and sympathy is highly valuable to campus leaders and doesn't have a price tag attached. When every campus leader, from president and provost to department chairs and Title IX officers, has a built-in community of practice they can turn to, support for the consortium can be bolstered by an appreciation of benefits that don't appear on the annual operating budget.

To help understand how collaborations can operate and how intertwined the costs and benefits can become, it's worth describing the nature of so-called Five College academic programs. A Five College major or certificate is essentially a curriculum collaboratively developed by faculty from multiple campuses that draws on courses from multiple campuses. It is not necessary for all five campuses to participate—some "Five College" programs are in fact a collaboration among three or four campuses. To become a credential that can be awarded to a student, the curriculum must be reviewed, approved, and offered by each participating campus and must at times be adapted to fit that campus's policies. As such, a Five College program might in fact look slightly different on each participating campus. What distinguishes these shared academic programs is the difficulty, if not impossibility, for a student to complete them with courses from a single campus. From an accreditation perspective, the nonprofit entity called FCI does not offer credentials—we facilitate the ability of the student's home campus to offer a credential it could not on its own. Although these programs are described as "Five College" programs, then, they are not offered by FCI, and no campus is compelled to participate in them if doing so does not fit their priorities, needs, or resources.

Cross-registration, also called course interchange or simply interchange, is a critical feature of many shared academic portfolios.[36] In simplest terms, cross-registration is the ability of students from a member campus to enroll in and receive credit for courses from the other member institutions without needing to apply for admission to the other campuses. The details of how that cross-campus enrollment works vary among the consortia that offer it. At FCI the courses are not treated as transfer courses. Each campus has a grade equivalency system that enables the courses to appear on the home transcript with a grade (as opposed to just the credits, as is typically the case with transfer courses). The courses are denoted as having been taken through the Five College system but are otherwise treated as home campus courses for most purposes. In the Five College setting, too, no tuition dollars change hands as a result of these cross-registrations, and no attempt is made to restrict or balance the exchange of students. This is possible in large part because for our consortium cross-registration is just one initiative in a large portfolio. It is difficult, therefore, to assess the costs and benefits of cross-registration as a stand-alone initiative.

Another mechanism for extending an institution's curricular offerings through the consortium is faculty sharing. This can happen through joint appointments, in which a faculty member has teaching and advising obligations on multiple campuses. These professors are housed on a single campus for the purposes of personnel and tenure policies, but the participating campuses each contribute a share of the salary, and input is sought from the partner campuses on reappointments, promotion reviews, and the like. Anyone who has managed cross-college faculty appointments within a large university will find many of the details and pitfalls familiar. Evenly split appointments (50/50 or 33/33/33 and the like) are challenging when it comes to determining where a faculty member should dedicate their service contributions, for instance, so having one campus hold a larger percentage of the appointment than the others is generally best. Similarly, it is the rare (usually senior) faculty member who can be split across five campuses and succeed. Pre-tenure faculty will need attentive and supportive tenure committees and deans or provosts to navigate a split appointment seamlessly. But for all these challenges, joint faculty and staff appointments can help in meeting the needs of a group of campuses each of which requires (or can afford) less than a full-time position. Although we follow certain principles (avoid 50/50 and 5-way appointments, articulate advising and service obligations up front, etc.), each new joint appointment requires a new round of negotiations and there is no single template for what such a shared position will encompass.

Building on joint appointments, the member campuses of FCI also "borrow" faculty from one another, sometimes for a single course to fill an unexpected gap, other times as a visiting appointment for several years. This mechanism supports the campuses in using more tenured and tenure-track faculty and fewer adjuncts. We also manage a spousal/partner-hire initiative that supports dual academic career couples. The provosts have a long and successful history of working with one another to seek out positions for partners of incoming faculty, and a standard funding model enables the two campuses and FCI to share the cost of such positions for a year or two. These partner hires were originally restricted to faculty and lecturer positions, but we have begun to experiment with supporting the placement of partners in administrative and academic staff roles as well. Again, the details, the structures, and the measures of success must be discussed anew each time, though practice and well-tended relationships make the process easier.

We've noted already the importance of having all the right circumstances align—the time, interest, and people to do the work necessary to launch a project. We've mentioned, too, the importance of ongoing commitment in the success of a venture. In addition to serendipity and commitment, optimism, goodwill, and trusting relationships are all essential components of a successful collaboration. Before diving into a new venture, it's important to consider two legalistic caveats as well.

First, a caution should be offered about contracts, memoranda of understanding, service-level agreements, and all manner of written agreements. On the one hand, there is surely value in coming to enough consensus to enable the terms of an agreement to be documented, and there is value, too, in the participants each making their portion of the commitment explicit. As one consortium coordinator put it, "It serves as both a reminder of that commitment and the aspirations of the collaborative venture and remains a useful point of referral when the rocky terrain of collaborative relationships may need to be negotiated."[37] But there is also a risk in translating collegial collaborative intent into impersonal protective legalese, which is too often written with deep suspicion and mistrust. We sign a prenuptial agreement in case the commitment goes south. We sign a legal contract to ensure our business partners don't renege on their commitments and leave us holding the bag. As one participant in a study on consortial trust noted, "Sometimes I feel like when you get down to negotiating contract language, trust is out the door. That's when people bring in their lawyers and it's all about making sure that you can't take advantage of me. None of that is based on trust." A tightly written contract for collaboration can prevent the sort of ongoing adaptation that is critical to success in these ventures. A well-crafted agreement, by contrast, can provide a shared foundation. As another participant in that same trust study saw it, "All they're [attorneys and contracts] trying to do is level the playing field and make sure that everybody plays properly in the sandbox like we're in kindergarten. That's important."[38]

Many of the longest-standing consortia were built in an era when a handshake agreement was considered sufficient. Even among consortia that operate as registered 501(c)(3) organizations and thus have clearly stated missions and by-laws, few have a catalog of contracts for each and every initiative. As society becomes more litigious and as turnover quickens in academic leadership, these handshake agreements are unlikely to be sustainable. The right level of documentation will depend on local circumstances, on the nature of the agreement, and on the risks if something should go sideways. One helpful tip to support crafting language that articulates the intent of a collaboration without suggesting distrust is to envision writing for your successors rather than for the current participants. What would a new provost, director, or president need to know about this initiative? Doing so can enable everyone to assume goodwill in those who've been at the table, while documenting decisions, rationales, and commitments for those who come after and lack the benefit of these early conversations.

Another legal issue to consider is antitrust legislation. There are limits (some clear, some hazy) on what campuses can and cannot do together. The Sherman Anti-Trust Act of 1890 sought "to protect trade and commerce against unlawful restraints and monopolies." Standard Oil had pioneered the concept of a "trust," in which "stockholders in several companies transfer their shares to a single set of trustees [and] in exchange . . . receive a specified share of the consolidated earnings of the jointly managed companies." The Standard Oil umbrella organization could thus operate as a monopoly. This practice spread quickly to other industries in the late nineteenth century, and the Sherman Anti-Trust Act provided a mechanism for the federal government to dissolve these trusts. But as a history of the law explains, "The act was designed to restore competition, but it was loosely worded and failed to define such critical terms as 'trust,' 'combination,' 'conspiracy,' and 'monopoly.'"[39] This lack of clarity in the original language makes for a murky legal landscape today.

Originally targeted at for-profit industries, the first significant antitrust case in higher education came in 1993 around a group of universities "that had engaged in establishing uniform scholarship awards." Since that case, antitrust concerns have also arisen around early-decision admissions, mergers, and a host of other collaborative or potentially collusionary activities: "sharing of information within peer-group institutions, joint buying arrangements, joint establishment of financial aid, joint agreements regarding faculty, shared trustees or officers, licensing of institution-owned intellectual property rights, student housing, accreditation, joint establishment of admissions protocols, and more."[40] And yet one advisory document also notes that not all collaboration is collusion:

> Educational institutions often collaborate and share information with one another, be it formally or informally. Some of these collaborations are in the form of associations, such as higher education consortiums or athletic conferences. Others may be informal, such as the periodic gatherings of administrators from similarly-situated educational institutions. Antitrust laws recognize that competition and services may sometimes be enhanced when competitors collaborate and share information. For example, when competitors set standards or share best practices, the activities often are benign and may serve to benefit consumers.[41]

In short, campuses share lots of things, most of which are okay to share, some of which may not be.

I am not an attorney, nor a specialist in antitrust law, so I won't attempt to offer guidance on the legal implications of any specific collaboration except to suggest that leaders be aware that issues may arise and to seek legal counsel when in doubt. I can recommend a few sources to get a feel for the landscape. The Office of General Counsel at Stanford antitrust guidance memo issued in 2023 provides useful guidelines to consider. Phillip Yao's 2020 article in *The Journal of Law and Education* is instructive, as is a guidance document produced by the National

Association of College and University Attorneys in 2015 by Jennifer Zimbroff et al., as well as the other sources in the notes. The Stanford guidance memo offers this summary:

> As a general proposition, it is worth remembering that what the relevant antitrust laws prohibit is an *agreement* (expressed or implied) that restricts competition, such as an agreement among competitors *to fix prices* (i.e., to set prices at a certain level), or *to divide markets* (e.g., we will not recruit in X area if you do not recruit in Y area), or *to limit employee compensation or recruiting* (such as a "no poaching" or "no hiring" or "wage-fixing" agreement). The US Department of Justice also has an interest in the *information-sharing practices* of universities and hospitals—whether through formal surveys or more informal communications—concerning matters such as fees, salaries and financial aid.[42]

Within the bounds of these legal caveats, and with the caution that anything worthwhile takes effort, almost anything can become a collaborative project. It's important for each of the players to understand and articulate the goal, but it's not critical that all the players share exactly the same goal. Potential collaborators should understand that many factors need to align—a project that on paper is a great idea may take years to find the right moment, and a project that works for many years may need to be sunsetted when it has run its course.

FOR FURTHER EXPLORATION

Step 2. Choosing Things to Be Done

Remember that it's important to engage deeply in the believing game first, approaching the possible with optimism and the confidence that a thing worth doing can be done. Having agreed on a specific motivation behind building a new consortial effort, the brainstorming can begin in earnest. Given the motivation identified in step 1 (at the end of Chapter 1), consortial leaders can begin by generating a list of several potential projects or initiatives to meet the shared goal, knowing they will likely pursue just one of them in the first year or so. The units and functions listed on campus organizational charts can provide some broad areas to consider. As an alternative, the following categories of collaboration cataloged by the Association for Collaborative Learning in 2010 might be helpful in generating ideas:

- Professional and faculty development
- Cross-registration
- Academic, library, and international programs
- Purchasing and information technology (IT)
- Emergency preparedness and planning
- Economic development and sustainability programs
- Legislative and public advocacy
- Faculty appointments and faculty exchange
- Programs to enhance access to higher education

If, for instance, joint purchasing seems like a promising place to begin, planners might identify their five most expensive contracts, compile a list of contracts up for renewal or renegotiation in the next 12–18 months, or identify a particular unit (e.g., dining services or IT) where collaboration seems promising (perhaps because costs have been rising there, or because substantial staff turnover is expected).

Once a vision has taken shape and a few options have been identified that seem worth exploring, is it time to turn to the doubting game, at least briefly, to consider constraints, budgets, logistics, and legalities. At this stage it's helpful to have a tool to guide discussion about the relative merits of each possibility.

The project screening tool worksheet provided in Table 2.2 can be used to build a custom screening rubric for a given place and time and set of partners. The resulting screening tool is meant to help focus conversation and prioritize activity, not to prematurely reject an idea that might have unconsidered benefits or that might respond to an emerging and unanticipated need. The rubric doesn't help gauge the quality of the initiative or how well it's carried out; it helps analyze whether the initiative could benefit from being done collaboratively. Note, too, that the rubric is not intended as a formula to plug options into and then mindlessly act based on numerical values. The intent is to support structured conversation about either an individual initiative or a set of options, to help guide decision-makers' thinking about where to put resources and where to prioritize efforts.

The worksheet should be completed by the leaders guiding this work or drafted by a trusted team for review by the leaders. First, the group should agree on a list of factors that are important to the participating institutions. The worksheet provides some examples, which can be adopted, edited, or amended to suit the team's priorities. Second, the group should agree on a range of descriptors. What would make staffing or facilities or funding favorable or unfavorable toward collaborative effort on a given project, for instance? The worksheet includes four columns, but the group certainly might choose more or fewer categories; the categories might each be assigned point scores as well, though making the tool more quantitative can give the impression that it is more precise than it's meant to be. Third, the group should consider the relative weighting of these factors. Are they all (roughly) equal in importance, or should some loom larger in decision-making?

Consensus is important in creating this rubric, but the tool can be refined along the way, so it's best not to get too bogged down in wordsmithing. The purpose of the screening tool is to help decision-makers on the campuses agree on when it's best to carry out a project together. What conditions must be met for collaboration to make sense? Given our shared motivation, what specific projects, initiatives, or programs can help us achieve our goal? If we already share some activities, how do we determine whether they're still the right ones for our purposes?

Most campus leaders are familiar and comfortable with the notion of peer competitors—those institutions you compete with for students, for faculty, for grant funding, and for other resources. This concept encourages and enables institutions to compare themselves to those peers: Are we spending as much on dining services as our competition: Do we offer comparable employee benefits? Is our admissions office doing outreach in the same range of communities? For a consortial effort, the competition isn't other consortia; it's the member campuses of the consortium itself. The competition we often talk about is between campuses acting alone and campuses acting in collaboration, and this assessment is what the screening tool is designed to support. Can we enact this program

Table 2.2 Project Screening Tool Worksheet

This sample matrix is intended as a rough draft of a screening tool that will support campus decision-making.

Step 1. Agree on factors to consider when assessing whether to pursue or continue a program/initiative/activity.

Step 2. Agree on descriptors for each level of favorability. Note that very few opportunities will score strongly across the board.

Step 3. Consider whether all factors should be weighted equally or whether some will weigh more heavily in decision-making.

Step 1	**Step 2**				**Step 3**
Factors	*Strongly favorable*	*Moderately favorable*	*Neutral*	*Unfavorable*	*Weighting*
Mission alignment	Closely aligned with our mission.	In keeping with our mission.	Neither aligned nor opposed to our mission.	In opposition to our mission.	
Staffing/ expertise	We already have the necessary expertise on staff, with capacity to do this.	We could readily find the needed expertise and/or provide capacity to do this.	We could find and hire experts in this area, but not quickly.	It's unclear that the expertise exists or could be recruited.	
Facilities	We already have the facilities needed to do this (or no special facilities are needed).	We could readily find the facilities needed to do this.	We could create/ build the facilities to do this, but it would take time/money.	We would need to acquire property to even consider building such facilities.	
Funds	The cost to do this would be minimal (or funds are already dedicated to it).	We could readily find the funds to do this.	We could raise the funds to do this, but it would take time and effort.	Donors have told us they won't fund this.	
Competition	. . . does not exist locally (or anywhere).	. . . exists to some extent, but not nearby.	. . . exists, but capacity exists for new offerings.	Others are well established in this space, and there is no capacity for new offerings.	
Audience/ enrollment	The audience already exists (e.g., prospective students are eager for program X).	Audience/ enrollment could be readily built and not interfere with existing programs.	Growth here would come at the expense of our other programs.	No one wants this.	
Timeline	This program could be established quickly.	It would take months to establish this program.	It would take a year or more to build this program.	It's unclear how long this would take—maybe forever.	
Stakeholders	. . . are on board and enthusiastic.	. . . could be persuaded.	. . . are indifferent.	. . . are actively opposed.	
Other (e.g., risk?)__________					
Other__________					
Other__________					

more cheaply or better together than apart? If we pool resources, can we accomplish a goal that would be impossible to do alone?

Once the screening tool is ready, it's time to evaluate the possible collaborative projects against each other. Ideally, a group of decision-makers will individually complete the screen for each potential project and then use the resulting ratings to guide a conversation. Did everyone score the same initiative the highest? Does that agreement pass the gut test, and does it "feel" right or surprising? If disparities exist (as they likely will), why did some scorers view a project more favorably than others? Even for projects that received uniformly low scores, it is often helpful to spend a few minutes examining that uniformity. Did we suspect that project was unlikely even when we included it on the original list? Did it seem viable until we considered all the factors (e.g., the time frame required is longer than we can afford to wait for a payoff)?

Ideally, the rubric helps the team compare potential projects or rate an individual one. It can also help leaders articulate why one project may be chosen or funded over another (especially one that may be popular with a group of stakeholders). If it becomes too complicated to use or if you find yourselves routinely ignoring the resulting scores, it's time to revisit and refine the rubric.

CHAPTER THREE

Governing Together (Generosity)

What goes around . . .

THE MOST WELL-ESTABLISHED consortia in the United States are structured as nonprofit organizations, typically led by an executive director, president, or other chief executive officer hired for the purpose and reporting to a board of directors made up of campus leaders. The choice of which leaders is usually determined by the nature of the collaboration. The Boston Consortium's focus on procurement is consistent with its board of chief financial officers (CFOs). The Big Ten Academic Alliance is guided by the provosts of the member institutions, in keeping with its focus on faculty development and academic programming. The Five College Consortium's board of presidents and a chancellor is in line with the comprehensive nature of its portfolio. Given its focus on libraries and digital literacy, the AMICAL Consortium of American-modeled institutions is guided by representatives from relevant departments on the member campuses. Consortia with large numbers of members tend to use a representative structure, such as the NELLCO Law Library Consortium, which operates under the guidance of a subset of the member library directors.

At first glance this sort of structure will seem familiar to campus leaders who have experience with oversight from a board of trustees or regents, and to be sure there are some commonalities, not least of which is a focus on higher education. Though this experience with governing boards is helpful, it can also be problematic in a consortial context because the structure of a consortial board and the nature of consortial work pose special challenges. And the differences do not exist solely at the level of the board. The presence of an executive director and consortial staff can add complexity to the landscape, as can the nuances of how shared governance and incentive structures operate across the member campuses.

These unique features can, of course, be managed and even provide advantages, but members need to acknowledge them, accept them, and then adapt to them. Those engaged in consortial leadership, from whatever vantage point, should be aware of the differences in this collaborative setting, must accept that those differences are an inherent part of the landscape that cannot be avoided or ignored, and would do well to design roles, structures, and goals that can function in this setting where leadership is distributed, shared, and networked. This acknowledgment, acceptance, and adaptation all benefit from a spirit of generosity that is often lacking or less emphasized in single-campus leadership. We need, then, a different model and a different mindset to understand and undertake leadership, decision-making, and strategic planning in a consortial setting.

In this chapter, we'll explore the unique aspects of collaborative leadership, consider the roles of boards of directors and executive directors and their relationship to each other, and look at the forms strategic planning and governance can take in this uniquely shared environment, highlighting the importance of generosity in navigating this unusual space.

Higher education, broadly speaking, wasn't built for this sort of collaborative work. If it were, we wouldn't need the lure of external funding or the fear of financial crisis to be interested in cross-institutional partnership. Frank E. Vandiver, one-time president of Texas A&M University, ascribed the widespread reluctance to collaborate to "habit, history, and hubris," though a contemporary consortial leader cautioned in response that "their relative absence does not necessarily make cooperation easy."[1] Another student (and supporter) of consortia warned against overly lofty expectations of cross-campus collaboration: "Claims that consortia can bring about substantial institutional change, revolutionize the current delivery model, or overcome the institutions' inclinations to compete with one another are not only unrealistic but also may be perceived as threatening to potential consortium members."[2] As one ACE report explained, daily academic decision-making is already complicated, but the governance of shared academic programs is even more challenging "because such alliances are uncharted territory for most academic leaders," and these leaders are attempting to navigate this new territory across different cultures, environments, processes, and procedures.[3]

In 1974, Franklin Patterson (the first president of Hampshire College) surveyed the landscape of higher education and highlighted the "notable phenomenon" of the burgeoning consortial movement: "It flies directly in the face of the historic pattern of institutional isolationism and independence which has dominated higher education until the present time. This movement constitutes something new in education: at the very least, a rhetorical and nominal commitment to cooperation, where before had existed a kind of friendly anarchy among colleges and universities."[4] Managing collaborative work, it must be said, cannot be done alone. As one faculty member involved in a cross-campus academic program put it, "You have got to get everybody on board and you have to get their investment in the process and their enthusiasm and willingness to put in the extra mile [or] they could kill it in a heartbeat."[5] But adding more people to the decision-making mix rarely simplifies the process. Let's consider, then, how leadership and governance structures in higher education operate in a consortial setting.

Guides on how to engage in board service as a trustee are easy to find.[6] Often these manuals summarize the role of college and university governing boards as "noses in, fingers out," highlighting the importance of arms-length, third-party oversight of campus operations that supports (and at times questions) but doesn't interfere with the work of senior staff. Many campus leaders also serve on outside boards, perhaps for a local community service organization, a national charity, or a corporation. All this guidance and experience can make it easy to assume that the work of being on a consortial board will follow a familiar pattern and set of expectations.

The Association of Governing Boards (AGB), for instance, developed its "Principles of Trusteeship" to help members of higher education governing boards better understand and carry out their roles.[7] AGB describes nine principles, grouped under three guidelines, as shown in Figure 3.1: Understand Governance, Lead by Example, and Think Strategically. This guidance is both simple and comprehensive, with the principles constructed to be easily digestible to board members new to their role and rich enough to provide useful reflection points for seasoned trustees.

But a closer look at the reality of consortial board work reveals significant differences between trustees and consortium directors in their selection, perspectives, and obligations. Some of the unique features of consortial board service are left unaddressed by popular guides for trustees, and other aspects run counter to generic best practices. If not recognized and accounted for, these differences can damage an otherwise promising collaboration. Campuses interested in partnerships with other institutions would do well to add a fourth guideline to the AGB rubric, as shown in Figure 3.2: Behave Generously.

Before exploring the principles behind behaving generously, let's consider the ways in which the nature of consortial board service differs from the work of boards of trustees. Like many consortia, Five Colleges, Incorporated (FCI) is a 501(c)(3), governed by a board of directors—made up of the college presidents and university chancellor—that has legal and fiduciary responsibilities for ensuring the well-being of the organization. In some ways this nonprofit board is similar to a board of trustees, and the AGB guidance for boards is broadly applicable. Expectations around being prepared for and attending meetings, developing effective relationships with staff, and undertaking fiduciary responsibilities with care, for example, are common across many

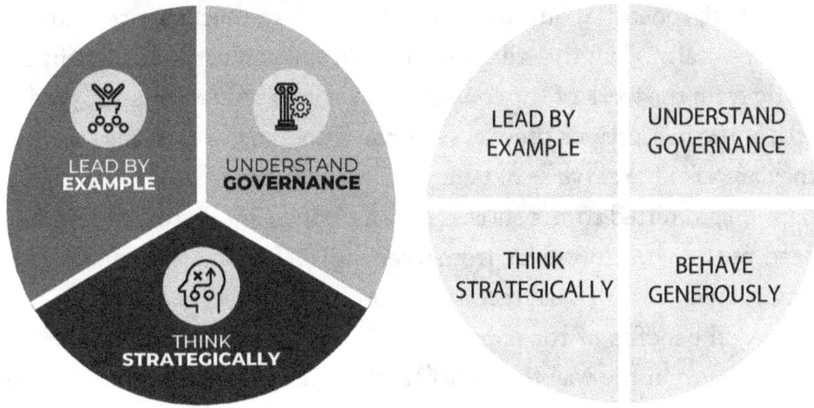

Figure 3.1 Principles of Trusteeship
From https://agb.org/principles-of-trusteeship/. © 2021 Association of Governing Boards of Universities and Colleges. Reprinted with permission.

Figure 3.2 Principles of Consortial Governance
Figure created by the author.

boards, consortial ones included. But at least three significant departures shape the work when done in a consortial setting.

First, consortial board members are not vetted volunteers but ex officio directors. Trustees (like the board members of many nonprofit organizations) are generally either selected or appointed, and some attention is paid to the skills, resources, and attributes they bring to board service, both as individuals and as a collective. Consortial directors follow a different pattern. In some consortia, board members are presidents and chancellors; in others they may be provosts or principal financial officers. Whatever their title, they serve the consortium because of their role in leading an individual campus, not because they were invited to serve, not because they volunteered to serve, and not because they demonstrated a commitment to the cause of the organization. They may be well suited to the role and committed to the consortium, but if they are it is generally by happy accident. The search process for these campus leaders may not include information about this role in the job prospectus, and the role is rarely the subject of questions during the interview process, despite the significant leadership, supervisory, and fiduciary duties that consortial board work entails.

Second, consortial directors are not interested third parties who can operate at arm's length—they are invested stakeholders who benefit directly from the work of the consortium. Though trustees may be graduates of the institutions they serve or have other loyalties to the campus, they are asked to serve as outside advisors and overseers. They are (one hopes) committed to the success of the campus but do not receive (indeed, are typically forbidden from receiving) direct material benefit from that success. Consortial directors, by contrast, are deeply engaged in the work and benefits of the consortium. Board members cannot serve at arm's length in the way that most trustees and directors are advised to do—consortial directors bring in not an outsider's perspective but a participant's self-interest. They are not consultants but stakeholders. The very member organizations they represent are, by design, beneficiaries of the work of the consortium, and therefore these ex officio directors all have a "baked in" conflict of interest between their role as director and their role as president or chancellor (or treasurer or provost or other campus representative). If the consortium is successful, the directors' campuses are the primary beneficiaries. By its very nature, a consortial board presents a conflict of interest for each of its members as they serve both their home campus and the shared organization. In many ways these interests are aligned, though some decisions will benefit either the campuses or the consortium, but not both.

And third, consortial board members face a set of time and attention constraints beyond that of a trustee. New consortial board members are simultaneously learning a new executive-level job, leaving little time to devote to engaging deeply in consortial onboarding activities. Trustees, by contrast, choose to commit their time to board service and can do so at moments in their careers when they have the capacity to fill the role responsibly. New trustees may be asked to participate in substantive orientation or training, and the AGB principles call for deep learning about the governance role being undertaken. Consortial orientation for new directors is often piecemeal and always secondary to their campus orientation, leaving little opportunity for a nuanced introduction to the special challenges of this work. Consortial board members are responsible for the oversight and health of the consortial organization, and yet this obligation will always take a back seat to their responsibilities on their home campus.

In short, a consortium cannot assume new campus leaders will come to the work with an interest in communal operations. Those new campus leaders cannot fully set aside their self-interest in their home institutions, and their day jobs limit the time and attention they can commit to the collaborative effort. Leading a consortium thus means adapting our thoughts about board-level governance structures and principles.[8] A 1969 study of "interdependency and conflict" found that consortial work "contradicted some basic assumptions of organizational analysis" and therefore required thinking differently about how to lead such efforts, "not the least of which is a determination of how to interrelate the corporate management model often used within institutions and the political management model which is seemingly more appropriate within the consortium."[9] One scholar of consortial leadership takes care to distinguish between collaboration and collaborative management, to highlight that the former may be the goal, but the latter is the process used to achieve that goal. It is one thing for a group of campuses to agree to partner but quite another when those autonomous campuses actively "manage a relationship in which they have made a commitment to work together to build on commonality and complementarity within a recognised [*sic*] collaborative framework."[10] Collaborative management, in other words, takes intentional, thoughtful effort.

Returning to AGB's principles (Understand Governance, Lead by Example, and Think Strategically), how does adding our fourth principle (Behave Generously) help to address the unique challenges of leadership in a consortial setting? What skills are needed to act with a consortial mindset? We can view Behave Generously as encompassing three guidelines not found in AGB's guidance (see Table 3.1).

First, do no harm to others. The typical advice for trustees is to prioritize the institution you serve, as in AGB's Principle 3, which calls on trustees to "be an ambassador for your institution and higher education." That prioritization is appropriate from a legal, fiduciary, and practical standpoint. A consortial mindset doesn't replace that commitment

Table 3.1 Expanded Principles of Leadership

			Principle of consortial boardship
Understand governance	**Lead by example**	**Think strategically**	**Behave generously**
Principle 1 Embrace the full scope of your responsibilities.	**Principle 4** Conduct yourself with impeccable integrity.	**Principle 7** Learn about the mission, constituents, culture, and context.	**Principle 10** Do no harm to others.
Principle 2 Respect the difference between the board's role and the administration's role.	**Principle 5** Think independently and act collectively.	**Principle 8** Focus on what matters most to long-term sustainability.	**Principle 11** Think collectively and act individually.
Principle 3 Be an ambassador for your institution and higher education.	**Principle 6** Champion justice, equity, and inclusion.	**Principle 9** Ask insightful questions and listen with an open mind.	**Principle 12** Give as well as get.

Source: Based on AGB Knowledge Center, "Principles of Trusteeship," https://agb.org/principles-of-trusteeship/.

but asks that directors *also* consider the impact of the institution's activities on others, even when acting alone. If my campus does X, can I ensure that it will either help or be neutral to the other campuses? If my benefit can only come at the expense of another institution (or the community in which we sit), is there an alternative to consider? Don't acquire all the moving boxes unless you mean to share.

Second, think collectively and act individually. Integrity and consensus are at the heart of AGB's existing Principle 5: "Think independently and act collectively." Judgment, diplomacy, and the willingness to speak up are important for all boards, as is a commitment not to undermine a collective decision once made. Consortial work asks that we simultaneously flip this guidance on its head, thinking collectively while acting individually. Directors in a consortial setting must bear the group in mind, even as they contribute individual resources to consortial initiatives. Put another way, consortial directors, while they certainly want their home campuses to benefit from shared initiatives, will aid the collective effort by considering long-term, big-picture cost-benefit analyses. Each campus may contribute a bit more or less toward individual projects than might be appropriate if viewed narrowly, but consortially minded directors assess the value of the consortium based on the overall benefit of the full portfolio. If you want a shared project to succeed, what will you and your individual campus do to contribute to the group's success?

Third, give as well as get. Principle 9 of the AGB model, for instance, encourages trustees to "ask insightful questions," "listen actively," and "bring genuine curiosity." This information-seeking behavior is important to consortial board work as well. But whereas trustees are focused on benefiting the institution they serve (and expect little in return), consortial directors are tasked with benefiting the organization that will in turn benefit them. This communal and even circular reliance means that consortial directors have an obligation to be open and transparent with one another and to do so as early and frequently as possible. In this spirit of reciprocity, what do your counterparts need to know so you can all do your best work together?

These principles are easier to state than to uphold. Given the unique characteristics of consortial board members, let's consider, too, five activities to address the challenges of welcoming new board members (and other new campus leaders with key roles to play) to collaborative work: prioritizing orientation, setting expectations, illuminating conflicts, streamlining meetings, and emphasizing relationships.

Because board members are assigned to service on behalf of their institutions, rather than selected for their personal interest in or commitment to the organization and its mission (as is generally the case for trustees and nonprofit board members), intentional orientation and onboarding are critical, not only to help them appreciate their legal and fiduciary responsibilities for ensuring the well-being of the organization, but also to persuade them of the value of the consortial enterprise. Early on, it's important to define terms, even apparently straightforward ones. In my setting, for instance, "Five Colleges, Incorporated" (or "FCI") generally refers to the nonprofit organization, its staff, and its budget—the separate entity the board of directors oversees. The "Five College Consortium" is the term we use to refer to the collective—the portfolio of shared activity and the entire community that consists of the member campuses' students and employees (and at times the FCI staff as well, as members of and contributors to this larger community). We use Five College (singular) to refer to consortial programs, as in Five College Risk Management or Five College grants, but since "Five Colleges" (plural) can be confusing when used as shorthand, we try to avoid that phrase in favor of "the member campuses" or something similar. "The Colleges" in our setting generally refers to the four private, undergraduate institutions, which in some cases collaborate without the state university. Your language will vary, of course. The point here is that confusion can abound, and careful communication is important.

The staff who support campus leaders are tasked with managing and protecting the schedules and commitments of these leaders, and they can be either advocates or roadblocks, depending on their understanding of the consortial role their leaders are expected to play. Orientation, therefore, may need to include not just the new board member but key members of their team as well. As early as possible after a new director has been identified, consortial staff should ensure this leader receives an explicit introduction to the organization's values, norms, and traditions and a review of its hallmark characteristics and unique basic values. They and their schedulers and staff will need to know the expectations for engagement, support, collegiality, time, and funding. There should be time set aside for an initial welcome and early onboarding, but the full orientation process is likely to take a year or more.

Many organizations supplement their formal by-laws and other governance documents with guidelines for board service that explicitly spell out what is expected of board members, and such documents can help directors appreciate and navigate their special role in consortial governance. FCI does this with a "Statement of Board Member's Responsibilities" (see pp. 98–100), much of which will be largely familiar to leaders who have served on other boards. The sections on "Meetings," "Relationship with Staff," and "Fiduciary Responsibilities," for instance, offer guidance that mirrors what directors will have experienced with other boards: come prepared, contribute to effective relationships, exercise fiscal prudence, and the like. But the FCI version also strives to recognize the unique features of consortial board service. The section on "General Expectations" calls on directors to learn about and serve the mission of FCI, recognizing that directors may not have a deep knowledge of the consortium and its work in advance of being assigned to service. The "Avoiding Conflicts" section acknowledges the need to juggle roles when serving in the capacity of director and cautions against behavior that would place FCI or the other institutions at a disadvantage. In my organization's case, directors receive but are not asked to sign this set of board expectations. The document describes the level of commitment and the quality of the interactions that will best serve the organization, but because directors are ex officio, they do not have the option to decline service, so the board expectations are necessarily advisory rather than obligatory.

Board members in any setting are typically expected to complete a conflict-of-interest review, in which they are asked to list potentially competing obligations, commitments, and investments. In addition to this traditional set of questions, our conflict-of-interest form names the inherent conflation of interests that consortial board members face. Our process does not call for mitigation or management of the conflict, however, since we cannot cure it. We simply ask each director to recognize and consider the multiple hats they wear in each meeting. Am I acting on behalf of College X, or the consortium as a whole, or the organization called FCI? More important than the form itself is ongoing, thoughtful attention to the roles being reflected during deliberation and decision-making, to help ensure that the directors are acting in the best interests of the organization when conducting board business.

Board guidance often emphasizes how to focus on governance rather than management, noting the tendency of boards to meddle.[11] The challenge in a consortium, by contrast, is often how to engage the board more fully—not to micromanage but to participate with enough attention and care to shape the organization. We noted in Chapter 2 that although opportunities abound for individual projects to emerge and succeed, fewer openings exist to plan strategically and set eyes on big goals, as broader conversations take time and are more difficult to do

Five Colleges, Incorporated ("FCI")
Statement of Individual Board Member's Responsibilities

I. General Expectations

A. Know FCI's mission, purposes, goals, policies, programs, services, strengths, and needs.

B. Support FCI's mission in the community by serving as an organizational advocate and liaison with interested persons and groups.

C. Serve in leadership positions or undertake special assignments willingly and enthusiastically when asked.

D. Follow trends in the organization's field of interest and bring them to the attention of the Board.

E. Bring a commitment to collaboration and a sense of humor to the Board's deliberations.

II. Meetings

A. Prepare for and participate in Board and committee meetings, including appropriate organizational activities.

B. Notify the Executive Director in advance if unable to attend Board or committee meeting, if feasible.

C. Ask timely and substantive questions at Board and committee meetings consistent with your conscience and convictions, while supporting the majority decision on issues decided by the Board.

D. Maintain confidentiality of the Board's proceedings and speak for the Board or the organization only when authorized to do so.

E. Suggest agenda items periodically for Board and committee meetings to ensure that significant policy-related matters are addressed.

III. Relationship with Staff

A. Contribute to effective relationships between the Board and the FCI Executive Director and staff.

B. Avoid asking for special favors from other Board members and FCI personnel, including special requests for information, without at least prior consultation with the Board or committee chairperson.

IV. Avoiding Conflicts

A. Fully comply with FCI's Conflict of Interest Policy and execute the Conflict of Interest Disclosure Form on an annual basis.

B. Be aware of and sensitive to the dual roles played by Board members, serving their home campuses and FCI (the Consortium) as a whole.

C. In your role as a member of the Board, serve the Consortium as a whole rather than any special interest group or constituency, or any organization in actual or potential competition with FCI, including the campus you represent.

D. Do not use your status as a Board or committee member, or information gained by such service, for unfair, material personal or individual campus benefit.

E. Avoid even the appearance of a conflict of interest that might embarrass the Board or FCI, and disclose any possible conflicts to the Board in a timely fashion.

F. Maintain independence and objectivity and do what a sense of fairness, ethics, and personal integrity dictate.

G. Never accept (or offer) favors or gifts from (or to) anyone who does business with FCI.

H. Share with the Board and the Executive Director in a timely manner any campus developments that may have a material effect on FCI or its programs, and avoid non-disclosure agreements where they may prevent such timely notification.

V. Fiduciary Responsibilities

A. Exercise prudence with the Board in the control and transfer of funds.

B. Faithfully read and understand the organization's financial statements and otherwise help the Board fulfill its fiduciary responsibilities.

C. Ensure timely payment of your campus assessments and special program fees as agreed to by the Board.

piecemeal. Given the significant obligations of campus leadership roles, our consortium strives to minimize the time board members must commit to consortial business while simultaneously allowing space for exploratory conversation. We have an informal rule that briefing memos must be no more than one page (even if many pages of addenda are required), and our agendas clearly highlight which items require a vote or other action, which allows board members to review materials as easily, quickly, and efficiently as possible. With the exception of the meetings in which the board reviews audit materials or accepts the consortium's tax return forms (which can run to 50 or more pages), our typical briefing book comes in under 20 pages, and the board meets for formal business just four to six times each year. These time-saving practices are hardly unique or revolutionary, but they play a particularly significant role in a consortial setting by lowering a few of the many barriers to participation and engagement.

Orientations, written expectations, signed conflict-of-interest forms, and other formal policies and procedures are helpful. We also recognize, however, that consortial agreements are highly dependent on shared motivations and mutual trust, neither of which is readily built through infrequent short meetings. At FCI, board meetings have returned to happening in person (generally over dinner), and fully half of each board meeting is dedicated to "campus updates"—our term for unstructured time in which the campus leaders compare notes, find common ground, seek advice, and (importantly) learn about one another. We also meet via teleconference every two to three weeks for a quick check-in—no agenda and no notes, just a brief opportunity to catch up on emerging issues or to share significant news. And of course there are email exchanges and text threads that help keep the group connected. We work to broaden the base of collaboration by leaning on advisory boards of provosts and financial officers who can support the board in its decision-making, but these folks are themselves ex officio, self-interested, and busy.

It is also important to think about which conversations are appropriate for which venues. During COVID-19, for instance, we developed an unwritten rule that campus leaders could (and should) question each other either in private or during closed meetings—about why and how they were implementing testing or if they believed their isolation plans were adequate, or any of the thousand other decisions that needed to be made. In public, however, each leader deferred to the others' judgment, noting that although they were all being informed by the science, their individual decisions needed to be suited to their local circumstances. An isolation plan might depend, for instance, on how many of a campus's residence hall rooms were single-occupancy, or how many students lived within driving distance of home. This was a means of demonstrating mutual respect for the difficult job of being a campus leader: It's okay to push, question, and critique one another as peers but don't throw anyone under the bus. In short, we rely on a great deal of generosity and goodwill.

Obviously, these particulars have evolved over time (and through various presidents and executive directors) to suit FCI's needs. More geographically spread campuses would find the frequency of our in-person meetings challenging, for instance, and consortia with a dozen or more members would find regular "campus updates" more time-consuming. Whatever the local circumstances, attending to orientation, expectations, conflicts, meetings, and relationships can help address the unique aspects of consortial board service.

A consortium relies on generosity, asking each president to shift from their day job as CEO of a campus, responsible for management, reputation, and fundraising, to their role as board member of a collaborative effort, responsible for the well-being of the consortium as an organization. They must consider the best directions for the consortium rather than for the constituent campuses, and yet they cannot set aside their own campus's interests. These two roles can never be fully separated. As one campus leader put it in a study of collaborative management, consortial leaders are "not joined together to be together, but joined together to remain detached."[12] The board members must focus on the health of the collective yet also go home to lead organizations that must contribute resources to the success of collaborative initiatives. It's a strange circularity.

In good times it's easy to wear both hats and easier to be generous with time and resources. During times of crisis for one of the members, the board must come to the rescue—not of the injured campus per se, but of the group. Consider the Hampshire College crisis, when the campus abruptly decided not to accept an incoming class in the fall of 2019. What at first seemed an unfortunate situation for a single institution was quickly followed by the realization that Hampshire's pain could hurt the others. If Hampshire did not survive, certain intertwined programs and contracts would have to be unwound, renegotiated, or even dismantled. If Hampshire employees left the valley, they would take spouses, partners, and family members away from the other institutions and from key community organizations. Given the history of Hampshire's founding, the other campuses' reputations would be at risk if the campus they created did not survive. The initial instinct was to pull back, to protect oneself first—not in the "own mask first" sense of staying safe in order to help others but in the "distance from the drowning" sense of keeping clear of the trouble to avoid getting pulled under too.[13] It took effort and not a few difficult conversations to surface these and other issues and to find paths forward that felt appropriate to all the players.

Crisis often comes in the form of conflict. In my experience and based on research on failed (closed) consortia and other collaborations, these conflicts tend to arise under three conditions: when there's bad news on one campus, when a crisis affects multiple campuses, and when a campus develops an outside interest.

First, the bad news. This might be a financial crisis (Hampshire and Wheelock provide two examples), and a campus facing such woes amid wealthier sister institutions often pulls back from collaborations, perhaps because nondisclosure agreements are needed or perhaps simply because attention is focused inward and on survival. As the consortium director Fritz Grupe noted in 1975, "Financial exigencies are as likely to destroy a joint effort as they are to nurture it."[14] Or it might be a public relations problem on a campus, which can lead to embarrassment, shame, fear, a focus on fixing the issue, and a desire not to escalate the problem. Or it could be a crisis that doesn't carry a reputational risk—an unexpected death, for instance—but that still requires focused attention and encourages a campus to turn inward. In any of these cases, it's important to note that the sibling institutions might be willing and able to help but remain unaware or unasked.

Second, conflict might arise because of a crisis affecting multiple campuses. We are all too familiar with the pandemic. Even on a single campus, too many cooks were already involved in most decisions, and those decisions needed to be made quickly. Bringing others into the conversation often felt like one step too far, with no time to explore consortial approaches to procuring tests or managing isolation space or coordinating faculty development to support the abrupt shift to online teaching. One campus leader, for instance, told me they needed to order their testing kits independently to convince their board they were taking direct action to protect their students. Even for campuses that have long been committed partners, this sort of a shared crisis can ironically encourage campuses to push out, shut out, and tune out extraneous voices in order to focus on the urgent, immediate, pressing need to protect their home campus, even when collective action might strengthen their response.

Third, competing outside interests can draw attention away from an existing collaboration. Many campuses belong to multiple consortia, often without drama, but an invitation to join another more elite or unique group or initiative can result in a pulling or shifting away of attention. Campuses in financial peril that are seeking a partner with whom to merge (again, see Hampshire and Wheelock Colleges) may need to focus on the potential new collaboration at the expense of an existing one. In either case, other members of a once-collaborative effort may be left behind or pushed aside, feeling betrayed by a sense of disloyalty.

It's important to remember that crises don't encourage people or institutions to behave any better or worse than they typically do. Rather, crises highlight existing characteristics. As sociologist Eric Klinenberg memorably put it, "Institutions have a tendency to reveal themselves when they are stressed and in crisis."[15] Who we are on a good day remains who we are on a bad day. As is so often the case, then, the best time to prepare for a crisis is long before it happens, building habits that will serve us well day-to-day and in moments of heightened stress. In our daily consortial work, we can tamp down the sense of interinstitutional competition, encouraging each campus to compete with itself but not with others. We can strive to minimize comparisons among member institutions, instead emphasizing that each campus contributes meaningfully to the shared enterprise and framing differences among the institutions as benefits enriching the whole, rather than as weaknesses or challenges. We can practice the habit of consideration, of thinking about those who might be affected by what we do, even in small daily decisions, so that when the larger, more dramatic decisions loom, we have exercised our collaborative muscles and honed our consortial instincts.[16] We can, in short, build our ability to behave generously.

A half century ago, an early leader of FCI with the distinctive name of North Burn noted that because collaboration is voluntary, "institutional self-discipline" is necessary in a consortium. Our campus settings may encourage us to behave as individuals and to compete for students, for funding, and for recognition, but can we behave with enough control and intention to pause before acting on those competitive instincts? Can we behave generously? Consortially? Leadership in a consortial setting, Burn urged, relies on "rigorous application of the principle that resources at the other institutions and cooperative possibilities be examined before institutional decisions on staff, facilities and course offerings are made."[17] Essentially, can we remember to look outside before acting inside?

We've been speaking thus far mostly about the role of campus leaders, but many consortia also have an executive director or comparable position—an employee of the nonprofit tasked with leading the organization and its work. The job of the executive director or president of a consortium is to support the board and other campus leaders in the process of shared governance, helping guide the organization to a strategic vision and plans for the future but not dictating that vision.

When asked in my interview for the executive director role what my vision was for the consortium, I replied, half-jokingly, that the job of executive director was not to have a vision but to follow the lead of the campuses and serve their interests. This is true, to a point. The organization exists to serve and support the campuses, and thus the vision for what we do should come from them. But it's also worth distinguishing between a vision for the organization (e.g., the nonprofit entity called Five Colleges, Incorporated) and a vision for the collaborative work that organization makes possible (e.g., the community collectively called the Five College Consortium). My job as executive director is surely to have a vision for the organization—that we should be professional and trustworthy and nimble; that the campuses should want to bring their collaborative ideas to us for execution; that we should steward our resources (which are really the campuses' resources) carefully.

I do hold those goals for the organization that is FCI and for its employees. But it is also true that my team and I help shape the vision for the consortium. What role should FCI be playing at any given moment? What should be out of bounds? How should FCI pick and choose which initiatives to pursue? Which campus voices should be prioritized? What is the overarching strategic plan that guides the investments and activities of the group? My vision for the nonprofit organization is largely set by me and my direct reports, though it is certainly informed by my interactions with the campuses and my understanding of our context. The vision for the consortium, by contrast, is a collective effort that requires input from campus leadership, tempered by the recognition that these leaders have a hundred other priorities and by the reality that the consortium is a loose federation whose component parts are independent and autonomous, though they find value in collaborating on some activities. As one study of executive directors explained, "Unlike the leaders of higher education institutions, consortium directors have little or no power over the member institutions, yet these directors must identify institutional needs, lead change to meet those needs, and build collaborative and cooperative partnerships to make change happen."[18] Executive directors must also manage a dizzying array of relationships (and the varied power dynamics accompanying each) with administrators and staff at all levels of each campus and with partners from outside higher education. A 1974 article offering guidance on "The Management of Consortium Priorities" noted a dozen different types of relationships required for accomplishing different forms of collaboration:

1. Exchange of information (discussion of long-range plans).
2. Interpersonal friendship (invitation for classroom lectures).
3. Altruistic assistance (one-way agreement to permit library access).
4. Coordination of efforts (non-competitive proposal development).
5. Sale/purchase of services (contract for use of a special facility).
6. Exchanges on a quid pro quo basis (cross-registration of students).
7. Sharing of non-expendable resources (inter-library loan).
8. Sharing of expendable resources (use of laboratory chemicals).
9. Joint acquisition of new resources (hiring a development officer).
10. Joint action to conserve resources (consolidated computer center).
11. Integration of resources (joint language department).
12. Establishment of common position (joint position on legislation).[19]

In addition to managing all these consortial relationships, the executive director who heads a nonprofit entity is also managing a small to mid-sized business, with its own employees, budget, facilities, obligations, and so forth.

It is a challenging role, calling folks to the table to do work that is hard, and doing so without any formal authority, amid what a former leader of the Colleges of the St. Lawrence Valley called "spasmodic and conflicting pressures."[20] The effectiveness of executive directors and their staff thus "flows not from [their] ability to punish recalcitrants," one study found, "but rather from the depth and relevance of the knowledge and the persuasiveness of the vision and logic [they] can bring to bear on a given issue."[21] And they must do this delicate leadership dance not only without authority but also "without much visibility, and often without much credibility in the eyes of academics."[22]

It is not surprising, then, that transformational leadership, which seeks to deploy influence and persuasion, should be so common in consortial settings. In contrast with tactical and strategic leadership, transformational leadership "focus[es] less on making decisions or establishing strategic plans, and more on facilitating organizational collaboration that can help drive a vision forward."[23] Or, as another scholar defined it, transformational leadership "seeks to change the perspectives of followers with innovative ideas and vision, while being attentive to their needs."[24] This leadership model requires a practitioner to be a motivational speaker, a charismatic representative, an intellectual peer, and a compassionate listener. It is leadership from the middle, and it is leadership that adapts to the needs of the current audience in the present moment, ideally while being grounded in some immutable guiding principles.

According to one summary of the skill set needed to manage a consortium and its portfolio of activity, "Consortium directors must be visionaries and agents of change. They must be able to set and attain goals. They must influence member institutions to work towards goals that extend beyond the institutions, and to recognize the individual benefits for having done so. They must not lose sight of the individual needs of each institution. They must be knowledgeable about the broader field of higher education, so that they are viewed as experts. They must put the success of others first."[25] If they can also walk on water, that would presumably be welcome too.

We noted that new campus leaders require orientation to this unfamiliar landscape of consortial oversight and leadership. The challenge is in some ways even greater for a new executive director, who is often left to their own devices to get oriented to the nonprofit, the member campuses, and the collective work. There is little preparation for this exact combination of duties, which include running a nonprofit business, navigating campus governance procedures, and learning about the full range of projects in the portfolio, from academic programs to insurance and fiber-optic networks. Particularly for executive directors with a small (or nonexistent) staff, a single morning can require moving back and forth between engaging with presidents and chancellors as peers in one moment and negotiating the purchase of a new photocopier in the next, followed by mediating a dispute between academic departments on multiple campuses and then writing a grant proposal or filing a tax return. With luck, we have colleagues on the campuses who can advise and support us in this wide array of duties, and those of us who have chosen this work tend to enjoy the variety and the challenge. Few outside of this setting, however, can appreciate the mental gymnastics required to navigate these many roles while retaining a firm grip on the core mission as well as our sanity.

This complex landscape helps explain why a study of the factors necessary for consortial success cited "personalities and the development of rapport" as very important. As one researcher explained in his summary of survey responses from consortial leaders, "A consortium position is a 'lonely job' because you do not belong to any institution. You must be 'insightful,' 'flexible,' and able to 'deal with ambiguity' to work well in a consortium."[26] A description of the Colleges of Central Kansas consortium noted how the success of the consortium ebbed and flowed with the abilities of successive directors: "An early period of growth was ushered in by a strong, aggressive executive director but stagnation followed under limited leadership when the next director was not able to work effectively with the consortium board and other institutional partners. Yet, in challenging times of limited funding, the third director restored credibility to the consortium by revitalizing old programs, starting new ones, and refocusing attention on the needs for a cooperative effort that would support the needs of the member institutions." An analysis of a failed consortium found the fault lay in part with the executive director, whose "need for recognition . . . was seen as coming before the public acknowledgement of how others contributed to the consortium. He was not self-motivated and did not show initiative in developing programs that would benefit the members."[27] As two veteran consortial leaders noted, "A lot of institutional and individual goodwill and vision are crucial to effective 'consorting.'"[28]

Given these challenges—that collaboration is hard, that campus presidents have a hundred other things to do, that consortial staff have little to no authority, that progress takes time and energy—how should we think about leadership and strategic planning in this setting? Aside from approaching this work with a spirit of generosity, and an appreciation for how challenging it is on the best of days, some conceptual models can help us function in this setting where leadership is distributed, shared, and networked.

One model for this sort of shared visioning comes from "collective impact," a concept in social change and community service in which individuals from a variety of different organizations, agencies, or sectors come together to address a specific issue. In a collective impact project, participating organizations operate together as a network, retaining their independent identities, rather than under an umbrella organization that guides their shared work, although a "backbone organization" may provide some coordinating support. Consortia similarly operate as networks of autonomous institutions (which makes them distinct from, say, state systems of higher education, in which the individual campuses report to a system office in some degree or another), perhaps with some central consortial staff who can nurture (but not dictate) the shared activities.

One guide to collective impact describes 10 ways things can go off the rails, including number 8, "Managing a Network like an Organization," which cautions that the experience of leadership in a single organization does not fully carry over to these networked efforts:

> Most institutional leaders have mental models for governing, managing, and building organizations that do not apply to a networked collective impact effort. . . . Rather than a hierarchical organization to be centrally managed, their job [in a networked setting] is to support alignment and commitment across a network of diverse actors who participate by choice. Steering committee members are stewards of the common agenda and their role is to nurture alignment, encourage shared leadership, and hold leaders and partners accountable to it. The role of the backbone leader is not to build an organization but to facilitate, coordinate, manage commitments, build capacity, and celebrate members to advance the common agenda.[29]

Executive directors of consortia can serve this role of backbone leader, focusing not on building the nonprofit entity for its own sake but on designing it to support the campuses' collaborative work. And board members can play this role of supporting alignment and commitment.

In doing this backbone work, executive directors walk a bit of a tightrope, offering suggestions of a vision without forcing one onto the campuses for which they work.[30] As two seasoned consortial leaders described it, "Cooperative efforts are seldom led in the traditional sense. They are achieved by a complicated process of cultivation and cross-validation, and they result from a consummate sense of timing. . . . Consortium decision structures need to provide a balance between the capacity to act with decisiveness and the capacity to sustain a decision process through long routes to a successful conclusion."[31] An executive director can serve as something of a funnel and a mirror. I am the only person who attends faculty meetings on all five of my member campuses, for instance, which means I have a perspective on cross-campus concerns and interests that no one else can be expected to have. I then have the opportunity to reflect back what I hear to the board, to the provosts, to the chief financial officers, and to others. They can bring the desire to collaborate, but I can bring a bird's-eye view of the landscape, ideas, and examples for them to react to and an understanding of the logistics required to pull off a new partnership. It is, in a sense, a dance—a back and forth as I listen deeply to what moves them, share it back for their reactions, adjust, step back when I haven't quite connected, and press forward when there seems to be an opening.

This distributed, shared, networked leadership structure presents challenges for an organization looking to craft a traditional strategic plan with benchmarks, targets, and quantifiable goals and deadlines. Strategist David LaPiana noted such challenges in crafting his concept of a "strategic road map" rather than a plan, as he explains in *Nonprofit Strategy Revolution*. LaPiana argues that in the fast-paced world of nonprofit leadership, 10-year plans are unrealistic and quickly out of date, requiring too much time from leaders for too little useful payoff. He presents instead a strategic planning model built on a set of worksheets—bite-sized activities that can be completed by a board or planning team in short bursts and adapted or updated piecemeal as needed. As I've described LaPiana's road map concept to some colleagues, it's like having access to a live image of the landscape and hazards via GPS instead of a printed set of directions to a single destination from an old-school AAA TripTik. With a GPS-style road map, you can plug in your preferences (avoid toll roads, for example), identify nearby sites (restaurants or gas stations, for instance) as you need them, and adjust on the fly when something unexpected comes up (an accident ahead or a sudden craving for a coffee), rather than following an immutable set of directions. And if you find that your destination is no longer appropriate (that beach is closed today), GPS can help you find an alternative destination. Similarly, with a strategic road map the result is not a predetermined and static plan but a dynamic road map that can adapt to the moment—a document that describes an overarching mission; articulates shared resources, constraints, values, and context; and lays out the principles the group will use to make decisions about which initiatives to pursue, even as the landscape changes.

In a similarly adaptive vein, "logical incrementalism" is a management philosophy in which "strategies develop over various small decisions evaluated periodically, and not by a one-time decision."[32] In essence, an organization using this approach is likely to have a guiding mission or overarching function (as most nonprofits do), but the path to fulfilling that mission of necessity must be built one logical step at a time. The path will depend on circumstances, opportunity, and instinct about what the correct next step, initiative, or action should be, as the organization navigates through the realities of capacity, resources, distractions, and political will. Although this approach has been maligned as "muddling through," its originator, James Brian Quinn, said that such leaders "arrive at their strategic goals through highly incremental processes, rather than through the kinds of structured analysis often prescribed or 'required' according to management dogma." It is a flexible, adaptive approach that can be highly effective in an unstructured, messy setting such as a consortium. Or as one *Harvard Business Review* author described it, a leader using this approach "is an opportunist, and he tends to muddle through problems—although he muddles with a purpose."[33]

Whatever their shape and size, consortia fundamentally exist because something motivated campus leaders to come together for their campuses' mutual benefit. But overcoming the daily habits of mind that can interfere with collective effort requires commitment to a spirit of generosity. Research on collaboration and teamwork suggests that a shared sense of purpose and mutual trust are essential elements of effective consortial work and as such can feed generosity.[34] Having this shared purpose is necessary but not sufficient. Developing mutual trust requires more intentionality—building respect, openness, and confidence takes time. Research on psychological safety also suggests that consistency is critical and "affects people's willingness to engage in experimentation, a behavior integral to innovation."[35]

Building this sense of psychological safety is part of the responsibility of the executive director (for those collaborations fortunate enough to have a dedicated staff member). True, the consortial board in part manages and advises the executive director, but the executive director also supports and encourages the board. At FCI, the semiweekly board conversations, campus updates during board meetings, shared meals in one another's homes, and other interactions we encourage among the board members are intended to support building and sustaining the trusting relationships necessary to a healthy consortium. This relationship building may feel peripheral. I mentioned that fully half of most FCI board meetings are taken up with campus updates. In a strict sense, no formal, official work is done during this portion of the meetings. And yet this part of the conversation provides context and strategic insight and a (vague) record of topics that are top of mind for the presidents. It helps the executive director hear what the presidents are thinking, and it gives the directors space to vent and share and seek advice. Does this sharing actually support the mission of the organization? Yes, if it strengthens the sense of shared purpose and psychological safety.

We aren't built to do this ("collaboration is an unnatural act"). As individuals, and as organizations, we face an uphill battle. We're built, structured, and rewarded to compete. And cross-campus collaboration will nearly always come second—the campuses must exist before they can partner. Presidents, provosts, trustees, CFOs, faculty, and students will all focus on their own campus before they think about the consortium. That makes sense. And yet good collaboration takes time and attention, and a willingness to set aside pure self-interest. So how can we find the inspiration, the motivation, and the incentives to add to already overfull plates? It's critical that member institutions feel they are getting their money's worth. And it's even more critical that institutional leaders feel they are getting their time's worth. As the consortial leader Stanley F. Salwak said, "Fundamentally, cooperation is not a matter of institutions; it is a matter of people."[36]

Recent research has found that collaboration isn't unnatural, though it does exist in tension with its opposite, "deflection." Deflection has short-term advantages, which make it so tempting. But the actions of neighbors and colleagues can help shift the balance toward cooperation. The immediate gratification of deflection can be offset by punishment for overly selfish behavior (or reward for collective behavior), and if tended to consistently, "a phase transition occurs in which cooperation spreads through the population like wildfire."[37] But if left untended, collaboration can easily lose out to self-interest. In other words, collaboration may not be our default setting, but it can become our norm.

For those of us working within a consortial organization, it's crucial to remember that in every meeting, we are the only ones whose full-time day job is thinking about this collective work. The mismatch between campus-focused leaders and collaboration-touting consortial staff can be stark and at times disheartening. For this work to be successful, we must overcome habit, history, and hubris, and build new practices, new patterns, and new confidence. We must remember that we can be better with one another without needing to be better *than* one another. We must develop the mindset of asking: What opportunities might exist if we worked across institutions? How might we be better with instead of better than? It's not a Pollyanna set of questions. It's remembering that this tool is in the box and available for use; don't let it get rusty.

FOR FURTHER EXPLORATION

Step 3. Governing Together

We've noted that higher education, broadly speaking, isn't built for collaboration. With that in mind, it's critical to approach consortial work with intention and to name the distinctions between these shared efforts and our more individual daily practices.

- Who will guide and govern this process? Presidents? CFOs? Student affairs officers? Note that these decision-makers are unlikely to be the folks who will be doing the day-to-day work of contributing to consortial efforts. For the moment, our focus is on the people setting the vision for the consortium. If the consortium already exists and has a governance structure in place, is there a clearly understood distinction between those with fiduciary responsibility (the board and perhaps an audit or investment committee, for instance) and those with advisory or management roles?

- Will a director or another individual coordinate the vision? If the consortium already operates as a 501(c)(3) or if the vision is to create such a nonprofit entity, who will oversee that organization? How much autonomy will this director have? Are they expected simply to carry out the assignments of campus leaders, or are they a thought partner in the work, bringing potential projects and innovations to the group for consideration? How will the director on the project have access to leadership? Will they be expected to function independently or under close supervision? There is no right answer as long as everyone understands their role, and the structure as a whole is sufficient to support the work.
- If there is no separate consortial entity or if that entity has (or will have) just one or two staff members, how does their role compare to the work of campus leaders? A truly collaborative effort cannot be the sole responsibility of any one individual (though many collaborative efforts benefit from one or two especially charismatic and committed leaders). How much autonomy will that staff member have? Are they expected simply to carry out the assignments of campus leaders, perhaps ensuring the leaders meet on a regular basis, preparing agendas, and taking meeting minutes? Or are they a peer collaborator in the work? How will staff on the project have access to leadership? Again, there is no right answer as long as everyone understands their role, and the structure as a whole is sufficient to support the work.
- Decision-making authority, duties, and reporting lines for all participants (including leaders, managers, and support staff) should be clear and ideally in writing. Has someone been tapped to document this information and share it with the group?
- We should expect and plan for personnel changes, so how will we cover consortial roles when departures happen? How will we welcome and orient new members or participants to this work?
- Will this work have a web presence? If so, who will design, build, and maintain the website? Will it be tied to one campus but

linked to all? Will it have a unique URL distinct from the campuses?

- Where will files be stored? Will a shared cloud drive be used? If so, who will design, build, and maintain the drive? Will it exist on one campus's network but be shared with others? Is there a backup owner in case of changes in personnel?
- How often will the leadership team meet? Monthly, quarterly, weekly? In person or electronically? Will someone be tapped to take notes or minutes and schedule the next meeting, or will this duty rotate among members? No meeting should end without some plan for convening the next meeting and deciding what attendees should do in the meantime. This is true in most settings but is particularly important for cross-institutional work that can too easily fall off the radar in the storm of daily activity on the home campuses.
- Does the board (or equivalent group) have, or can it create, rules of engagement? (A set of board responsibilities is one version.) What do we expect of one another? Even if the consortium has no staff as yet, a set of shared expectations remains important.
- Where can we build this collaborative work into campus policies and structures? For instance, can our tenure and promotion guidelines and our campus definition of "service" include cross-campus collaboration? If the consortial focus is on procurement and each campus has a documented process for contract renewal, can that process include a requirement to consider cross-campus collaboration before signing new individual agreements? Given that consortial efforts can weaken when personnel inevitably change over time, it can be helpful to bake collaboration into the daily routines on campus. This sort of institutionalization also signifies campus commitment to the work.
- Do we have skills in transformational leadership, mediation, logical incrementalism, and other areas that will be important to our success, or can we build these skills? (See also the list of skills on p. 106.) What training or facilitation can we seek

out to support this collaborative work? For instance, the Association for Collaborative Leadership offers a variety of professional development opportunities relevant to cross-campus partnerships.

- Who else needs to be educated about our efforts? For instance, do our boards of trustees understand why we're engaged in this partnership? Are our provosts and CFOs as committed to this collaboration as we are? Do our graduates need information about why we're pursuing consortial efforts?

Because we have or are building an effort that both cuts across campus lines and operates outside traditional campus operations, it's important to take time to articulate and reinforce the governance structures that will guide and support collaborative work.

CHAPTER FOUR

Building a Backbone (Commitment)

Support it like you mean it.

LONGTIME CONSORTIUM LEADER Donn Neal's definition of a consortium from Chapter 1 included three elements: structure, staffing, and funding. Neal described "a semi-permanent organization [with] financial contributions from its members, that employs a professional staff whose sole responsibility is to encourage and to facilitate cooperative activities."[1] These elements—structure, funding, and staff—are prescriptive as well as descriptive. Research on collective impact initiatives similarly describes "the five conditions of collective success": "a common agenda, shared measurement systems, mutually reinforcing activities, continuous communication, and backbone support organizations."[2] By contrast, literature on and case studies of failed collaborations point to a lack of commitment as high on the list of key factors. Inadequate staff, insufficient funding, and inattention by the board and other leaders can all be signs of this lack of commitment. Consortia as Neal described them provide the backbone support that fosters the collective success of the member institutions.

The structure of a consortium, as we discussed earlier, is a manifestation of the motivation and vision of the leaders, reflecting the nature of the collaborative effort being undertaken. The staffing and funding reflect commitment—that this project is worth doing, that it's worth doing well, and that it's expected to continue for an extended period of time. The staffing and funding also serve as counterbalances to the obstacles facing collaborative work. They signify campus leaders' willingness to put people and money in place to facilitate, manage, oversee, and administer consortial activities, even (or especially) when those leaders themselves cannot routinely be at the table.

There is a danger in this last point. When consortial or campus staff are making collaboration happen, whether it is cross-registration or pooled insurance or a jointly managed Title IX program, those outside the minutiae can find it too easy to start taking these activities for granted, or even for the activities (and at times the people) to become invisible. Students take classes, insurance pays claims, Title IX cases get resolved. When these things happen well, who remembers the mad paddling under the water that makes the serene view above the surface possible? Two longtime leaders noted this challenge: "It is almost universally accurate to say that the institutional members of academic consortia do not fully understand the nature and operations of the consortium. The broad purposes served by the consortium are somewhat remote from the daily experience and needs of most of these individuals. As a result, it is not unusual for consortium staff to have to justify repeatedly what the organization does, why it costs so much, and why the institutions should continue to support it."[3] Collaboration is not a quick fix. And it does not happen by magic, although an element of serendipity is involved. Much of the press coverage of consortia and many op-ed pieces encouraging partnership focus on cost savings as the primary reason for campuses to explore collaborative work. While collaboration can save campuses money, those benefits can take time to achieve, and they require dedicated effort and, frequently, investment up front before the savings can be realized.

This chapter describes a range of existing staffing and funding models in US consortia. The goal is not to advocate for a particular structure or budget model but to argue that these administrative underpinnings should be chosen with and driven by purpose. As we'll see, even existing consortia adapt over time to serve the needs of the moment.

Let's begin with staffing. Who is needed to do this work? Some collaborations, such as the Higher Education Consortium of Central Massachusetts; or Wellesley, Olin, and Babson outside Boston; or the Tri-Co consortium in Philadelphia, have no staff per se. These consortia can and do function, the latter two without the administrative structure of a separate 501(c)(3). The partnership is limited in scope, and the mechanics of, say, cross-registration are handled by existing staff on the campuses, from registrars to advisors. For a more comprehensive and mature collaboration such as the Claremont Consortium or the Lehigh Valley Association of Independent Colleges (LVAIC), a dedicated staff provides and coordinates the wide portfolio of shared services, though the size of Claremont's staff is many times that of LVAIC.

To be clear: Additional work must be done in both models to make the collaboration happen. Consider the elements of cross-registration, for instance, which some campuses manage without a formal consortial structure underpinning the work. Allowing a student from one campus to take (and receive credit for) a course on another campus requires that students have access to a course catalog outside their home institution. They must receive guidance about which courses are available and appropriate. They must have a mechanism to indicate they want to take a course, which might require a log-in or credentials for the host campus or might involve their home registrar passing along requests to a colleague. They must have an identity on the host campus that allows them to appear on a class roster, have access to a learning management system, and receive a grade. They may also need key or card access to a classroom building, library, or laboratory. They may need access to dining services on the host campus if their course falls near a mealtime. They need the ability to receive emails from instructors, notices of snow days and emergencies, access to course evaluation portals, and other routine communications. A mechanism must be in place to transfer their credits to their home campus, and if (as is the case for the Five College Consortium campuses, for instance) the courses are treated as in-residence courses rather than transfer courses, the home campus will need a process to assign not just credit but a grade.

A diagram of the Five College cross-registration process (Fig. 4.1) illustrates the complexity of a collaborative program, though the details will vary by project and setting. Documenting the workflow for a shared program can help articulate which personnel are responsible for which steps, identify where communication and handoffs need to occur, and highlight potential problem areas.

All of this takes work. Whether that work is added to the duties of existing staff on the campuses, is assigned to new campus personnel hired for the purpose of coordination, or is undertaken by consortial staff hired by a separate entity, there is work. And if the work is "outsourced" to consortial staff, work is still required of on-campus personnel—advisors, registrars, provosts, and the like—to ensure that cross-registration is successful.

The work *can* be done with existing staff and often *needs* to be done with existing staff, at least for a time. It's important for campus leadership to recognize this labor and invest in it—not necessarily with dollars per se but with attention, with commitment, and with frequent vocal reminders to the entire community that these efforts are important and are valued by senior leadership. Consortial meetings share a common dynamic. A group of peers in some position or another—it could be procurement directors or Title IX coordinators or chief information officers or any of a hundred other examples—meet and talk about their overlapping interests and needs: to keep service contracts affordable, to respond to ever-changing compliance rules, to better serve a new population of students. Again, it could be anything. There will come a moment in the conversation when the obstacles appear. Our timelines aren't the same. Our scales are different. Our duties and titles and reporting lines don't align, so we don't all have the same authority or access to leadership. We are busy. This is extra. It is too much. The brief glimpse of what a collective approach could offer isn't tangible enough to withstand the doubts. If consortium staff exist, even they cannot easily keep the ethereal vision in the room long enough to battle the doubts that begin to creep in. You don't know my day job.

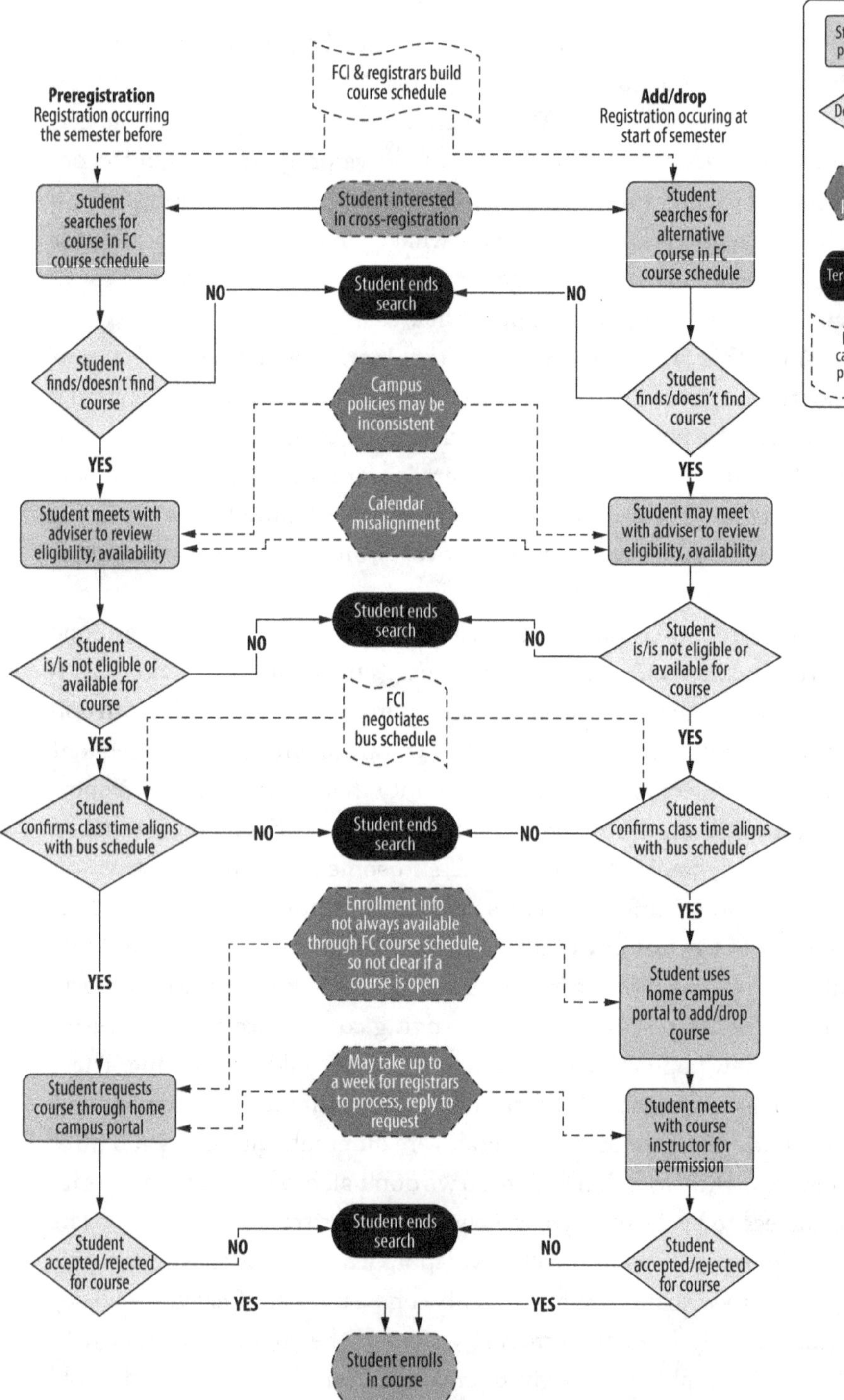

Figure 4.1 A Student's Five College Journey: Mapping the Cross-Registration Process
Diagram created by Kevin Kennedy, Ray Rennard, and Tom Brennan for Five Colleges, Incorporated.

You're not my supervisor. This doesn't fit with what I'm expected to do on my home campus. I'm tired. This is extra. The moment passes, the conversation moves on, the meeting ends, and we all return to our routines, familiar and inertial. This is where campus leadership matters deeply. A president who says, "We can and should do this. I want you to do this. I expect you to take the time to figure out a way to do this. Other things will not get done and I understand. Staying with this dream long enough to make it tangible, to bring it to reality, is a worthy goal and one I support." This encouragement, which can feel like so little as it's being offered, can be the turning point for those hearing it.

At all levels of the campus, from leaders to faculty to front-line staff, it's helpful to make space for cross-campus communication, carving out times when the purpose is simply to share news, concerns, personnel changes, personal challenges, successes, plans, and priorities. The goal is not to force collaboration but to engage in regular communication that builds knowledge, familiarity, and, importantly, trust. Senior leaders who are aware of each other's landscape are more likely to see opportunities, and leaders who like and respect each other are more likely to want to help. I'm reminded of an early experience I had upon joining the consortium, standing at a reception with a senior campus leader when their counterpart from another campus joined us, turned to his colleague, and asked with sincere interest and concern, "So, how many protesters are outside *your* office this week?" It was an odd but touching moment of connection between two leaders facing similar challenges on very different campuses (and it did not escape my notice that they were willing to share this potentially vulnerable moment within my earshot). That brief exchange reflected a sense of camaraderie. These leaders knew and respected each other, and they recognized the similarities in their work in spite of their different roles and campuses.

In August 2007 the I-35 bridge over the Mississippi River in Minneapolis collapsed, killing 13 people. After-action reviews of the collapse noted that, devastating as the collapse and the deaths were, the response to the collapse was extraordinarily effective and should serve as a model for emergency response elsewhere. The 13 deaths were just a fraction of the 190 travelers on the bridge at the time of the collapse, and all but one person rescued from the site survived. That rescue operation represented a highly effective collaboration across multiple response units on two sides of the river—fire and police departments, ambulance units and hospital personnel, HAZMAT teams, the Occupational Safety and Health Administration, the US Coast Guard, electrical crews, dispatchers, communications teams, and more. It was a collaboration that "could have been a multi-jurisdictional nightmare." When asked what had made the response so notable, Minneapolis Fire Chief Jim Clack credited "an already existing working relationship between agencies as a vital link to the successful immediate response and recovery phase."[4] Many of the responding personnel had trained together in exercises and simulations, had existing working relationships, and, notably, had one another's cell numbers programmed in their phones. The FEMA report noted, "Key players not only knew each other, but were familiar with the operations and disaster assignments of others. When it came time to pull together efficiently as a team—they did."[5] Each leader knew who to call, knew the person who would be on the other end of the line, and knew what they could expect of their partners in the effort.[6] The on-scene medical responders "all followed a one page incident response plan that is shared in common with the 24 EMS agencies in a seven county area" that had taken years to develop.[7]

To be clear, not everything worked well (it never does), and the FEMA and National Transportation Safety Board reports identified areas for improvement, but existing relationships and effective communication proved key to what did succeed.[8] As one news story reported, "Ask those who were there and their testimony is uniform: Success was the result of human ties—ongoing personal connections that already existed between members of the area's many responder organizations. These connections and their foundations were laid long before the bridge went down."[9] Such relationships happen because they are built. In the case of Minneapolis, FEMA noted, "The city had invested heavily in the development of those relationships, which were built through plan development, universal NIMS training, appropriate use of exercises and strategic planning over several years."[10]

Effective consortial leaders share this belief with emergency managers: Relationships are critical and require time and investment to build.[11] Even national and international alliances require relationships. As one leader of the Great Plains IDEA collaboration explained it, "You have to know your partners. You can't just walk in randomly and say let's take these ten schools. There has to be a real reason for the partner to be there. You have common interests. Some of you have worked together before. You have to have some history, or at least some members that have history. You are going to rely upon that history to carry you through some tough times. You don't just look them up in the phone book."[12] In a study on trust in consortial settings, one leader described striving to help their colleagues conceive of the effort required for collaboration as essential rather than extra, "to combat . . . the perception that collaborative work is extra work" and instead encourage participants to see "collaborative work *is* your work." Investing in time to build relationships can be more powerful than investing direct funding.[13] Collaboration expert Deb Mashek reported one nonprofit leader saying "Good people figure out how to get it done with the tools available to them, even if the tools are crappy. . . . They find a way to get it done."[14]

Again, the folks tasked with managing collaborative activities need not be outside the campuses, although great benefit can come from having a neutral third-party helping facilitate the work. What's critical is that someone be tapped as "responsible for putting the combined interests of the group ahead of individual interests, treating every institution as equal, and creating a level playing field for the discussion and debate of issues and programs." One summary of the work of consortial staff explains:

> Their tasks can vary from scheduling meetings (no small undertaking) to developing vendor relationships and managing shared contracts. They might put together newsletters and offer faculty development workshops for participating institutions and the larger higher education community. In most cases, consortium

staff must accept that, for the participants, the consortium is a low priority in the context of campus issues and day-to-day job responsibilities; yet staff must help keep consortium groups focused and on task. The consortium staff also provide stability in the face of staff turnover on the campuses; they provide continuity to the effort and are there to orient new representatives of member institutions.[15]

To help understand the work of consortial employees, consider, in broad terms, three categories of consortial staff: core administrators, consolidated service providers, and shared staff. First are the core administrators, or those responsible for managing the nonprofit entity. In a large consortium, this category might include an executive director, treasurer, human resources staff, grants manager, and the like. These folks manage the operations of the nonprofit entity if one exists, working with the board of directors, hiring and overseeing staff, managing contracts and financial records, and generally facilitating the collaborative work. The majority of their work is (arguably) for the shared organization. When the consortium receives grant funding to support a shared project, for instance, the core administrative staff is responsible for stewarding and distributing the funds, coordinating with the project leaders, and ensuring that reporting obligations are met. If there is no formal nonprofit entity, these roles are either unnecessary (no consortial human resources office is needed if there is no stand-alone organization hiring employees) or are filled by existing staff on the campuses (e.g., campus business offices directly billing one another without a dedicated consortial treasurer). In a small consortium, even one with nonprofit status, some of these duties might be outsourced to one of the member campuses. For example, a nonprofit with only three staff may operate as an external agency affiliated with one of the campuses so that the staff are employees of that campus. A shared grant might be technically managed by a single campus on behalf of the group.

A second category comprises staff who are consolidated (often neutral, and often team-based) service providers. They are employed by the nonprofit to provide or oversee a shared program, such as risk-management functions, a fiber-optic network, a joint police force, facilities management, or multicampus academic programs. They might negotiate contracts or help design academic credentials or support information technology (IT) functions. The majority of their work provides a direct benefit to the campuses, though some might also contribute to the leadership of the nonprofit (e.g., a director of shared academic programs or a director of shared IT might also be considered senior staff of the nonprofit). In the case that no formal nonprofit organization exists, these roles are typically still needed on the campuses. The campuses will either have individual risk-management offices or will share a single office, for example, but they usually can't do without this function. Sharing such functions effectively shifts them from the campuses into the consortium (or creates them within the consortium, if they are emerging roles).

The third category, shared staff, includes personnel with appointments or duties directly on multiple campuses. For example, several institutions may opt to share a team of production assistants that support fine arts performances on multiple campuses. Or the campuses may each need a few hours a week of an accessibility specialist or emergency manager or Title IX investigator and find it beneficial to share a single position. These hires generally have no direct obligations to the nonprofit entity per se but are on the consortium's payroll for convenience's sake. Shared faculty, it's worth noting, typically follow a slightly different pattern, with a professor's appointment split, say, 50/25/25 across three campuses. This individual would be hired by one of the campuses and effectively loaned to or bought out by the other participating campuses. They are tenured and receive a paycheck and benefits from a single campus, but the other campuses contribute their shares of the compensation via the nonprofit entity, which tracks the obligations and bills the campuses appropriately. In the absence of a separate consortial entity to serve as the employer for shared staff, the campuses could certainly directly share such positions. The consortial structure can help ensure that shared employees are equitably serving the participating campuses, streamline management of the finances, and provide orientation and support for employees who will need to navigate multiple campuses (obtaining credentials, computer accounts, building access, parking passes, and so forth). But strictly speaking, a consortial entity isn't a prerequisite for such collaboration.

These three categories of staff are helpful in envisioning what sort of budget is required for collaboration. "Shared staff" often fill roles that are desirable but not essential; they are often positions that campuses want to have but would struggle to fund alone. The collective investment makes them attractive and affordable. "Consolidated service providers" generally emerge from functions that campuses have been providing on their own and opt to combine in order to either reduce expenses or enhance services. These functions, then, are often already in the campus budgets when discussion of sharing begins. "Core administrative staff" are the outliers in this budget picture. Outside of a consortial setting, five campuses that each have a business office do not have a financial incentive or an individual business need to create a sixth one, for instance. And yet if those campuses have a consortial structure to lean on, they can unlock the benefits of shared staff and consolidated services. The consortium staff can, as noted above, convene the meetings, build the funding models, draft the sharing agreements, submit the grants, and facilitate the conversations needed to arrive at a plan for sharing a function.

It is possible, therefore, to explore and do collaborative work without start-up funds, but seed money can be helpful. And just as a consortial structure should be driven by mission, funding models should derive from the intended purposes and desired structures of collaboration.

For many consortia, foundation funding provided incentive to form and expand. The New York Six consortium, for instance, was founded in 2009 with funding from the Mellon Foundation, which "provided the presidents of six liberal-arts institutions in upstate New York with a planning grant to explore potential areas of collaboration with an eye toward cost-saving and efficiency through academic and administrative collaborations."[16] Additional grants supported specific initiatives on libraries, IT, and academic collaboration. The Five College Consortium's long-standing joint faculty program began with Mellon funding "to support cooperation in the joint appointment of faculty across its participating institutions."[17]

The Mellon Foundation funding database lists 270 consortial projects funded between 1977 and 2024, with grants from under $50,000 to more than $5 million, to support collaboration in library services, graduate programs, student services, study abroad, and more.[18] This sort of seed funding can be powerful, but grants require proposals, which necessitates thoughtful work on the part of campuses *before* that external funding is in place and a willingness to commit human resources to the task of exploring what campuses might do together.

What can such external funding provide? First, an influx of external funding can lend focus and deadlines to efforts. It's easy to fantasize about what it would be like to share insurance coverage or professional development or study abroad, but time and effort are required to determine the right people to get in a room (or on a video call). The folks with the authority to approve collaborations are often not the folks with the in-the-weeds knowledge necessary to build a viable structure, so early on a group of provosts or presidents or chief financial officers need to have an idea (or be convinced that an idea is worth pursuing), and they (or someone) must identify a task force, working group, or ad hoc committee to explore and design a plan. Membership on such a committee is not straightforward. It's easy enough to say that my campus leaders are four presidents and a chancellor and to gloss over the fact that their titles are different. It's reasonably straightforward to talk about chief academic officers, though at FCI we recently renamed our Deans Council to the Provosts Council because campus terminology had changed (though no one term has ever been accurate across all the schools). But if you want to collaborate on Title IX staffing, or food contracts for dining services, or emergency preparedness functions, things can get complicated quickly. The equity and inclusion office on one campus might be responsible for student and employee issues, while on another campus student concerns might be managed through student affairs (which might be called a dean of students office or a dean of the college or something else entirely), and faculty issues might report through the provost, with staff issues assigned to human resources. Contracts, whether for food or batteries or insurance, might be managed centrally on one campus but distributed more locally on another. Emergency management might be an entire unit at a large university campus, one person on a well-resourced smaller campus (with any number of possible reporting lines), or shared across multiple people on another campus. At some colleges, it may be a line item in someone's job or not explicitly called out at all.

Consortial staff find ways to work around or through such disparities. We remind committee members of their purpose in this particular meeting or group, regardless of their home campus title, translating across differences in terminology, structure, and culture. We engage campus leadership early and often to ensure that wherever staff and their supervisors are situated, the senior leadership team on their campus acknowledges, supports, and (ideally) rewards their efforts. Above all, two features are critical: communication and flexibility. Communication is necessary because information needs to flow from the cross-campus group to the home campuses and back again. Who needs to be aware? Who might be affected? Whose support is necessary? Flexibility is a must because the structure that works for today's topic might not be up to the challenge of tomorrow's. FCI's emergency preparedness group, for instance, has a large number of members who tap in and out based on the topic of the day (a tabletop exercise on a cyberattack requires different voices than a response to a meningitis outbreak). Indeed, our entire portfolio of committees changes on a regular basis to adapt to changing needs. At FCI we established a committee taxonomy (see pp. 131–33) to help explain our array of committee types, from formal and legally required governance bodies (board of directors, audit committee, investment committee) to structured program and project management groups to informal and self-directed communities of practice. Claremont uses the term "intercollegiate committees," and the Atlanta University Center Consortium uses what it calls "administrative councils" for similar purposes.[19] Whatever the labels, intention and clarity are important.

Obviously, this level of detail is hardly necessary for an early or straightforward collaboration. But whether the collaboration under

Sample Committee Taxonomy

The Five College Consortium manages a diverse array of committees, but in broad terms these groups can be classified as falling into one of three main categories: Governance & Strategy; Program & Project Management; and Community Building. The lines between the categories are not always clean, and each group may engage in work outside its primary focus area, but the descriptions below are intended to provide guidelines and common terminology across Five College activities.

Governance & Strategy Committees

Committees, councils, and boards within this category have clear authority over the direction of Five Colleges, Incorporated (FCI)—the nonprofit corporation that administers the consortium—or some well-defined and substantial subset of Five College activity. The Consortium's existence is highly dependent on the regular engagement of these committees, and the service provided to them by Five Colleges is accordingly high. Three governance bodies are required by the Five College by-laws: the Board of Directors, and two Board committees—the Investment Committee and the Audit Committee. Two additional committees provide key leadership to Five Colleges and advise the Board in its actions, though they are not considered "governance" bodies per se: the Provosts Council (formerly Deans Council) and the Principal Business Officers (PBOs). Other leadership committees oversee specific areas of collaboration across the five campuses. These committees are typically composed of senior leaders on the campuses, who serve on a Five College committee ex officio (e.g., Library Directors or Chief Information Officers).

Program & Project Management Committees

Committees in this category have been given responsibility by one or more Governance groups for a specific program, task, project, or event (either one-time or recurring), typically with a set deadline and clearly articulated outcome, and/or a defined scope of work. These groups may be ongoing or ad hoc, but typically their scope and scale of responsibility is more focused than that of Governance and Strategy groups. These workgroups are responsible for activities and initiatives that have been identified as important to the mission of the Consortium, and their charters or charge letters should thus include a detailed description of the (financial and human) resources required to accomplish their assigned task, including what support (if any) is expected from Five College resources.

Community Building Committees

Committees in this category serve primarily as "affinity groups" or "communities of practice," gathering together colleagues from across the campuses to share expertise and build collegiality. Typically, these groups consist of individuals filling similar roles on their respective campuses. In some cases these groups include individuals from outside the consortium. Community and collaboration are central to the mission of Five Colleges, and these groups can help to build networks and relationships that serve the broader aims and activities of the Consortium. Their informal nature means they can often be self-guided and/or can convene with minimal use of Five College resources. When these groups meet during work hours, members/attendees should seek supervisor approval prior to participation. Groups that wish to be formally recognized as Five College committees (to be able to refer to themselves as a "Five College" group, be identified on the Five College website, be eligible to apply for funding, etc.) are expected to do so in collaboration with Five College staff, and commit to adhering to Five College standards of conduct and inclusion. Affinity groups may, from time to time, be called upon to undertake a specific project and thus temporarily move into the category of Program & Project Management. A list of recognized Five College Community Committees will be posted on the Five College website and reviewed annually.

A Note on External and Inactive Groups

In addition to the groups described above, some groups are largely external to or independent of Five Colleges but have an affiliation agreement for specific engagement or services and/or provide an ex officio role for a member of the FCI staff. Some groups existed at one time but are currently inactive or meet so sporadically that no schedule can be discerned.

consideration is the establishment of an entire new campus or simply jointly sponsoring a high-profile speaker, it's important to approach collaboration with purpose, thinking carefully about who needs to be in the room and who needs communication with those in the room.

Beyond pilot or seed funding, a time will come when collaborating campuses must consider the ongoing contributions necessary to institutionalize collaboration. Essentially four funding models are used for cross-campus collaboration: distributed, assessments, dues, and in-kind. To illustrate the differences, consider as an example the relatively straightforward collaboration of three campuses inviting a guest speaker, with an anticipated budget of $3,000: $1,000 each for the speaker fee, the on-site costs, and the speaker's travel expenses.

Under a distributed funding model, one campus might pay the speaker fee, another campus might cover the site rental and catering costs, and the third campus might pay for the speaker's travel and lodging. As long as all three campuses agree that their payments are either roughly equal or otherwise acceptable (e.g., based on the number of expected attendees from each institution), no funding needs to be transferred. This model is ideal for one-off events because it requires no special accounting and is also an easy starting point for new collaborators who have little collaborative infrastructure. Even well-established consortia use this model from time to time, such as when an event is planned after the annual budget is established.

Under an assessment model, the three campuses would determine how best to split responsibility for the $3,000 budget and would pool the funds in a central location (one of the campuses or a consortial entity), which would then pay the bills. This model can simplify planning by centralizing it, and the speaker can receive their honorarium and reimbursements from a single entity. This model also enables each campus to support the event as a whole, rather than a particular portion, which can be helpful—as, for instance, if one campus's funds have a restriction against deploying them for food, or the speaker wants to use an airline not reimbursable under one campus's policies. This model can work for small-scale collaboration, including one-time events, with two campuses simply transferring funds to the coordinating campus. If an event is significantly over or under budget, it's helpful to have discussed in advance how that will be dealt with. Is the coordinating campus (or consortial entity) responsible for keeping to the planned budget and thus on the hook for any overages? If the event ends up costing just $2,000, will the campuses be reimbursed the extra $1,000?

This assessment model can also work for much larger collaborations. FCI has a roughly $10 million annual operating budget, some 70% of which comes from assessments (the remainder largely comes from grants and our endowment). Each of the hundreds of collaborative initiatives that FCI manages has a budget line and is split in some agreed-upon fraction—sometimes equally across all five campuses, sometimes with one campus paying a greater or lesser share. The bus service that connects all five campuses is split in fifths. The supplemental bus service that connects just two of the campuses is split evenly between those two. A faculty line that is shared by three campuses might be split 50/25/25, with one campus serving as the home institution and thus paying the larger share. Another collaboration at FCI includes 10 area museums, with 3 museums on a single campus and another 3 that are independent entities adjacent to but not owned by any campus. The budget for their shared work is divided roughly by the scale of each museum, and the campus with multiple museums is responsible for several shares—one for each museum. The consortium's complete portfolio of projects for each year is determined in advance. If expenses are less than budgeted, the campuses receive refunds proportional to what they paid in on the relevant line item. In the rare event that expenses are more than budgeted, FCI must tap its reserve funds, find alternative funding, or go back to the campuses to cover the overage. This elegant but complex model works well for FCI and its member institutions, providing transparency and accountability, but requires significant accounting work.

FCI uses the decision tool depicted in Table 4.1 to determine how costs are divided among member campuses. For programs that will be funded with dollars (as opposed to in-kind, for example), the cost will be split among member institutions based on one of the available allocation formulas, often referred to in FCI parlance by the fractional share (e.g., "on the sevenths"). These formulas are grouped into three broad models:

1. All participants share equally.
2. A two-tiered scale.
3. A three-tiered scale.

The two- and three-tiered scales allow the institution size and/or level of participation to be recognized in the assessment allocation in varying ways. In addition to assessments determined by these three categories, other items are "by agreement"—that is, allocated on an ad hoc basis driven primarily by member participation. Such agreements are necessary, for instance, when campus engagement is significantly skewed, and/or external partners engage in and pay for programming. (One example at FCI is Museums10, mentioned above, which consists of seven campus-based museums, including three on a single campus, and three community-based museums.) The formula to be used should be chosen at the time the program is approved but may be adjusted if circumstances change.

For FCI, the "fractions" model allows for flexibility without overemphasizing scale or calculating participation to exact percentages. This rough division of costs is workable in a consortium where the portfolio is large enough that fine differences come out in the wash—a campus that pays a bit more than its "true" share in one area often pays a

Table 4.1 Allocation Fractions at FCI

Category	Rationale	Calculation	Notes/examples
Equal	5 campuses share equally	5ths	All FCI administration and many program costs
	4 campuses share equally	4ths	Center for Women and Community—UM excluded from fees as host campus
2-tiered	5 campuses participate; 1 pays half of other 4	9ths	Fiber-optic network—HC pays half share
	4 campuses participate; 1 pays half of other 3	7ths	Risk Management—UM does not participate and HC pays half share
	5 campuses participate; 1 pays 2x the other 4	6ths	*Massachusetts Review*—UM pays double share as "owner"
3-tiered	5 campuses participate; 1 pays half and 1 pays 2x the other 3	11ths	Libraries and Bunker and Annex storage facilities—UM pays double share, and HC pays half share due to relative size of collections
Agreement	By agreement: joint appointments		Usually proportional to share of teaching (e.g., 50%/25%/25%)
	By agreement: other		Museums 10 includes 4 campuses with 1 museum each, 1 campus with 3 museums, and 3 community-based museums; museums differ significantly in size of collections.

bit less in another. A smaller organization with fewer initiatives may find it both workable and desirable to calculate contributions more precisely. The important thing in choosing any model is ensuring that the participating campuses agree the model is fair, whatever "fair" may mean in the local context.

A variation on the assessment model is the fee-for-service model, or what the Association for Higher Education of North Texas (AHE) called a "subscriber" model: "Although occasional grants are accepted for specific development projects, AHE does not actively raise funds, so it is not in the position of competing with its member institutions for foundation monies. Participants' membership dues make up less than 7 percent of AHE's operating budget. The lion's share of revenues comes from fees for services, paid by both members and subscribers."[20]

Under a dues-paying model, the partnering campuses each pay a membership fee into a central pot, which may be managed by one of the institutions or a separate consortial entity. In this funding scenario, whoever is managing the funds could decide to spend $3,000 of the annual budget on this speaker event. In this scenario, the decision regarding this particular event affects the rest of the portfolio—money spent here reduces what is available to support other activities. The amount of the dues may be set according to the anticipated portfolio of activity, but it is not tied to specific line items. Each campus may pay an equal share, or the shares may be determined by a formula based, say, on enrollment. The Big Ten Academic Alliance, the Colleges of the Fenway, Great Lakes Colleges Association, Associated Colleges of the Midwest, and Associated Colleges of the South all follow versions of this model, though with widely disparate dues amounts. A variation on this model is a budget supported by sponsorships, as in the case of the Baltimore Collegetown Network consortium, whose aim is to "attract, engage, and retain students, raise the profile of Baltimore as a college destination, and help colleges share resources."[21] For this sort of "booster" consortium, contributions from a chamber of commerce or local employers can make sense as part of the budget picture.

Most campuses are familiar with in-kind funding, and many consortial collaborations make use of such contributions, even when they follow one of the models above. In the speaker scenario, one campus might waive its usual site-rental fee, for instance. The staff time required to coordinate and manage the event is generally provided in-kind as well, though staff providing catering, sound and lighting, security, and the like may require a line item in the event budget. For consortia with dedicated staff who require offices, the space is often provided in-kind or through an arrangement where there is no rent, but building maintenance (cleaning, pest control, plumbing repair, and the like) may be paid by the consortium.

For a limited partnership, in which a group of campuses coordinate on a small and well-defined set of initiatives, the budget (and thus the funding) may be fairly straightforward, and all expenses can be directly tied to a particular project or event. For more mature and complex consortia, administrative and overhead costs need to be considered. In an assessment or dues-paying model, whoever is responsible for building the budget will need to take into account salary and benefit obligations, office supplies, computer equipment, software subscriptions . . . everything required to run any small office business. If the consortium administration is a single staff member supporting collaboration across three campuses, it might be that one campus agrees to provide an office and the necessary accoutrements (an email account and phone number, access to a printer and a conference room, payroll accounting, access to a health care plan and retirement benefits, etc.) while the other two split the cost of the salary and benefits (which they pay to the "host" campus).

FCI, with its 40–50 staff, has offices in a dozen locations across the campuses and in one FCI-owned facility. The campus locations are provided rent-free, with varying agreements on maintenance costs. If the campus is providing an office or two within a larger campus-occupied and managed building, janitorial services, snow removal, and the like are paid by the campus. The FCI mailing address is a stand-alone house converted into office space, which is owned by one campus but fully occupied by FCI. Costs to maintain this building and the landscaped property on which it sits are shared between the host campus and FCI (which is in turn, of course, funded by all the member institutions).

Whatever structure and amounts are chosen, an organization's budget represents its values and priorities. Phillip DiChiara, describing The Boston Consortium, offers several recommendations in establishing financial support for a consortium, among them these two. First, "the recurring overhead of consortium management must be equally borne." This supports every campus having an equal seat at the table as decisions are made that affect the whole. Second, support for these core administrative costs should not be shifted onto or reliant on grants: "Soft revenues from grant support act as venture capital for new ideas, not as support for the core consortial vehicle."[22] Longtime consortial directors Baus and Ramsbottom noted, too, the invisible investments of time and energy and the intangible benefits that can accrue from collaboration and argued that consortia should take both monetary and nonmonetary costs and benefits into account in designing an allocation of contributions "that is perceived to be fair and equitable to the paying customers."[23]

When money and people are involved, it is also important to consider how management—the day-to-day decisions and authority to sustain elements of the portfolio, as distinct from the high-level strategic decisions and institutional commitments of the board of directors—will work. A report supported by the American Council on Education identified three specific governance issues that arise in cross-institutional collaborations. First, uncertainties about who is responsible for decision-making. For example, if, as is generally understood, "the faculty are responsible for the curriculum," which faculty are responsible for shared curricula, and what role do other campus leaders play in facilitating collaboration? Second, the need, when designing shared programs, to satisfy multiple campuses' requirements and incentive structures. Potential mismatches in an academic collaboration can arise on everything from course structures and teaching expectations to curricular support and program review. On the administrative program front, mismatched budget models can, for instance, frustrate efforts to share things like procurement if cost savings do not accrue comparably across campuses. And third, the challenges inherent to any collaborative undertaking. How will goals be identified, problems addressed, resources allocated, and responsibility shared, not just at the outset but for the duration of the collaboration?[24]

Similarly, an analysis of cross-campus work in two sample consortia highlighted three decisions unique to collaboration that institutions need to be aware of and address early in the partnership. First, how will joint operations be managed? Essentially, who will identify the work to be done, who will do the work, and who will oversee it? Second, how will the costs and benefits of the collaboration be shared? What investments are needed and in what proportion by each campus, and are there limits on how much each campus can access the shared resource or program once it has been built? And third, what are the boundaries between the individuals and the group? What responsibilities and benefits remain with each campus, and which are shared by the collective?[25]

The fact that decisions like these need to be made in an environment built on competition and individual achievement further complicates matters. Pretending that competition doesn't exist is not the answer. One short-lived consortium found that "competition and secretiveness remained more characteristic of inter-university relations than were co-operation and candor."[26] Another consortium leader, mindful that the drive to compete is so ingrained it can't be entirely avoided, describes her campuses' work as "collabetition"—a sort of collaborative competition in which partnering with nearby institutions can help each campus compete in the wider landscape for students and resources.[27] (A 1996 book coined the term "co-opetition" with the same intent.[28]) One description of early consortia "cautioned that conflict and competition could only be controlled if they were viewed as functional," accepting them as necessary and even helpful features of collaborative work.[29] As the director of the CIC (the Big Ten Academic Alliance's precursor) once explained, "The enthusiastic participation of members and faculty is essential to the success of projects; but so is the responsible dissent. . . . There is an abrasive quality in such discussions which is constructive. . . . What others are doing inevitably leads to a self-evaluation: 'What are *we* doing?' "[30] The director of the Associated Colleges of the St. Lawrence Valley in 1975 was more blunt: "Colleges do not work together to cooperate. They cooperate to compete."[31] In this way of thinking, conflict and competition serve as traffic lights, at times signaling a need to slow or pause before moving forward, but they are never barriers completely blocking the road ahead.

As a study of failed consortia explained, "Conflict avoidance increased the level of ambiguity in the consortia and resulted in even less trust and more suppressed conflict," and "The inability to deal with conflict . . . proved to be a serious shortcoming" in the failed consortia studied.[32] Similarly, a *Harvard Business Review* article on collaboration characterized conflict as not only inevitable but also important: "The disagreements sparked by differences in perspective, competencies, access to information, and strategic focus within a company actually generate much of the value that can come from collaboration across organizational boundaries. Clashes between parties are the crucibles in which creative solutions are developed and wise trade-offs among competing objectives are made. So instead of trying simply to reduce disagreements, senior executives need to embrace conflict and, just as important, institutionalize mechanisms for managing it."[33]

Conflicts may also arise at the level of an individual initiative or program, when campus policies affecting a shared program do not align. Consortial management in this case needs to recognize the conflict and identify a path forward. One option is to negotiate a new policy, either specifically for the shared program or (less commonly) for the institutions generally. Consider room reservations, for instance, where on-campus personnel may have priority and be able to book rooms at no cost, while off-campus individuals have lower priority and may be charged a fee. Consortial partners may agree to a middle tier that elevates requests from members of sister institutions above those coming from fully "off-campus," but at a lower fee, thus still giving preferential treatment to on-campus users. This middle ground is most likely to work when the policy in question is not deeply embedded in campus culture and where the authority to approve the new policy is clearly delineated.

A second option is simply to acknowledge the lack of alignment and leave the decision to each campus. Promotion and tenure, for instance, are likely to vary across institutions, and generally it is preferable to identify a single "home" campus for a joint faculty member rather than to build a unique set of expectations or policies that may not be respected by either campus and that are likely to lead to confusion and frustration for the candidate. Student conduct policies similarly vary by school, and students might be subject to discipline by both their home campus and the campus on which the offending conduct occurred. Another cross-campus collaboration "decided to avoid potentially divisive issues, such as how partners should allocate alliance revenue internally, or compensate and reward faculty teaching in the program," by leaving each campus to make such decisions independently[34] This approach is likely to be most appropriate when the policy in question is key to each campus's culture and where adapting it will result in inconsistencies and a lack of fairness that extend beyond the program.

A third approach is to agree to follow the strictest policy relevant to the program. For instance, during the COVID-19 pandemic, the FCI campuses agreed that for students to participate in cross-registration they needed to comply with either their home or host campus testing policy, whichever was the most stringent (but that tests taken on one campus would be accepted on any other campus). Another collaborative reported choosing this approach when building shared academic programs, agreeing to adopt "the partner's policy that was most strict and had the least amount of flexibility" (such as the minimum number of courses required for a credential).[35] Choosing the strictest policy is likely to be the best option when health or safety are involved or when the policy may have legal, financial, or compliance ramifications for a participating campus.

Whichever approach is taken, it needs to be actively, intentionally, and mutually chosen and then documented and communicated to those who need to know (and reviewed periodically) because collaboration is a team sport. In addition, negotiation about any individual policy needs to keep the bigger picture in mind. Is this the battle I want to fight, or is this one I'm willing to concede in order to keep a partner in the room? As one collaborating dean cautioned, "When you don't have any room to compromise, alliances fall apart."[36]

Chapter 3 discussed the importance of setting expectations for consortial board members. Guiding principles may also be necessary for the staff, faculty, administrators, or other partners involved in a specific collaboration or initiative. One American Council on Education report recommends "written and agreed-upon guiding principles that outline parameters and set responsibilities," ideally written by the participants and supported by campus leadership. These principles should address what each partner institution will contribute in people and funding, how decisions will be made and communicated, and what specific functions each participant will be responsible for within the initiative. They may also cover any special arrangements or understandings that are fundamental to the collaboration. The Great Plains IDEA program, for instance (a 10-campus collaboration offering online programs in human ecology) specifies that courses included in the program are exempt from transfer credit policies, that faculty qualifications are established by their home campus and carry over to other campuses without additional review, and that students admitted to the program by one campus will be accepted by all the other campuses. Similarly, an international group of business schools jointly offering an executive master of business administration degree through a program called OneMBA notes that core courses must be completed on the student's home campus, that shared courses will be taught in English, and that each campus will contribute "in an equitable manner" to cover the shared cost of governing the program but will otherwise manage its own revenue and expenses for participation.[37]

There is no free lunch. Consortia are not quick fixes or cash cows. Time and attention must be invested. Beware of outsourcing either the work or the funding, either by expecting consortial staff to act alone, without campus engagement, or by relying on external funding to support initiatives, with no institutional contributions. Even if the shared goal is to save money (e.g., by sharing a resource), time and effort are needed to achieve those savings, so it's important to invest in relationships as much as in projects. Consortial staff can coordinate logistics and manage projects; keep folks coming back to the table; and facilitate through obstacles, hiccups, and turnover, but they cannot replace campus willingness to engage in the hard work of collaboration. That commitment must be fed and sustained, both at the outset and over the long haul.

FOR FURTHER EXPLORATION

Step 4. Mapping Workflows and Building Budgets

The diagram of the cross-registration process in Chapter 4 (Fig. 4.1) illustrates the complexity of a collaborative program. Documenting the workflow for a shared program can help articulate which personnel are responsible for which steps, identify where communication and handoffs will need to occur, and highlight potential problem areas. Software tools are available to help depict workflows but are not essential to the process. A hand-drawn sketch will suffice to help us gauge whether we're prepared to provide the structure, funding, and staffing needed to support our envisioned collaboration.

- For any given project, can we map the workflow of collaborative effort required? Indeed, we may need two maps: one for the implementation stage and one for when the project is off the ground. For instance, if the goal is to share a new contract, we need a map for the work entailed when negotiating terms with a vendor, including the logistics of executing a cross-campus agreement. A second map will show the work of managing that contract once it has been signed. Who needs to contribute to creating each map to ensure its accuracy? What campus governance or review steps will be required? How long will each step take? Is our overall timeline realistic? Are all the contributing players listed, and are they aware of the work entailed (or does the workflow include a communication plan to get them up to speed)?
- What skills are needed to do this work? Communication, negotiation, change management, attention to detail, optimism, and so forth will be needed in most initiatives. Are there legal, financial, academic, or other specific skills? In general, individuals tasked with consortial effort should be determined enough to pursue success in the face of obstacles but flexible enough to adapt as conditions require, and they must have relevant subject matter knowledge or ready access to those who do.
- Given the skills required, who exactly will be tasked with the work? Who will guide the work, establishing goals and budgets? Who will do the work, designing or executing details of the program? Who will support the work, scheduling meetings, keeping minutes, dealing with logistics? If hiring or assigning staff, is their role administrative, clerical, managerial, or something else? If staff are or will be employed by a single campus, how will they report to the group?
- What instructions will these staff be given? Find a way at any cost? Prepare a white paper on how to do this? Dive in and give it a try for six months and prepare an evaluation report?

- For each step in the process, will there be a cost? What resources will be needed? The financial contributions may (need to) be small, especially at the start, but they must also be in line with the goals and the complexity of collaboration (which often requires more time and effort at start-up than a solo version of the same project). Will any incentives be provided to those doing the work? Administrative support, access to space, a course buyout or summer stipend, food for meetings, or a bonus if successful?
- Do the partner institutions expect to benefit equally or proportionally? Are we all contributing monetary resources to this shared work? If an external funder is providing the majority of the support, how can each of us as participant leaders demonstrate our commitment to the collaboration?
- Will campus financial contributions be structured as dues or as cost-basis assessments? In other words, do we want to build the budget as "Do what you can with X amount" or "Do Y and we'll each pay our share of the necessary cost"? Will this structure be true for all collaborations between these partners, or will each project need to negotiate this? Will any partners be providing in-kind contributions instead of direct funding? Remember that any funding structure and allocation can work as long as all the contributors believe the arrangement is equitable.
- What other resources are available to support the work? Can leaders attend the ACL Summer Institute? Have any other consortia attempted something similar? Is grant or seed funding available to get the initiative off the ground?

Very few cross-campus collaborations come with an extensive staff (even 5 is uncommon, and 50 or more is rare) or an extensive budget ($5 million is unusual, particularly for new consortia), but the successful ones all benefit from material contributions and investments of time and attention if not dedicated staff or expendable cash.

CHAPTER FIVE

Cautionary Tales from the Consortial Front Lines (Attention)

Take care, for delicate things are more easily broken than mended.

"THE APPALACHIAN COLLEGE ASSOCIATION could have disbanded." So began a 2017 *Inside Higher Ed* article about this regional consortium founded in 1993.[1] There was, the story explained, a sense among the 35 member institutions that the consortium "was drifting," particularly after "it had burned through several presidents and interim presidents in the years since longtime president Alice L. Brown retired in 2008." But after nearly a decade of faltering member engagement, the board approved a new mission and strategic plan, shifting from its original focus on strengthening academic offerings on the campuses to engaging with the member campus communities and supporting the K–12 systems feeding their enrollments. The board noted, too, the importance of hiring a new leader for the consortium: "Because of [the] pressure on presidents and provosts to take care of their own institutions, if you don't have a strong consortia [*sic*] leader, the [campus leaders] won't come forth, and the organization won't come forth and be successful and make a difference. . . . So the leadership of a consortium seems to be absolutely critical to its success." As one member institution leader cautioned, "Institutions who don't constantly look at redefining themselves and assessing where they are, are going to be in trouble."[2]

Collaboration is a delicate thing. Not even the largest, longest-standing consortia are immune to change, disruption, or the risk of closure, whether of a single campus or the entire venture. I say this not to dissuade potential collaborators but to caution that this work never becomes automatic or straightforward. I often describe what we do at Five Colleges (FCI) as looking like either a jellyfish or a complicated extemporaneous dance. Our portfolio expands and contracts, and the relationships between our campus leaders become closer and more distant, like a jellyfish floating in water. But a jellyfish has only so much room to expand or contract—it's a controlled range of movement. So perhaps an improvisational dance is more apt—each partner reading the other (and the surrounding music) and responding in sync, moving in and away, creating new movement in the moment, testing out new configurations that sometimes work and sometimes fall away in favor of a different approach.

In 1998 the Colleges of Worcester Consortium (CWC) executive director cowrote a piece on how that consortium had lasted three decades. Fifteen years later, the CWC split into two entities, leaving a weakened structure behind. Another decade on (and, like the Appalachian consortium, facing leadership turnover) and the successor consortium is still finding its new footing, with an additional restructuring underway.[3] The Atlanta University Center Consortium, too, has evolved over its century-long history. Its origins date to 1912 and the establishment of the Atlanta Federation of Schools, which became the Atlanta University Center (AUC) in 1929. Shortly after one of its founding members lost accreditation in 2002, resulting in it leaving the consortium, the AUC officially dissolved and reincorporated as the Atlanta University Consortium, Inc.[4] The history of the Great Lakes Colleges Association describes "the consortium's major organizational crisis" coming a decade after its founding, when faculty on the campuses began to take on leadership of the shared international program "at a time when the central office was understaffed [leading] to extreme decentralization and erosion of authority at the center" and a second similar challenge with the women's studies program another decade on.[5] When Hampshire College stumbled in 2019, contingency plans needed to be discussed in the event that Five Colleges needed to become Four Colleges again. Change happens, and no consortium can last without continually renewed effort and attention.

None of what we do should be taken for granted. Every new campus leader, every new fiscal challenge, and every new demographic trend that affects enrollments and student interests can tip a consortium from robust to faltering. We began this volume with a definition that emphasized the voluntary nature of consortia as an essential characteristic. That feature can quickly become a fault. As collaboration expert and advocate Deb Mashek advised, we should "take a step back from the full-throated celebration of collaboration that's often present in many workplaces, instead acknowledging that collaboration can be really difficult to do well and that it is often fraught with disappointment, frustration, and worse."[6] Indeed, Mashek lists two dozen ways that collaboration can go off the rails, from underpreparation to overload. Or, as another team of collaboration scholars noted, "Here's the thing about consortia—they involve people. People bring aspirations, common interests, and good will. They also bring biases, frailties, and conflicting interests."[7]

One provost in 1977, concerned by what he saw as a tendency to look too optimistically on the promise of consortia, cautioned: "There have been many successful consortia. Yes, consorting can be great fun. New talent might be located and hired. Creative new programs may be produced. Colleagues may find whole new career interests. Or, as too often happens, institutions may work very hard and still feel they have been cheated."[8] These are reminders that things do not always go well. And they certainly cannot be expected to go well if care isn't paid to the ongoing health and evolution of the venture. As noted at the outset of this book, successful consortia require five elements: motivation, optimism, generosity, commitment, and attention. Time and space must be intentionally set aside to return to these basics, particularly in times of organizational stress or changes in leadership.

1. Motivation: Check in with one another on the why. Do the partners continue to share the same motivations? Has the landscape or leadership changed so much that a reset is needed? Have new members been welcomed into the existing motivations and goals and invited to help shape them for the future?
2. Optimism: Are the optimism and confidence in the collaboration still there? If doubts have begun to creep in, what factors are providing them entry? Can the faith be recaptured, or is it too badly fractured? Have new collaborative ventures been undertaken lately, or is the organization coasting on long-standing but potentially stale partnerships?
3. Generosity: Is everyone clear on their roles in supporting the collaboration, or is frustration emerging? Have members begun to pull back into their own institutions at the expense of the partners? Institutions should be allowed the space to put their own masks on as needed but should also return to helping others once their own essential requirements are met. Are leaders willing both to ask for help and to offer it in times of stress?
4. Commitment: Are the relationships strong enough? The leaders needn't be the best of friends, but there should be respect and care and a commitment to sustaining the relationships and the work they enable. Are bills being paid in full and on time? Are experienced staff being retained and new staff being added and trained as needed?
5. Attention: Is this work of checking in ongoing, or is it happening in cycles of near crisis? Is there a regular routine of touching base about expectations, needs, and perceptions? Are mechanisms in place to make adjustments when needed?

Interpersonal and organizational relationships flow, drifting apart and then back together, ideally with a core set of commitments and values keeping things from drifting too far. Some of this drifting is natural and necessary, but are people at the core attending to the drift and helping corral things back in before attention has been elsewhere for too long? Sustaining an organization is hard, but rebuilding one is harder and sometimes impossible.

We have no detailed recent statistics on the number of consortial partnerships that are attempted each year, nor the number that fail once launched. One study in the early 1980s reported that "nearly one of every three consortia in existence or developed since 1973 had ceased operation by 1984."[9] Another scholar in 2007 reviewed the available data and reported "a persistently high failure rate for collaborative activity; it is estimated to average at least 50%, with consortia likely to disappoint in 90% of cases."[10] But no comparable studies have been conducted since that time. We might, however, glean something from the data about small businesses. The Bureau of Labor Statistics reports that nearly 20% of small businesses fail within 1 year of opening, half fail after 5 years, and after a decade, roughly 65% have closed.[11] Data on nonprofits looks similarly bleak, with a plurality of closures happening between 6 and 15 years after founding.[12]

Research on small business closures notes the importance of building a customer base, which takes time and becomes easier with experience and reputation.[13] For consortia, the "customer" is the member campuses, and the "competition" is those campuses choosing to go it alone (or, occasionally, choosing to partner without the benefit of the consortial structure). Research on why nonprofits fail highlights the common pitfalls—lack of a clear plan, poor organizational development, insufficient time spent on understanding the context in which the work is being done, and lack of trust and communication.[14] In these respects consortial organizations are no different than any other nonprofit. A study of one successful higher education collaboration found similar challenges, even after more than two decades of operation: "a lack of clear, shared goals and objectives; a lack of fundamental principles to guide and evaluate collaboration; the absence of a clear communication framework to provide mechanisms for the partners to engage; the lack of both a funding model and an incentive model that are built for [the organization's] collaborative structure."[15]

As one scholar noted, given the relatively high failure rates for such collaborative work one wonders why new attempts continue to emerge and how existing ones remain healthy.[16] A case must continually be made for why this structure is aligned with stakeholder needs and worth the effort.

The caution for both new and long-standing consortia is simple: A group of committed and well-meaning presidents can establish a new consortium, but unless they build support for the collaboration at multiple levels within their campuses, the structure will be fragile and may not survive presidential turnover. By contrast, a consortium that has existed for decades has typically become deeply embedded in the work and culture and awareness of faculty and staff—"being part of the institution's DNA," as members of the Council of Public Liberal Arts Colleges (COPLAC) call this—and these folks can help advocate for the collaborative work as new leaders enter the community.[17] But even long-established consortia can face existential challenges if care isn't taken to communicate the value and feed the commitment.

Let's talk about some times that collaboration didn't go so well, as a reminder that these relationships should not be taken for granted or treated as cure-alls. Not surprisingly, tales of failure are harder to come by than documentation of successes. The closure of a campus or the contraction of a consortium is typically not a subject for sharing widely. Prompted by the lack of research exploring why the failure rates of consortia seemed to be high, Michael Offerman undertook a study of higher education consortia that had closed by the early 1980s. He began with a list of 38 "terminated" consortia and selected 3 to study in detail.[18]

The Consortium for Urban Education, a group of 16 member institutions in Indianapolis (not all of them colleges or universities), was founded in 1969, incorporated in 1975, and "substantially curtailed" operations in 1980. As Offerman explained, it relied on federal and foundation support and "was designed to unite resources of higher education, business, government, cultural, and community service agencies to find solutions to urban problems and to promote interinstitutional cooperation among its academic members." The Rochester

Regional Planning and Education Center consisted of 10 higher education institutions in Rochester, Minnesota. Founded in 1973, it ceased operating in 1981. While it functioned, it relied on state, federal, and foundation support "to offer courses and degrees to residents of Rochester, Minnesota whose educational needs were not being met." The University of Mid-America, in Lincoln, Nebraska, brought together 11 Midwestern state universities with member, federal, and foundation support in 1974 and ended the collaboration in 1982. The consortium "was designed to develop and experiment with educational alternatives for adults in a regional open learning system which utilized teaching at a distance."[19]

Offerman found that the end of funding was but one reason for the demise of the Consortium for Urban Education (CUE). One of the institutions grew rapidly and "unilaterally announced a program very similar to LIC [one of CUE's signature offerings]" and "even from the outset, there were varying levels of commitment to CUE by its member institutions." In addition, although the organization's by-laws had allowed for dues to be charged, they never were. That no-dues model was sustainable for a time, while grant funding was plentiful but left no backup or bridge and created burnout for those chasing funds. "At one point," Offerman found, "the institutions' business officers jointly stated: 'We can cooperate on everything except on sharing or allocating of students and in the use of institutions' funds for cooperative ventures.'" In other words, the "commitment" among these institutions was only to cooperate as long as it required no actual obligations or contributions. Offerman also noted a lack of consensus in the organization's mission: Was it to be program centered, or was it to facilitate cross-institution communication and cooperation more generally? At the same time, the organization lacked a functional governance structure, with even officers of the corporation unclear as to its purpose and their role and with each new director bringing a different emphasis to the mission. The lack of clarity in goals left success difficult to measure.[20]

Rochester, Minnesota, home to the Mayo Clinic, did not have a comprehensive public university to serve the community, but local leaders wanted one. The Rochester Regional Planning and Education Center (also called the Southeastern Minnesota Education Consortium, or simply the Rochester Consortium) had aimed to fill the need by developing a partnership among small private colleges in the area and several campuses with branches or extension centers in Rochester. It was one of three regional consortia formed by the Minnesota Higher Education Coordinating Board. As Offerman explained, "The development of the consortium was, in part, appeasement for the lack of a university. The demise of the consortium occurred, in part . . . because 'there were community board [Task Force] members who really wanted it to fail' so that they could then try again for a four-year institution."[21] An initial review of the three regional Minnesota consortia had been promising, noting that they had increased access to higher education and "satisf[ied] the education objectives and purposes set forth by the legislature." And yet a year later, a new governor proposed budget cuts to address shortfalls, including ending funding for the consortium in spite of the governor's earlier support for the work and his personal ties to the region of the state where Rochester is located. The governor argued that the earlier funding had established coordination that could continue without ongoing support from the state.[22]

Offerman cautions that although the closure of the Rochester Consortium can be seen merely as the result of political expediency, "the funding cut came in the midst of a much more complex set of circumstances." The institutions, although they valued the consortium, did not believe in it strongly enough to defend it from political attacks. It was a nice-to-have, but when asked in one hearing whether its closure would significantly alter their operations, every institution replied no. Offerman cited "lack of mission clarity, little articulation of goals and efforts, and limited communication between its committees" as contributing factors.[23]

Offerman notes that echoes of both the Consortium for Urban Education and the Rochester Consortium continued even after their "closures." A version of the Consortium for Urban Education, for instance, exists today with eight partner institutions and an emphasis on academic collaboration. Most notably, the early efforts provided a sort of proof of concept for interinstitutional collaboration: "The accomplishments highlighted at each consortium included the belief that the consortia had initiated a process of collaboration that had not previously existed and had demonstrated that cooperation in higher education can work."[24]

Offerman's third case study, the University of Mid-America (UMA), was a far grander and more widespread plan for public campuses across seven states to offer a regional open-access curriculum. Tellingly, he notes that these campus presidents "were persuaded to join together in this effort"—a description that doesn't suggest enthusiastic or self-driven engagement. Federal funding supported the effort to the tune of $14 million, along with additional grants for specific initiatives. UMA had three goals—produce courses, provide a mechanism for a regional degree, and conduct research on distance education in lifelong learning—goals that Offerman described as "deceptive in their apparent clarity." Six years into this undertaking, an evaluation described "contentiousness" between the consortium organization and the member institutions, as well as between the consortium and its federal funding agency, "due to serious differences of opinion on what UMA's proper role was within higher education in its region and how it was to function as a consortium."[25]

Even as these concerns were being documented, UMA was beginning efforts to build the American Open University (AOU), a new institution designed to grant degrees and credits made possible through the collaboration. In effect, "UMA had addressed the issue of its role by moving squarely into the domain of its member institutions." If UMA had overreached, a lack of clear engagement and support from those member campuses, at both the presidential and faculty levels, brought the situation to a head: "The institutional presidents on the Board had allowed the creation of AOU but would not be a party to its operation." UMA officially closed two years later.[26]

Offerman cites eight factors that affected all three failed consortia and a ninth factor that affected some of them. The first two factors are "funding policy" and "institutional commitment and support," two sides of the same coin. Essentially, each of these consortia began with external funding and no internal financial commitments; the external funding also came with expectations that did not necessarily align with the members' interests. When external funding disappeared, little incentive remained to institutionalize the efforts, and when interests diverged, the campuses had little leverage with their funders to realign purposes. "The institutions were apparently unwilling to view membership as a reciprocal arrangement in which advantages and resources were to flow to and from the consortium. Instead, membership appeared to be measured in terms of the amount of advantage to be gained with little or no investment."[27] By contrast, most consortia with long track records of success receive significant funding commitments from their members, with external funds used to seed and pilot new programs rather than to supplant internal commitments.

The next three factors—"mission clarity and articulation," "organizational structure," and "effectiveness"—all indicate a lack of shared understanding of the purpose of the effort. In the failed consortia, missions were not concisely stated, shared, or reviewed. Without clear missions, it was difficult to establish "organizational structures appropriate for attainment of consortium objectives." Without clear articulation and agreement on mission, and with the pull of funders' views, it was difficult to agree on accomplishments. More troubling, but not surprising, "any accomplishments were selfishly viewed by the members as resulting from institutional rather than consortium efforts. There were both usurpation and cooptation of consortium achievements and innovations."[28] As we've noted, most consortia take a back seat to the campuses in receiving credit for their successes, but in long-standing consortia, there is a clear understanding of what the consortium is permitted to do (even if that scope is sometimes quite broad) and agreement about what activities are off-limits.

Three further factors involved a lack of appreciation for the unique features of collaborative work: by leaders, by the institutions they represented, and by the communities the consortium was meant to serve. The board members possessed little clarity regarding their roles in shaping the goals and activities of the consortium, limiting the effectiveness of the staff tasked with day-to-day management. As Offerman realized, "These presidents were selected by their institutions for assumed abilities to manage traditional education organizations but those abilities may not be the same ones required for leadership of collaborative, innovative ventures." Confusion at the leadership level about the role of the consortium as well as their role in guiding it translated into institutional uncertainty: "The unwillingness of the institutions to allow the consortia to define a domain in which to operate was a pervasive and debilitating problem. . . . Rather than utilizing the consortium to manage or control competition, the institutions came to view the consortium as one more source of competition."[29] Without a clear mission, role, and domain, these failed consortia struggled to identify, much less engage, a supportive set of stakeholders. The unique features and demands of consortia are always present, but in the most established consortia, at least some attention is paid to managing and mitigating these challenges.

Offerman's last factor—member complementarity—is somewhat misleading. He noted that to a greater or lesser degree in all three cases, the failure could be tied to "dissonance amongst members . . . in terms of perceived status, resource wealth, and levels of ownership and commitment to the consortia."[30] Note, though, that these disparities exist in many successful consortia and that a strong alignment of these characteristics can spur competition that damages collaboration. In short, differences among institutions are not inherently problematic, but respectful relationships must be nurtured, and equity must be designed into shared systems.

A decade after Offerman's study, an analysis of a seven-year, multimillion-dollar computing collaboration that led to "disappointment at failure to deliver what was expected" uncovered five lessons about collaboration that Offerman would have recognized:

- Collaborative groupings should generally be voluntary with no element of moral compulsion to participate.
- Collaboration tends to work best on a small scale.
- Collaborative groupings work better if they have shared interest and philosophies, and geographical proximity is useful.

- Whatever the size of the collaborative grouping, it must have clear project management processes and disciplines by which members must agree to be bound.
- Members must accept that they will not be able to obtain all of their user requirements from a collaborative project and will have to undertake in-house adaptation on their own for a considerable proportion of what they need.[31]

Although the fifth lesson from this failed computing initiative sounds specific to information technology (with its reference to user requirements, for instance), the notion that collaboration requires adaptation and a willingness to accept and manage cross-campus disparities holds true for any partnership.

These lessons are reflected in the more recent experience of a Western Pennsylvania consortium that failed before it launched. In the fall of 2023, a news report emerged that as many as 17 private colleges in Western Pennsylvania had been working with a consultant to explore the formation of a consortium to share administrative services. Some of these campuses already belonged to the Pittsburgh Council on Higher Education, a general-purpose consortium with a successful portfolio of activity, including the Pittsburgh Scholar House. Within weeks of the news report on the new exploratory work, several campuses told *Inside Higher Ed* they were no longer pursuing the consortium "despite participating in the study to explore the benefits of such an agreement." Although the consultant suggested that collaboration could provide cost savings and reduce personnel, one campus spokesperson said, "Our aims and those of the consortium weren't aligned, and not in any way reflective of our original intent." They also noted that they were not the only campus withdrawing from the process. A second campus's representative was more explicit, noting that "collectively negotiated purchasing agreements" continued to be of interest, but the campus was less enthused "with the consultants' ideas for consolidating operations that would result in employee layoffs." The news coverage suggested that campus leaders had pursued the potential for collaboration largely in secret and that faculty and staff on the campuses had been surprised and alarmed at the prospect of staff reductions. One faculty member was quoted as saying "It's never been, 'Hey, let's all get together and talk about what a consortium even is.' We all learned about it from the [WESA] article."[32]

We've noted the importance of creating time and opportunity for relationships to form for campus leaders and also for key peer groups on campus—a department chairs meeting or a multicampus faculty-of-color reception or a new faculty meet and greet can allow relationships to begin. These relationships support dreaming together, identifying potential projects, building collaborative muscle. In the Western Pennsylvania exploration, the lack of transparency made it difficult to persuade employees that the goal of collaboration was to become better. Instead, the conversation among campus leaders (or at least the conversation as guided by the consultant) seemed focused only on becoming leaner. The common themes in research on collaboration include trust, shared goals, funding clarity, flexibility, and knowing when to end a collaboration.[33] In this case the campus leaders' failure to attend to the first four themes effectively ended the collaboration before it began.

A few ill-timed departures can also impede a group's ability to play well together. In describing the conditions that led to Wheelock College's separation from the Colleges of the Fenway and absorption into Boston University, Mary Churchill (the last vice president for academic affairs at the stand-alone Wheelock) noted that "between 2004 and 2016, six different vice presidents for academic affairs at Wheelock arrived and departed." Making matters worse, leadership among the Colleges of the Fenway was in flux in 2017, with three of the then–six-member campuses operating with interim provosts.[34] Leadership changes such as these are difficult for a single institution to navigate when finances and enrollment are stable. Attempting to address challenges collectively with a rotating cast of characters becomes nearly impossible.

Turnover in leadership will happen. Some of it will be predictable; some will come unexpectedly. In the space of a single year, FCI saw the departure of three (of five) directors who had each served for more than a decade in their role as president or chancellor. We knew it was coming and were making plans to manage the transition. In the midst of this preparation, a fourth director got tapped for a dream job and left before any of the three planned departures. Presidents and provosts and other campus leaders retire, get sick, get chosen for other roles, and get removed from office; the same is true with executive directors and presidents of consortia. Institutional memory helps sustain partnerships, and loss of that memory can damage them. When departures are planned, those on their way out can help orient their successors to the roles and procedures of an existing collaboration. But even in the best of circumstances, new campus leaders are learning their own campus community, and attention to collaboration or a consortium can be a low priority in the early days.

If the transition is planned, certain steps can help support the organization through the change. Begin by communicating with the search committee and/or search firm so they understand the place of the consortium in the role they are looking to fill. If the new president will be a member of the board of directors, for instance, it's important that candidates know their legal and fiduciary obligations before they accept a position. Provide the committee or firm with language that can be included in a position precis or job narrative. Make sure the consortium website is up to date and inviting so that candidates and committees can easily grasp the organization's activities. Consortial staff need to remember, though, that the search belongs to the campus. I offer information and let search firms know I'm available if they or candidates have questions about what we do, but I also make it clear that I understand the hiring authority is not mine. The process is generally a bit more open at a public institution, but still challenging.

Once a new president, provost, dean, or other key leader has been named, or once we know an announcement is coming soon, a new opportunity to engage presents itself. On some campuses I've been invited, as executive director of the consortium, to be present at the public introduction of the new leader, joining trustees and other dignitaries in welcoming the president-elect to campus. The presidential transition team on a campus may, however, view the consortium as one external obligation among many, akin to the local Rotary club or chamber of commerce—respected, perhaps, but not central. If this is the campus's view, it's unfortunate, but the period leading up to the transition is generally not the time to attempt a reboot of this relationship. It's better to focus on getting access to the president as early as possible and making that first impression a pivot point.

At FCI we have developed an onboarding book for new presidents, chancellors, provosts, and chief financial officers (CFOs), as well as for senior staff hired at the consortium. Each group's version is slightly different (the CFOs get more budget information than the others, for example), but the overall structure remains similar. (It can easily be adapted for other new leaders as well—chief information officers, library directors, heads of student affairs, and so forth.) The book includes a few key items:

1. A brief overview of the organization—this begins with a small brochure that provides a high-level overview. Given the breadth and scope of our portfolio, we also designed a roughly 40-page mini-encyclopedia designed to be read once (in under an hour) or skimmed (in as little as 5 or 10 minutes) and referred to as needed later. It briefly describes our history, structure, and key programming.
2. Governance documents—our by-laws, articles of organization, and agreement of association documents (all required under state law) that lay out the basic legal functions and obligations of the organization and its leaders. We expect very few leaders will read these carefully, but it's important they know this is a 501(c)(3) with legal and fiduciary responsibilities and that they have these documents on hand, even if they don't recall the details.
3. Strategic road map—as described elsewhere, this is our version of a strategic plan, and it allows us to agree on strategy and priorities while also enabling FCI to adapt quickly to changes in campus needs. This entire document is less than 20 pages long.
4. Budget documents—this section includes a snapshot of the current fiscal year budget and a 1-page overview of the budget

process. Provosts also receive a summary of all the jointly appointed faculty, with their campuses' respective shares of and responsibilities for each one.

5. Risk management—although risk management is just one of hundreds of collaborative initiatives we manage, it's important that presidents know about this feature of our work early since emergencies and crises can happen at any time.
6. Resource information about our password-protected portal, contact lists, and meeting schedule—because our work depends on communication and relationships, we make sure that campus leaders have ready access to their counterparts, and we highlight upcoming meetings that will be important for them to attend.

We schedule a one-hour orientation for each new leader, ideally over lunch. One or two of us from the consortium join the campus leader. We strive to offer a warm welcome to the community, highlighting our role in helping each new leader achieve success. We describe the benefits and activities of the consortium and their role in the work. And we briefly talk them through what's included in the binder as resources for them to refer to later. We answer as many questions as we can in that first hour together and ensure they leave with my cell phone number (and I with theirs).

When leaders turn over, it isn't simply that a new widget gets inserted into the mechanism of the consortium. New leaders come with new perspectives, priorities, and prejudices. They are chosen for the alignment of their vision with that of their new campus, not necessarily because of their appreciation for the work of the consortium. The most resilient consortium is one that has a solid enough core mission to be compelling to new leaders but is also flexible enough to adapt to new viewpoints without breaking. Discussing, documenting, and routinely revisiting a few core principles can help build a resilient foundation, as in the FCI example below.

Another challenge in onboarding new leaders is related to measuring and celebrating success. Consortia generally exist to make their member

The Five College Core Principles

This consortial way of thinking is supported by a set of values. For Five Colleges, these values find expression in our Core Principles.

1. Collaboration
   Consortial work depends on collaboration, and that principle should be evident in our daily work with one another as well as in the cooperative programming we administer.

2. Trust
   Trust is an essential element to successful collaboration and is built over time and with experience. Our committees, communal events, and shared governance structures all aim to nurture and sustain the interpersonal relationships and transparent communication that enable the work of the consortium.

3. Equity
   Our campuses vary in scale, mission, and resources, but are equal partners in the consortium and deserve equitable benefits from their participation.

4. Interdependence
   While the campuses remain independent entities, the collaborative programs that make up the shared portfolio are highly interdependent. As a result, access to the non-funded benefits of participation in the consortium is dependent upon engagement in the funded portion—a campus cannot opt out of the funded portions of the portfolio but retain access to the unfunded programming.

5. Adaptability
   The work of the consortium occurs in the ever-changing intersection of the member institutions' interests and priorities. The staff of the organization commit to adapting nimbly to respond to the opportunities and needs of the moment, and to using our resources to support deliberative and thoughtful adaptation in moments of crisis.

institutions better, not to make themselves the stars. If consortial efforts are successful, the members will look better, and the consortium itself is likely to be invisible, or is at least expected to take a back seat. And if consortial efforts fail, it is easy to blame the consortial structure itself. Phillip DiChiara, the former director of The Boston Consortium, describes this as an attractive feature for the member campuses, allowing them to manage their "inherent risk aversion" by placing the risk in the consortial laboratory. "In effect, when the project was successful and adapted, the member institutions genuinely deserved the credit. If the project failed, it was just the consortium doing what it was set up to do: experiment."[35] While this mental model of the consortium may be attractive to campus leadership, it can be dispiriting to consortial staff, whose entire job is to enhance the campuses and yet who rarely receive thanks for their work. And if the consortium's positioning is typically behind the scenes, new campus leaders may understandably have difficulty grasping what the consortium does and why they should care or invest in its success.

It is a difficult needle to thread. As we saw in Chapter 3, the parallel challenge of identifying a strategic plan for the consortium is to draw enough attention to the collaborative organization to set a meaningful course forward without pulling undue attention away from the campuses' own strategic efforts. As Offerman described the demise of the University of Mid-America consortium: "Perhaps the most important aspect of the lack of institutional support for UMA was the fact that there was a fear of and resistance to UMA becoming a competing institution." He cited a board chair who cautioned, "You have to keep in mind that a consortium does not exist in and of itself even though they do develop a life of their own" and a dean who complained that "every consortium has this problem of seeking an identity of its own."[36]

Anyone entering consortial work should understand this dynamic, though it manifests differently in different settings. When in my interview I told the search committee it was "not my job" to have a vision for the organization, I understood it was what that committee wanted—even needed—to hear in that moment, given its recent history. That my ego would take a back seat to theirs. That the organization wouldn't wag the dog. That I understood the mission of the consortium truly was "to enhance the member institutions," not to highlight the role of the nonprofit in enabling that enhancement. The trick is to balance that invisibility with garnering respect for the important work being done.

How then ought we to gauge the success of a consortium and its efforts? Offerman, in summarizing the lessons of failed consortia, noted that "just as the consortium may require different approaches to leadership, it may also be appropriate to reconceptualize consortium evaluation." He argued that consortia had been touted for their "potential macroscopic, societal gains" but were typically evaluated "in terms of the individual institution's budget-management concerns." Campuses may claim to want to change the world, he suggested, but at the end of the day, they were swayed by more prosaic changes. But he conceded (as Davis had suggested in 1967) that "the failure to evaluate consortia in terms of societal benefits . . . may limit consortia to insubstantial accomplishments."[37]

One study found that leaders of existing consortia typically reported them to be successful, and yet when prompted to identify metrics that would demonstrate effectiveness at their mission or achievement of their goals, they almost universally failed to do so. A second study argued that consortia "are effective if they meet the needs of their members," which the author summarized as the five E's: "expanded student and faculty opportunities, promotion of greater managerial efficiency, promotion of experimentation and change, promotion of exchange through interpersonal contacts among the members, and entrepreneurship."[38]

While the first of these studies emphasized metrics (particularly numeric ones), the fact is that for most consortia the goals are not easily quantified. If the mission is, for instance, "to enhance the member institutions" or to promote various activities, the qualitative assessments and descriptions by campus leaders do reflect success. Quantitative metrics may make for nice graphics in an annual report, but they may be inappropriate to the work of a consortium.

In setting up a consortium evaluation or gauging the success of a collaboration, it's also worth asking whether we're aiming to measure the effectiveness of the consortial organization (the nonprofit entity) or the effects of the consortial portfolio. The organization is a structure that facilitates collaboration and manages the programs that the campuses have chosen to sponsor. Those programs should of course be evaluated, but this isn't the same as measuring the success of the consortial entity or structure. The questions are both valuable but shouldn't be confused with one another. Years ago, I team taught a course on research methods. One of my fellow instructors argued that double-blind studies were the gold standard, and in the medical setting that was her background her statement was quite true. By contrast, for my work as a historian double-blind studies don't exist. The questions we were asking were different. If we want to know whether medication X effectively treats disease Y, a double-blind, quantitative study is appropriate. If we want to know how physicians learned to diagnose that disease over the past century, we need stories and documentation, but there is no "metric" that will give us the answer. The right data and method depend on the goal. In evaluating consortia and their work, the best approach may be both/and. Quantitative measures of, say, how many more courses are available to students through the collaboration or how much money joint procurement has saved in the past year can help document the benefits of collaboration. (Though note that long-standing shared procurement becomes difficult to benchmark after an initial period of clear savings.) But stories of recruitment efforts helped by the existence of a spousal hire program, or quality-of-life enhancements thanks to a robust set of arts programming, are also signs of consortial success.

An additional item to consider is how to unwind a collaboration that is no longer effective or desired. If the purpose of the organization is to support the campuses, what's the plan if they don't play well together or are no longer interested in playing? What happens if the evaluation data, in whatever form, show that this simply isn't working? It's the rare organization that can find itself in trouble and disassemble itself with grace. Some consortia have rules about how much notice is required before a member can withdraw from the partnership (typically a full fiscal year or more, to facilitate planning). For FCI, because we're not a dues-paying organization, member institutions cannot simply withdraw from the consortium. They are charter members, and their withdrawal would effectively require dismantling (and perhaps rebuilding) much of the structure of the consortium. Still, it is worth (occasionally) considering what would happen if dismantling were desired or necessary, if only as a reminder of the value of staying together.

We follow a similar practice at FCI in individual initiatives. If you've signed on to share a faculty line or to support a multicampus program, you can't simply pull away. You need to give full notice and provide your partners with a chance to replace or otherwise accommodate your share. I won't lie: Things don't always work so smoothly. Someone forgets that a faculty line is shared and opts to remove it from their campus budget before they recall that it is not theirs to cancel. Or a faculty committee votes to close an academic program, forgetting that they are but one group of stakeholders in a collaborative venture. Or a unit makes a hire to fill a perceived gap, unaware that the "gap" is actually filled by a shared service. In general, such actions are inadvertent and don't come from any ill-will or desire to do harm. More typical is that the collaboration is so seamless or invisible that it's easy to forget that this faculty line or program is different from others. Or the committee making the decision doesn't realize this exception doesn't fall under their purview. It's also worth mentioning here that as important as presidential engagement is, one study cautioned that "some consortia have found their successes multiplied just to the extent to which their chief executive officers have *not* been involved in making program decisions."[39] Sometimes it's best to leave the details to others.

Offerman took the factors that he found led to consortial downfall and crafted them into a set of recommendations for success. They look remarkably similar to those identified by Jackie Pritzen, which she structured as a set of five questions to gauge "the degree of institutional commitment, and therefore the likelihood of cooperative success":

- Are the member institutions willing and able to define common needs and common goals?
- Is each member clear about what it hopes to gain through the cooperative program, and is there a reasonable expectation that these gains can be realized?
- Are the members prepared to provide adequate financial resources and administrative support to make the program work? Are they willing to furnish some "hard money" support?
- Is each institution willing to bend itself a little to adjust or revise some of its regulations, procedures, or policies in order to accommodate cooperative activity?
- Is each institution prepared to publicize its commitment to the cooperative program to its own constituencies—faculty, staff, students, and alumni?[40]

Pritzen's overall advice remains on point: Provide leadership through institutional commitment and clarity of goals, develop a coordinating structure, build a consortial community, and create incentives for engagement. These four tasks continue to hold true nearly 40 years later: commit, coordinate, commune, and incentivize.[41]

At FCI today, these questions are formulated in a set of organizational vital signs to gauge the consortium's health: a small number of easily measured characteristics that do not in themselves diagnose "disease" but do provide either quick reassurance that we are headed in the right direction or an early indication of issues that might need attention. The full description appears in Table 5.1, but in essence the vital signs are measured with just four questions:

1. How well is the board getting along?
2. How much do campus leaders trust the executive director and senior consortial staff?
3. How aligned are the academic calendars?
4. How much do campus leaders focus on the overall portfolio versus individual initiatives?

Table 5.1 Sample Organizational Vital Signs

	Exemplary performance *The organization is excelling, but the effort required may be unsustainable over extended periods.*	**Optimal performance** *The organization is healthy and should be able to achieve and sustain this level of performance.*	**Suboptimal performance** *The organization can survive for some time at this level, but action is needed to get healthy.*	**Unacceptable performance** *The organization is at existential risk. Action is urgently required and overdue.*
Board relations	The board members are deeply engaged with the work of the organization, attend all meetings, and exceed the Board Expectations. They communicate frequently with one another and the ED, even when not required or expected.	All board members are routinely engaged with the work of the organization, fulfill Board Expectations, and communicate with one another and with FCI when/as necessary.	Most members attend most meetings and are striving to fulfill the Board Expectations, but with some departures. Communication gaps exist but are generally minor.	One or more board members are significantly departing from the Board Expectations and/or are actively hiding information or sabotaging the health of the organization.
Executive director and senior staff performance	The ED and senior staff routinely exceed expectations as laid out in their job descriptions and performance reviews. They are recognized as experts in collaboration and are sought out as consultants and contributors.	The ED and senior staff understand and execute their jobs well and faithfully, serving the best interests of the organization and the campuses. They are engaged with peers outside the consortium.	The ED and senior staff mostly perform well, but some minor gaps in performance or weaknesses are evident in some skills or judgment. They are minimally engaged outside of FCI.	One or more members of the senior staff are performing significantly below expectations to such an extent that the organization is experiencing pain. Campus colleagues and peers may avoid working with them or the organization.
Academic calendar alignment	The campuses exceed the expectations of the Calendar Guidelines, with all five calendars in perfect alignment and effectively acting as a single calendar. Campus leaders communicate frequently to ensure alignment continues.	The campuses are in full compliance with the Calendar Guidelines, though key dates are not entirely aligned. Campus leaders communicate routinely and actively encourage their staff to mitigate gaps and their consequences.	The campuses are in compliance with some but not all Calendar Guidelines. Campus leaders communicate occasionally. Staff strive to manage gaps and their consequences, though perhaps with minimal support from leadership.	One or more campuses depart significantly on key dates and the value of alignment is not recognized. Leaders and staff rarely communicate about the misalignment. Students are left responsible for managing any gaps.
Portfolio vitality (perceived ROI)	Campus leaders view the effort and investment required to feed consortial activity (reflected in the annual proposed portfolio and budget) as highly beneficial. Campuses actively propose and seek new collaborations to extend this success.	Campus leaders view and can articulate the effort and investment required to sustain and build consortial activity as worthwhile and actively support new collaborations as appropriate and necessary.	Campus leaders continue to approve FCI budgets and to pay their assessments but with some significant questions about the value of one or more major FCI activities or collaboration generally. The portfolio is stagnant or shrinking.	Campus leaders view the consortium as requiring far more effort and funding than the portfolio is worth. Leaders frequently question project expenditures and administration and are actively disengaging.

Abbreviations: ED, executive director.

Board relations and trust in the staff are easily understood, and when the financial officers and others are looking more at the big picture rather than at line items, this, too, suggests trust and confidence in the organization's staff and initiatives. The emphasis on academic calendars may be more cryptic, but alignment of the schedule that dictates much of the flow of campus life is actually quite crucial. The calendars aligning well doesn't only make cross-registration easier; everything from bus schedules to cross-campus auditions to shared faculty development programs becomes easier. In addition, setting academic calendars is an intricate process on each campus, with multiple layers of review and approval needed, so when we *can* align calendars, we know we've managed to coordinate across all these layers, suggesting our interinstitutional cooperation and trust are strong.[42]

Each of our four vital sign questions is answered with one of four characterizations:

1. Exemplary performance: The organization is excelling, but the effort required may be unsustainable over extended periods.
2. Optimal performance: The organization is healthy and should be able to achieve and sustain this level of performance.
3. Suboptimal performance: The organization can survive for some time at this level, but action is needed to get healthy.
4. Unacceptable performance: The organization is at existential risk. Action is urgently required and overdue.

It's important to note that "exemplary performance" is not where the organization is expected to be at all times. We should strive for it, but like an athlete who trains for a competition, rest days are critical, and not every day is the Olympics. Assessment of these vital signs does not replace fiduciary reporting, program reviews, performance evaluations, and other assessments, but it provides a simple way to gauge the well-being of the collaborative undertaking as a whole.

The history of consortia is filled with tales of growth . . . and with change and failure. The most successful and long-standing consortia faced the same headwinds as the ones that fell apart. Offerman lists recommendations for success, and they remain important some four decades later. The developing, building, addressing, and assessing he recommends must all be done by humans. And often a very small group of individuals can either keep the plates spinning in the air or can introduce chaos and catastrophe very quickly. The history of successful consortia is filled, too, with stories of charismatic, dedicated, attentive individuals and small groups of close colleagues, with off-the-cuff conversations that led to remarkable achievements. The Claremont consortium at its founding consisted of a single campus and its president's dream, and the Atlanta University Center Consortium came about when a single president was simultaneously leading two campuses. This is not to diminish the breadth and depth of collaboration that have emerged in these two consortia over the past century but to highlight how fragile the beginnings can be. The ability to envision a different future is powerful, but collaborative efforts can just as easily be derailed by offhanded comments, distraction, and overwork. Whether a collaboration is new or long-standing, leaders should neither take the planning lightly nor take what exists for granted.

FOR FURTHER EXPLORATION

Step 5. Maintaining a Healthy Collaboration

With a clearly articulated shared motivation, an agreed-upon project (based on the project screening tool or a comparable evaluation), a detailed set of board expectations, and a dedicated budget and staff (even if quite small), the elements are in place for a successful collaboration. But ongoing vigilance remains important.

- How often will we revisit our shared motivation and goal? What data or process will help us determine if we remain in alignment?
- How will we know whether our project is living up to expectations?

- When and how will we review our board expectations and honestly assess whether we are living up to them?
- Who is overseeing the time and money being spent on this work?

We've noted that collaborations can be fragile. How do/will we know if our efforts are going well? What warning signs will we watch for? What safeguards can we put in place to protect against losing momentum as personnel change over? Can any policies and practices support this work? For instance, are boards of trustees aware of the key role of campus leadership in the consortium so that when a search is launched for a new president the consortium is included in the duties and expectations? Do annual reviews ask participants to reflect and report on the effectiveness of cross-campus initiatives?

One mechanism for documenting signs of wellness or concern is via a set of organizational vital signs, as in Table 5.1. This tool is intended to support the assessment of FCI as an organization and the consortium as a set of relationships. These "vital signs" are markers of the overall health of the organization; they don't diagnose or treat conditions but do serve as indicators when additional analysis or care may be needed. In each of these four areas, the organization has a written standard or formal process against which to compare performance. Note that the academic calendar alignment is important because it supports not just cross-registration, but also cross-campus collaboration more broadly. In addition, achieving alignment reflects significant effort on the part of many individuals and governance committees, which itself is a sign of healthy collaboration. As with other tools, the right vital signs are those that are appropriate to the nature of the organization and reflect the priorities of its leaders.

For your existing or desired collaboration, what three to five vital signs (or key performance indicators) would suggest that all is well or flag potential or emerging issues? This is not an all-inclusive list of the countless factors that need to align for success. It is a small set of critical aspects of the collaboration that can be readily tracked and then managed or explored further when necessary.

Having a list and using it are two different things, so how might we ensure that the list will serve its intended purpose? Leaders might choose to include the vital signs on each meeting agenda as a reminder to check in. Or the signs might be referenced in an annual report for the organization. Whatever the mechanism, its effectiveness depends on where we began—with the motivation to craft a path to success, the optimism that a path is possible, the generosity to contribute the necessary time and energy, the commitment to see the work through, and the attention to keep striving to be better than we are.

CONCLUSION

People, People, People, and Resources

We can become better than we are.

IF THE GOAL is to be better, the mindset must be new. This is the heart of consortial thinking in a competitive landscape. It begins with motivation, perhaps individually held at first but then articulated so it can be discussed and collectively shaped into a shared intention. This is not so that each participant can become more similar to the others but to enhance each member's individuality. It is fed by optimism, faith that the effort will be worthwhile, that obstacles can and will be managed, and that the payoff will come and be valued as well as valuable. Not naive, unrealistic, foolish optimism but the hope and confidence that committed, capable, inspired people can come together to do powerful things. It is nurtured with generosity of spirit, a willingness and even a commitment to think beyond self-interest while not ignoring the benefits that will be returned. Such generosity is easiest to offer from a position of strength and self-confidence, aware of areas in need of improvement, surely, but also secure in one's fundamental value. It is strengthened by the commitment of time, attention, energy, people, and, yes, funding. And it demands attention: continual care and feeding of the structure and relationships as well as of the portfolio of initiatives and projects. As two long-serving consortial leaders put it, "Starting an academic consortium is a serious undertaking. Sustaining a consortium is every bit as serious and much more complex."[1] In spite of all the ways in which this work is hard and unnatural, it is also deeply rewarding.

In my early days as an academic administrator, I worked for a seasoned and adept dean whose mantra of leadership was that to get anything done required people, people, people, and resources. His point being, if it hasn't become clear in these pages already, that people—their time, attention, wisdom, and relationships—are critical elements of collaborative work, whether that work is a research project, a curricular revision, or a multicampus consortium, and that those people must be given the resources (equipment, space, support) to do their best work together. But most important are the people. Hire (or appoint or promote or tap) the right ones and give them room, and they will find the magic together.

No book can identify or convene the people, people, and people required to do consortial work, but this one offers a few of the resources those people might need to do consortial work to the best of their ability.[2] The tips and practices and tools described in this volume are not formulaic. They're not intended to be used as plug-and-play workbooks. They're meant to support and encourage and give direction to conversations and negotiations, to help build consensus and shared motivation. As we noted at the beginning, if you've seen one consortium, you've seen one consortium; the guidance here must be read and deployed in a local context. A core precept in emergency management is that we build a strong foundation of planning and protocols, not because we can predict the future but rather to support flexibility in that moment of crisis when we must think on our feet. Establishing structures and practices we can rely on as a starting point helps to free up mental space for coping with the unique and unexpected features of the situation we're facing. And deep collaboration is nothing if not filled with the unexpected.

Further support is available for those who attempt such ventures. An excellent resource is the Association for Collaborative Leadership, a professional association of consortia and consortial leaders created in the early 1970s as the mid-century boom of consortia came online.[3] The organization offers professional development webinars, virtual coffee chats, an annual conference, and a biennial summer institute for those new or exploring entry to this work. They can be found at www.national-acl.org/. The consortial landscape is dynamic, and any list of organizations is necessarily incomplete and quickly out of date. The ACL directory is a useful reference, though it is limited to member organizations and thus does not include all consortia, either in the United States or around the world.

Jackie Pritzen, a former program director at FCI, described the evolution of expectations over the first few decades of the consortial movement: "Cooperative programs and agreements were the vehicles of growth and expansion during the 1960s; today (1988) they may be becoming the vehicles for consolidation, focus, and self-preservation."[4] With another three decades of experience now behind us (and a reminder that such collaborations did not begin in the mid-twentieth century), it may be helpful to think of consortial trends as cyclical and responsive, enabling both expansion and consolidation, growth and contraction, helping campuses continue to meet their needs as circumstances change. The consistent feature is consortia's adaptability to the moment.

What does the next generation of consortia hold in store? As in the Progressive Era a century ago, we are seeing both progress and backlash in civil rights, along with calls for greater efficiency in higher education. As in the 1950s and 1960s, campuses and the federal government are experimenting with mechanisms for increasing access and affordability, and student activism and expectations are evolving quickly. As in the 1990s, developments in information technology are again presenting new challenges for institutions—then it was desktop computers and the beginnings of the Internet; today it is virtual conferencing and generative AI.

Consortia have served as bulwarks, backstops, breakwaters, and buffers: They have offered a means both to protect what exists and to build what doesn't. They have been conceived, designed, and adapted to help campuses deal with the most challenging issues of the day. Moments of disruption, both in higher education and in society more broadly, have provided particularly fertile ground for exploring how we might be better with one another instead of better than one another. Predicting the future is a risky undertaking, but it does seem reasonable to think that, as was true in the 1920s and 1960s and 1990s, the current moment is ripe for a new round of consortial exploration. That we don't know where such exploration will take us is the point, so long as we trust that it will be somewhere good, where together we can become better than we are. Welcome to the work.

ACKNOWLEDGMENTS

I would be a poor consortial leader if I didn't recognize that many people have contributed to the ideas and insights in these pages. I'm grateful for the wisdom they've offered and responsible for the gaps that remain. This book and I are both better thanks to those listed here and too many more to name.

I am grateful to my predecessors and colleagues in this role at the Five College Consortium, in the Association for Collaborative Leadership, and beyond. Lorna Peterson and Neal Abraham each held this post before me at FCI and offered models for how to do this work while encouraging me to find my own approach. ACL members have welcomed me into the world of consortia since the day I was named executive director at FCI, and I am humbled by their commitment, grace, and wisdom. Claire Ramsbottom, Barb McFadden, Keith Marshall, Stig Lanesskog, Diane Dimitrov, and Cristin Toutsi Grigos are just a few of the many who deserve thanks. It is a joy to work with a group of colleagues so consistently dedicated to collaboration.

Five College Consortium board members past and present with a vision of what a consortium could be and the discipline to commit time and energy to bring that vision to fruition continue to inspire me. Among the many, I owe a particular debt to Chancellor Emeritus Kumble "Swamy" Subbaswamy at the University of Massachusetts Amherst, who served more than his fair share of terms in order to sustain the work of the consortium with minimal disruption, and President Emerita Kathleen McCartney of my alma mater Smith College, who chaired the search that brought me to this role. The provosts and principal business officers provide critical guidance and attention to detail, and I'm thankful for the good humor with which we've tried to do this work well and equitably. Timely advice from Michael Thurston at Smith College about maintaining writing habits while serving in a leadership role proved invaluable. Gary Hawkins at Hampshire College introduced me to the believing game, which so eloquently captures the particular and even peculiar optimism of our shared efforts.

I owe a special debt of gratitude to the many folks who do and have done the daily detail work of collaboration, including FCI staff as well as colleagues and students on the campuses. My favorite thing about being back on-site after the pandemic is spending time working and laughing with these wonderful humans. The creativity, integrity, and playfulness of the FCI leadership team make this hard work easier, and Julie Holt deserves special thanks for her efforts to keep us all on task. I would be remiss if I did not also acknowledge the debt I owe to four longtime colleagues and friends who modeled for me what generous, thoughtful, collaborative leadership could look like, long before I dreamed of joining a consortium: Jeff Russell, Mike Corradini, Bob Ray, and Daniel Kleinman. I strive to carry your wisdom and grace with me every day.

A long list of folks helped bring this project to publication, including the authors on whose shoulders I stand, but I will mention only a few, who each deserve a special callout: Greg Britton, who bore with me longer than I had a right to expect; the staff at Johns Hopkins University Press, who make things better every day; and everyone who reviewed a draft of this book, both known and anonymous. Brian Williams, Cole Woodcox, and Mickey McDonald gave their time generously and their feedback gently, and I owe them each a favor and a cocktail.

My friends and family have sustained me and exhibited enormous patience when this project has consumed me. Elaine Klein and Molly Davis Reinhard each helped me celebrate the official start of this project. Judy Houck and Lisa Saywell continue to make Madison feel like home, even when we're far away. Dina Venezky asks unexpected questions and helps me unwind the spring slowly. Jen Kushner inspires me with her resilience and wisdom. Carl Pfatteicher, Carolyn McDermott, and Linda Pfatteicher, thank you for helping keep Mom and Dad in our lives. Philip and Lois would, I hope, have enjoyed seeing this book. I miss them both and am glad to have you all. David Gregory, that goes for you too. Ian Conlin and Sharon Weissburg, this work is part of my effort to leave you a better world than I found it; I hope you'll pay it forward. And to Bob, who would prefer not to be mentioned, for nudging me along, if only so it would be done. I love you all.

NOTES

Introduction. Better Than We Are

1. Michael Anft, *Stronger Together Than Alone? Assessing College Leaders' Attitudes Toward Mergers and Other Partnerships* (Chronicle of Higher Education, 2021); *Strength in Numbers: Strategies for Collaborating in a New Era for Higher Education* (EY Parthenon, 2020), https://www.ey.com/content/dam/ey-unified-site/ey-com/en-gl/insights/strategy/documents/ey-strength-in-numbers.pdf; "Mergers and Major Cross-College Collaborations," *Inside Higher Ed*, accessed June 26, 2024, https://www.insidehighered.com/audio/2022/07/15/ep86-reprise-mergers-and-major-cross-college-collaborations.

2. James L. Shulman, *The Synthetic University: How Higher Education Can Benefit from Shared Solutions and Save Itself* (Princeton University Press, 2023); Sandra Abegglen, Tom Burns, and Sandra Sinfield, eds., *Collaboration in Higher Education*, 1st ed. (Bloomsbury Academic, 2023); Ricardo Azziz et al., *Strategic Mergers in Higher Education* (Johns Hopkins University Press, 2019); James Martin and James E. Samels, *Consolidating Colleges and Merging Universities: New Strategies for Higher Education Leaders* (Johns Hopkins University Press, 2017).

3. James A. Yankech, "Trust Within Higher Education Consortia—a Phenomenological Study of the Experiences of Directors and Leaders" (PhD diss., University of Nebraska, 2015); Robyn Dinicola, "Strength in Numbers: An Exploratory Case Study on the Impact of Conflict in Multi-Institutional Higher Education Collaborations" (PhD diss., Nova Southeastern University, 2023); Britany L. Affolter-Caine, "Going Beyond Traditional Consortia: Exploring the Collaborative Process Among Traditional Private Liberal Arts Colleges and Universities Engaged in Interinstitutional Consortia That Promote Curricular Joint Ventures" (PhD diss., University of Michigan, 2008); see also Michael Joseph Offerman, "Factors Leading to the Termination of Three Consortia of Higher Education Institutions: A Case Study" (EdD diss., Northern Illinois University, 1985), which includes an excellent bibliography of pre-1980 sources on consortia and collaboration.

4. John C. Cavanaugh, "Rethinking Higher Education Through the Consortial Model," *Inside Higher Ed*, October 22, 2019, https://www.insidehighered.com/views/2019/10/23/easing-student-transfer-challenges-through-college-consortia-opinion.

5. See la paperson, *A Third University Is Possible*, Forerunners: Ideas First from the University of Minnesota Press (University of Minnesota Press, 2017); Luis

Alvarez et al., *Another University Is Possible* (University Readers, 2010) for thought-provoking discussions of why this competitive and colonial underpinning is problematic and how it can be reimagined.

6. I add quotation marks here because the data show that this "crisis" has been growing since well before the pandemic and that the shortage of resources to support mental health has long been the norm rather than a wholly recent aberration. See, for instance, Betty Fleurimond et al., "College Students' Mental Health and Well-Being," *Deloitte Insights*, August 6, 2021, https://www2.deloitte.com/us/en/insights/industry/public-sector/college-students-mental-health-covid-19.html; and M. D. Victor Schwartz and M. D. Jerald Kay, "The Crisis in College and University Mental Health," *Psychiatric Times* 26, no. 10 (2009), https://www.psychiatrictimes.com/view/crisis-college-and-university-mental-health.

7. Catherine Pearson, "Text Your Friends. It Matters More Than You Think," *New York Times*, July 11, 2022, https://www.nytimes.com/2022/07/11/well/family/check-in-text-friendship.html.

8. "Nonprofit Trends Report, Fourth Edition" (Salesforce, 2021).

9. Clifton Conrad and Todd Lundberg, *Learning with Others: Collaboration as a Pathway to College Student Success* (Johns Hopkins University Press, 2022), 5. Their project was informed by their study of MSIs and leads them to propose that "the conventional understanding that individual learning should be placed at the forefront . . . falls far short of educating students not only to thrive in their personal lives but also to thrive and contribute in their workplace and their public lives."

10. Joel Cutcher-Gershenfeld et al., *The Consortia Century: Aligning for Impact* (Oxford University Press, 2025), 15, 9.

11. John Kania and Mark Kramer, "Collective Impact," *Stanford Social Innovation Review*, Winter 2011, https://ssir.org/articles/entry/collective_impact.

12. See R. Owen Williams, in Martin and Samels, *Consolidating Colleges*, 177.

13. See, for instance, Danielle S. Allen, *Talking to Strangers: Anxieties of Citizenship Since Brown v. Board of Education* (University of Chicago Press, 2004), a powerful treatise on the importance of finding common ground.

14. Lorna Peterson, executive director of Five Colleges, Incorporated from 1990 to 2009, was well known for this phrase, which continues to be used in the consortium and by many of her colleagues nationally.

15. Franklin Patterson and Charles R. Longsworth, *The Making of a College: A New Departure in Higher Education*, new ed. (MIT Press, 1975), https://compass.fivecolleges.edu/islandora/object/hampshire:1185 (originally published in 1966, this is a book-length telling of the story of Hampshire's founding); C. L. Barber, *The New College Plan: A Proposal for a Major Departure in Higher Education* (n.p., 1958) (this is the original planning document from 1958); Five College Long Range Planning Committee, *Five College Cooperation: Directions for the Future* (Five Colleges, Incorporated, 1969), http://archive.org/details/fivecollegecoopeoooofive. For a quick overview, see Wikipedia, https://en.wikipedia.org/wiki/New_College_Plan, accessed January 30, 2025. In 1965 the University of Massachusetts was still referred to

without the "Amherst" identifier used today to distinguish it from other campuses in the state system.

16. See, for instance, Ursula K. Toomey, *A Brief History of the Activities of the Committee on University Extension of the Connecticut Valley Colleges, 1914–1958* (Committee on University Extension of the Connecticut Valley Colleges, 1958); and George C. S. Benson et al., *A Brief History of the Group Plan of the Claremont Colleges* (Claremont University Center, 1993).

17. Lorna M. Peterson, *Glancing Backward: Twenty-Five Years of Cooperation: A Retrospective Report on Five Colleges, Incorporated* (Five Colleges, Incorporated, 1984); Stanley F. Salwak, "The Need for Cooperation and the CIC Response," *Educational Record* 45, no. 3 (1964): 308–16; Affolter-Caine, "Going Beyond Traditional Consortia"; Wayne Anderson, *Creative Collaboration: The Associated Colleges of the South*, n.d., https://www.acsouth.edu/wp-content/uploads/2020/09/acs-creative-collaboration.pdf; John Alexander Duke, "The Image of Oxbridge and American Universities: English Residential Colleges and American Research Universities, 1894–1980" (PhD diss., Indiana University, 1991); Judith Laikin Elkin, *The Great Lakes Colleges Association: Twenty-One Years of Cooperation in Higher Education* (Great Lakes Colleges Association, 1982).

18. Franklin Patterson, *Colleges in Consort: Interinstitutional Cooperation Through Consortia*, 1st ed., Jossey-Bass Series in Higher Education (Jossey-Bass, 1974); Donn C. Neal, *Consortia and Interinstitutional Cooperation*, American Council on Education/Macmillan Series on Higher Education (Macmillan, 1988); Lawrence George Dotolo and Jean Strandness, eds., "Best Practices in Higher Education Consortia: How Institutions Can Work Together," *New Directions for Higher Education* 1999, no. 106 (1999): 1–120. See also Naida C. Tushnet, *A Guide to Developing Educational Partnerships* (Office of Educational Research and Improvement, 1993) for still-relevant general guidance on partnerships, especially with noneducational organizations. Another still relevant source is Fritz H. Grupe, *Managing Institutional Change: Consortia in Higher Education* (Associated Colleges of the St. Lawrence Valley, 1975), though it may be less readily available than the others listed here.

19. See, for instance, Mary L. Churchill and David Chard, *When Colleges Close: Leading in a Time of Crisis* (Johns Hopkins University Press, 2021), 14–15, describing the challenge they faced at Wheelock in finding a consultant to help them through the process of finding a partner: "Plenty of merger partners existed, in theory [and yet] the consultant reviewed the landscape but couldn't offer a specific road map."

20. Ronald J. Daniels, *What Universities Owe Democracy* (Johns Hopkins University Press, 2021); Arthur Levine, *The Great Upheaval: Higher Education's Past, Present, and Uncertain Future* (Johns Hopkins University Press, 2021); Cathy N. Davidson, *The New Education: How to Revolutionize the University to Prepare Students for a World in Flux*, 1st ed. (Basic Books, 2017); Nathan D. Grawe, *The Agile College: How Institutions Successfully Navigate Demographic Changes* (Johns Hopkins University Press, 2021).

21. Danielle Melidona et al., "The American College President: 2023 Edition," American Council on Education, 2023, 8, https://www.acenet.edu/Documents/American-College-President-IX-2023.pdf; "Chief Academic Officer Survey: The CAO Job," American Council on Education, n.d., accessed February 16, 2025, www.acenet.edu/documents/chief-academic-officer-survey-the-cao-job.pdf.

22. Churchill and Chard, in describing Wheelock College's departure from the Colleges of the Fenway consortium and subsequent merger into Boston University, noted the increasing frequency of leadership turnover and remarked that "this lack of consistent leadership made academic collaboration among the consortium's member institutions more challenging." Churchill and Chard, *When Colleges Close*, 11.

23. For leaders interested in what a merger looks like from the inside, I recommend Churchill and Chard, *When Colleges Close*, by a former vice president and president of Wheelock College about its transition into Boston University. See also Rick Seltzer, "The Growing Role of Mergers in Higher Ed," *Inside Higher Ed*, 2018, https://www.insidehighered.com/content/growing-role-mergers-higher-ed.

Chapter One. Why and How We Collaborate (Motivation)

1. Lorna Peterson, longtime executive director of FCI, was fond of this phrase. Versions of this variety-but-commonality message appear in much of the literature on consortia. See, for instance, Jackie Pritzen saying "There is no set formula for guaranteeing success, since every consortium is in a real sense unique, with its own combination of problems and opportunities. Nevertheless, some broad generalizations are possible about ways in which institutions can actively develop the conditions under which cooperation is most likely to thrive." Donn C. Neal, *Consortia and Interinstitutional Cooperation*, American Council on Education/Macmillan Series on Higher Education (Macmillan, 1988), 42. Also Neal, p. 2: "There is no typical consortium"; Franklin Patterson, *Colleges in Consort: Interinstitutional Cooperation Through Consortia*, 1st ed. Jossey-Bass Series in Higher Education (Jossey-Bass, 1974), 10–29.

2. Neal, *Consortia and Interinstitutional Cooperation*, 1–2.

3. Neal's was hardly the first attempt to capture the key characteristics common to all consortia and to sort them into a taxonomy or typology. Examples and catalogs of these efforts appear, for instance, in Patterson, *Colleges in Consort;* Lawrence C. Howard, ed., *Interinstitutional Cooperation in Higher Education: Proceedings*, Conference on Interinstitutional Cooperation in Higher Education, Johnson Foundation Center at Wingspread, 1967; Michael Joseph Offerman, "Factors Leading to the Termination of Three Consortia of Higher Education Institutions: A Case Study" (EdD diss., Northern Illinois University, 1985).

4. See, for instance, membership data of the Association for Collaborative Leadership, https://www.national-acl.org/directory.

5. See, for instance, Offerman, "Factors Leading to the Termination of Three Consortia."

6. Deb Mashek, *Collabor(h)Ate: How to Build Incredible Collaborative Relationships at Work (Even If You'd Rather Work Alone)* (Practical Inspiration, 2023).

7. Simon Sinek, *Start with Why: How Great Leaders Inspire Everyone to Take Action*, repr. (Portfolio, 2011).

8. See also Stanley F. Salwak, "New Patterns of Institutional Cooperation: Compacts and Consortia," *Journal of Higher Education* 39, no. 9 (1968): 490–96, https://doi.org/10.2307/1980032, for additional examples.

9. "About CSCU," Connecticut State Colleges and Universities, accessed May 7, 2024, https://www.ct.edu/about; see also Nancy Zimpher's description of SUNY and other state systems in James Martin and James E. Samels, *Consolidating Colleges and Merging Universities: New Strategies for Higher Education Leaders* (Johns Hopkins University Press, 2017), 52–53.

10. Robyn Dinicola, "Strength in Numbers: An Exploratory Case Study on the Impact of Conflict in Multi-Institutional Higher Education Collaborations" (PhD diss., Nova Southeastern University, 2023).

11. "About the Mission and History of the AMICAL Consortium," AMICAL, accessed June 18, 2024, https://www.amicalnet.org/about.

12. Texas A&M University is in the process of closing its campus in Qatar. Liam Knox, "Cutting Off Qatar," *Inside Higher Ed*, February 16, 2024, https://www.insidehighered.com/news/global/us-colleges-world/2024/02/16/how-texas-ams-qatar-campus-suddenly-collapsed.

13. "Explore Qatar's Education City," Qatar Foundation, accessed June 28, 2024, https://www.qf.org.qa/education/education-city.

14. "Building a World-Class Education Ecosystem in Qatar," Qatar Foundation, accessed June 28, 2024, https://www.qf.org.qa/education.

15. "IAEM Universities & Colleges," International Association of Emergency Managers, accessed July 16, 2024, https://www.iaem.org/groups/us-caucuses/universities-colleges; see "National Intercollegiate Mutual Aid Agreement: White Paper," National Intercollegiate Mutual Aid Agreement/International Association of Emergency Managers, January 2021, https://docs.google.com/document/d/1YoBvk44nEAW_mAMTCtUed2ovYtc38-jvaq3aADjAAww/edit for more information.

16. "MHEC: New England's Premier Purchasing Consortium," MHEC, accessed June 18, 2024, https://www.mhec.net/welcome-to-mhec/; see also the Virginia Higher Education Procurement Consortium, which serves a similar purpose: "About the Virginia Higher Education Procurement Consortium (VHEPC)," accessed July 16, 2024, https://vhepc.org/about/.

17. Offerman, "Factors Leading to the Termination of Three Consortia," 28; Richard Bailey Lancaster, "Interdependency and Conflict in a Consortium for Cooperation in Higher Education: Toward a Theory of Interorganizational Behavior" (PhD diss., University of Michigan, 1969).

18. The collaboration continuum was originally developed by the National Institute for Technology in Liberal Education, which operated from 2001 to 2018. A version of the continuum is captured in Michael Nanfito, "The Collaboration Continuum," *Michael Nanfito* (blog), May 12, 2015, https://mnanfito.wordpress.com

/2015/05/12/the-collaboration-continuum/. A graphical version of the continuum is available on the Teagle Foundation website at https://www.teaglefoundation.org/Teagle/media/GlobalMediaLibrary/documents/resources/CollaborationContinuum.pdf.

19. Howard, *Interinstitutional Cooperation in Higher Education: Proceedings*, 110.

20. Howard, 110; Mary L. Churchill and David Chard, *When Colleges Close: Leading in a Time of Crisis* (Johns Hopkins University Press, 2021); Scott Jaschik, "Marlboro to Become Part of Emerson," *Inside Higher Ed*, November 6, 2019, https://www.insidehighered.com/news/2019/11/07/marlboro-will-become-part-emerson-college; Michael Vasquez, "Pennsylvania's Governor Seeks to Consolidate Most of Its Public Colleges—and Make Them More Affordable," *Chronicle of Higher Education*, January 26, 2024, News, https://www.chronicle.com/article/pennsylvanias-governor-seeks-to-consolidate-most-of-its-public-colleges-and-make-them-more-affordable; Marley Parish, "Three Consolidating State Schools to Become 'Commonwealth University of Pennsylvania,'" *Pennsylvania Capital-Star*, March 2, 2022, https://penncapital-star.com/briefs/three-consolidating-state-schools-to-become-commonwealth-university-of-pennsylvania/; Josh Moody, "Cuts Follow Consolidation at Vermont State," *Inside Higher Ed*, October 11, 2023, https://www.insidehighered.com/news/business/cost-cutting/2023/10/11/cuts-follow-consolidation-vermont-state-university; Roger C. Schonfeld and Jane Radecki, "Consolidating the University of Wisconsin Colleges: The Reorganization of the University of Wisconsin System. Case Study," *ITHAKA S+R*, August 30, 2021, https://doi.org/10.18665/sr.315853; Lisa Rathke, "Students, Faculty of Vermont State University Urge Board to Reconsider Cuts," *NECN*, November 14, 2023, https://www.necn.com/news/local/students-faculty-and-staff-of-vermont-state-university-urge-board-to-reconsider-cuts/3091316/; Erin Gretzinger, "Wisconsin's Warning for Higher Ed," *Chronicle of Higher Education*, January 8, 2024, https://www.chronicle.com/article/wisconsins-warning-for-higher-ed. As noted in Churchill and Chard (*When Colleges Close*, 33, 29), other recent examples include the Boston Conservatory and Berklee College of Music, School of the Museum and Fine Arts–Tufts University, the Mount Ida campus purchased by the University of Massachusetts Amherst, and Mills College (Oakland, California) and Colby-Sawyer College (New Hampshire) restructuring.

21. "Penn in the 18th Century: 1791 Union," University Archives and Records Center, accessed April 18, 2024, https://archives.upenn.edu/exhibits/penn-history/18th-century/1791-union/; "History," Radcliffe Institute for Advanced Study at Harvard University, accessed April 18, 2024, https://www.radcliffe.harvard.edu/about-the-institute/history; "Radcliffe: Merged and Ready," *John Harvard's Journal*, December 1999, https://www.harvardmagazine.com/sites/default/files/html/1999/11/jhj.radcliffe.html.

22. "Our History—Hobart and William Smith Colleges," Hobart and William Smith, accessed April 18, 2024, https://www.hws.edu/about/history/default.aspx; "Coordinate Heritage—Hobart and William Smith Colleges," Hobart and William

Smith, accessed June 28, 2024, https://www.hws.edu/about/history/coordinate-heritage.aspx.

23. Barb Brandes and Dan McKeown, "A Message from the Boards of Trustees," College of Saint Benedict & Saint John's University, accessed April 17, 2024, https://www.csbsju.edu/about/college-of-saint-benedict/update-on-strong-integration.

24. Five College Long Range Planning Committee, *Five College Cooperation: Directions for the Future* (Five Colleges, Incorporated, 1969), http://archive.org/details/fivecollegecoopeoooofive, 1.

25. Rick Seltzer, "Indiana University, Purdue University Lay Plans to Split IUPUI in 2 Years," *Higher Ed Dive*, August 16, 2022, https://www.highereddive.com/news/indiana-university-purdue-university-lay-plans-to-split-iupui-in-2-years/629721/; Michael T. Nietzel, "Indiana University and Purdue Officially Split Up IUPUI," *Forbes*, July 15, 2023, https://www.forbes.com/sites/michaeltnietzel/2023/06/15/indiana-university-and-purdue-officially-split-up-iupui/; Kennedy McCormack and Ashley Wilson, "The Great Divorce: The IUPUI Split and What Comes Next," *Campus Citizen*, February 21, 2024, https://www.thecampuscitizen.com/article/2024/02/the-great-divorce.

26. Described by J. Matthew Hartley and Alan Ruby in Martin and Samels, *Consolidating Colleges*, 91–92.

27. "HERC About Us," Higher Education Jobs—Higher Education Recruitment Consortium, accessed June 18, 2024, https://www.hercjobs.org/about-us/; "MHEC: New England's Premier Purchasing Consortium." MHEC began as the Five Colleges, Incorporated buying group before it spun off as an independent nonprofit organization.

28. Patterson, *Colleges in Consort*, 14.

29. Charlotte Cox, "Academic Consortia as Strategic Alliances," *AGB Reports* 33, no. 1 (1991): 22.

30. Neal, *Consortia and Interinstitutional Cooperation*, 3.

31. Frederick Baus and Claire A. Ramsbottom, "Starting and Sustaining a Consortium: New Directions for Higher Education," *New Directions for Higher Education* 1999, no. 106 (1999): 3–18, https://doi.org/10.1002/he.10601.

32. Patterson, *Colleges in Consort*, 4. Franklin Patterson, the first president of Hampshire College, should not be confused with Lewis Patterson, author of "Consortia in Higher Education" and compiler of several directories of consortia in the 1960s and 1970s.

33. Several concise descriptions of the history of consortia exist, including Patterson, *Colleges in Consort*, 1–9; Raymond S. Moore, *Consortiums in American Higher Education: 1965–1966, Report of an Exploratory Study* (US Department of Health, Education, and Welfare, Office of Education, 1967), https://files.eric.ed.gov/fulltext/ED051728.pdf; Lawrence C. Howard, "Interinstitutional Cooperation in Higher Education," *New Dimensions in Higher Education* 21 (1967); Howard, *Interinstitutional Cooperation in Higher Education: Proceedings*, 101–63, especially the comprehensive chapter "Survey and Analysis of the Literature Related to Interinstitutional

Cooperation in Higher Education." Howard (in "Interinstitutional Cooperation") and Offerman, "Factors Leading to the Termination of Three Consortia" cite examples of cross-campus collaboration dating as far back as 600 AD. This work is clearly not new.

34. Peter F. Drucker, "The Rise of the Knowledge Society," *Wilson Quarterly* 17, no. 2 (1993): 52–71, https://doi.org/10.2307/40258682.

35. Ryan Best, "Confederate Statues Were Never Really About Preserving History," *FiveThirtyEight*, July 8, 2020, https://projects.fivethirtyeight.com/confederate-statues/; Karen L. Cox, *No Common Ground: Confederate Monuments and the Ongoing Fight for Racial Justice* (University of North Carolina Press, 2021).

36. "The 1920s Education: Topics in the News," Encyclopedia.com, accessed June 28, 2024, https://www.encyclopedia.com/social-sciences/culture-magazines/1920s-education-topics-news#.

37. Rogers Hollingsworth, "Higher Education: The Making of US Academia," *Nature* 541, no. 7638 (2017): 461–62, https://doi.org/10.1038/541461a.

38. US Census Bureau, "Bicentennial Edition: Historical Statistics of the United States, Colonial Times to 1970, Chapter H: Social Statistics," 385–86, accessed June 28, 2024, https://www.census.gov/library/publications/1975/compendia/hist_stats_colonial-1970.html.

39. "History of AAC&U," AAC&U.org, accessed April 22, 2024, https://www.aacu.org/about/history-of-aacu.

40. "Alexander Meiklejohn," Brown University, accessed June 28, 2024, https://www.brown.edu/Administration/News_Bureau/Encyclopedia/Meiklejohn.html.

41. Benjamin B. Goldman, ed., *Handbook from the Experimental College (1927–1932)* (University of Wisconsin–Madison), 1928, https://ils.wisc.edu/wp-content/uploads/sites/135/2017/04/1927-32_Experimental_College_Handbook.pdf, p. 8.

42. Goldman, *Handbook from the Experimental College.*

43. Adam R. Nelson, *Education and Democracy: The Meaning of Alexander Meiklejohn, 1872–1964* (University of Wisconsin Press, 2001), 135.

44. "Integrated Liberal Studies," Integrated Liberal Studies, accessed April 22, 2024, https://ils.wisc.edu/.

45. Nelson, *Education and Democracy*, 133–34.

46. George C. S. Benson et al., *A Brief History of The Group Plan of the Claremont Colleges* (Claremont University Center, 1993).

Benson et al., *Brief History of the Group Plan*, 13.

47. John Alexander Duke, "The Image of Oxbridge and American Universities: English Residential Colleges and American Research Universities, 1894–1980" (PhD diss., Indiana University, 1991), 5.

48. "About the Claremont Colleges," Claremont McKenna College, accessed April 23, 2024, https://www.cmc.edu/about/about-the-claremont-colleges; "A Brief History of Pomona College," Pomona College, March 19, 2015, https://www.pomona.edu/about/brief-history-pomona-college; Duke, "Image of

Oxbridge and American Universities," 185; Benson et al., *Brief History of the Group Plan*, 15.

49. "History—Atlanta University Center Consortium," Atlanta University Center Consortium, accessed April 23, 2024, https://aucenter.edu/history/.

50. "History—Atlanta University Center Consortium"; See also "History of the Atlanta University Center," Atlanta University Center Consortium, accessed July 8, 2024, https://web.archive.org/web/20110719142723/http://www.aucenter.edu/history.php.

51. Neal, *Consortia and Interinstitutional Cooperation*, 33; Moore, *Consortiums in American Higher Education*, 4; see also Raymond S. Moore, *A Guide to Higher Education Consortiums: 1965–66* (US Department of Health, Education, and Welfare, Office of Education, 1967), https://hdl.handle.net/2027/uc1.c2847250; Offerman, "Factors Leading to the Termination of Three Consortia," 8.

52. Neal, *Consortia and Interinstitutional Cooperation*, 2; see also Patterson, *Colleges in Consort*.

53. Neal, *Consortia and Interinstitutional Cooperation*, 2.

54. "FAQ: National Center for Interstate Compacts," accessed April 25, 2024, https://compacts.csg.org/faq/; "Regional Higher Education Compacts—Federalism in America," accessed April 3, 2024, http://encyclopedia.federalism.org/index.php/Regional_Higher_Education_Compacts. South Dakota is listed as a member of both the Western and Midwestern compacts.

55. "NCIC Database—National Center for Interstate Compacts," Council of State Governments, accessed April 25, 2024, https://compacts.csg.org/database/. This MHEC (mhec.org) should not be confused with the MHEC purchasing consortium (mhec.net).

56. "Regional Education Compacts," NC-SARA, accessed April 25, 2024, https://nc-sara.org/regional-education-compacts; "About NEBHE," New England Board of Higher Education, accessed April 25, 2024, https://nebhe.org/about/.

57. Salwak, "New Patterns of Institutional Cooperation," 491; Sara Appel, Jenny Parks, and Everett Trechter, "Student Reciprocity Programs and MSEP in the 21st Century. Midwest Student Exchange Program (MSEP): Midwestern Higher Education Compact," Midwestern Higher Education Compact, July 1, 2021, ERIC database; "Regional Higher Education Compacts—Federalism in America"; "Regional Education Compacts."

58. Howard, *Interinstitutional Cooperation in Higher Education: Proceedings*, ix–x. The proceedings of this 1967 conference make for fascinating reading about Title III funding and its implications. Joselynn H. Fountain, *The Higher Education Act (HEA): A Primer* (Congressional Research Service, 2023), https://sgp.fas.org/crs/misc/R43351.pdf.

59. Neal, *Consortia and Interinstitutional Cooperation*, 34; Mary Frances Forcier, "Innovation Through Collaboration: New Pathways to Success," *AGB Trusteeship Magazine* 19, no. 5 (2011): 8–12.

60. Howard, *Interinstitutional Cooperation in Higher Education: Proceedings*, 109–10.

61. Elmo V. Roesler, ed., *Progress Report No. 1: First Six Months of Consortium Activities* (Appalachian Developing Institutions Consortium, January 1972), 6.

62. James Farmer and Robert I. Littel, *An Evaluation of the Small College Consortium, a Title III Project. Part I: Survey Results* (Small College Consortium, July 1977), 17.

63. "About the CMCC," CIBER Minority-Serving Institution and Community College Consortium, accessed June 20, 2024, https://cibercmcc.org/about/.

64. "About Phelps Stokes," Phelps Stokes, June 22, 2012, https://web.archive.org/web/20120622121305/http://www.phelpsstokes.org/About_Phelps_Stokes; "GuideStar Profile of Trustees of Phelps Stokes Fund," GuideStar, accessed April 29, 2024, www.guidestar.org/profile/13-1624208; Herbert A. Wilson, *The Cooperative College Development Program* (Phelps-Stokes Fund, 1969).

65. "AIHEC History," American Indian Higher Education Consortium, accessed April 25, 2024, https://www.aihec.org/vision-mission/.

66. "The Robert R. Moton Memorial Institute (Informational Flyer)," Smithsonian Institution, n.d., https://transcription.si.edu/view/8831/ACM-ACMA_06-010.3a; *Alfred P. Sloan Foundation: A Grantmaking History, 1934–2009* (Alfred P. Sloan Foundation, 2009), 28–29, https://web.archive.org/web/20120103145630/http://www.sloan.org/assets/files/general/sloan_hist_bk_text_version.pdf.

67. Howard, *Interinstitutional Cooperation in Higher Education: Proceedings*, 107; citing Alfred T. Hill, "Cooperation Among Small Colleges," in *Proceedings of the Workshop on College and University Interinstitutional Cooperation, Conducted at the Catholic University of America, Under the Auspices of the Director of Workshops, June 11 to June 22, 1964*, ed. George Francis Donovan (Catholic University of America Press, 1965), 34–46.

68. "What Is a Work College?," *Work Colleges Consortium* (blog), accessed June 21, 2024, https://workcolleges.org/about/what-is-a-work-college/; "Brief History of Work Colleges Consortium," *Work Colleges Consortium* (blog), accessed June 20, 2024, https://workcolleges.org/about/brief-history/; for more information about work colleges, see Louis Soares, Vickie Choitz, and Kelly Rifelj, *Exploring the Work College Model for Working Leaders* (American Council on Education, 2022).

69. Herman B. Wells, "A Case Study on Interinstitutional Cooperation," *Educational Record*, Fall 1967, https://btaa.org/docs/default-source/news-pub/history ofcic3abf.pdf.

70. Wells, "A Case Study."

71. Stanley F. Salwak, "The Need for Cooperation and the CIC Response," *Educational Record* 45, no. 3 (1964): 308–16; Wells, "A Case Study."

72. "History," Associated Colleges of the Midwest, February 15, 2024, https://acm.edu/about/history/.

73. "CAA Academic Alliance Programs," *CAA Academic Alliance* (blog), accessed June 18, 2024, https://www.caa-academics.org/programs/; "AEAC Frequently Asked Questions," America East Academic Consortium, accessed June 18, 2024, https://theaeac.org/about/frequently-asked-questions/.

74. Judith Laikin Elkin, *The Great Lakes Colleges Association: Twenty-One Years of Cooperation in Higher Education* (Great Lakes Colleges Association), 1982, 1–3, 7, 13; for more on the evolution of GLCA's programming, see Neil R. Wylie and Jon W. Fuller, "Enhancing Faculty Vitality Through Collaboration Among Colleagues," *New Directions for Higher Education* 1985, no. 51 (1985): 99–108, https://doi.org/10.1002/he.36919855110.

75. Baus and Ramsbottom, "Starting and Sustaining a Consortium," 6–7.

76. Eric Casey, "Central Mass. Colleges Downsize Consortium, Appoint New Board Chair," *Worcester Business Journal*, June 21, 2024, https://www.wbjournal.com/article/central-mass-colleges-downsize-consortium-appoint-new-board-chair.

77. Salwak, "Need for Cooperation," 309.

78. Mark E. Shelton, "Leadership Style and Outcome Behaviors of Higher Education Consortium Directors in the United States" (EdD diss., Johnson & Wales University, 2008), 14; Marybelle C. Keim, "Educational Consortia—a Longitudinal Study," *College and University* 74, no. 3 (1999): 31.

79. Judith S. Glazer, "Designing and Managing an Inter-University Consortium in a Period of Decline," *Journal of Higher Education* 53, no. 2 (1982): 177–94, https://doi.org/10.2307/1981494.

80. Richard H. Morgan, *Nashville University Center Report of the Executive Director, 1973–74* (Nashville University Center, September 1, 1974), https://files.eric.ed.gov/fulltext/ED101626.pdf; Maurice J. O'Sullivan, *Dynamics, Role, and Function in Inter-University Collaboration* (Higher Education Center for Urban Studies, July 1972), https://files.eric.ed.gov/fulltext/ED068044.pdf; Offerman, "Factors Leading to the Termination of Three Consortia," 51.

81. James A. Yankech, "Trust Within Higher Education Consortia—a Phenomenological Study of the Experiences of Directors and Leaders" (PhD diss., University of Nebraska, 2015), 21.

82. Baus and Ramsbottom, "Starting and Sustaining a Consortium," 3.

83. Nancy Weiss Malkiel, *Changing the Game: William G. Bowen and the Challenges of American Higher Education* (Princeton University Press, 2023), 266–67, https://doi-org.amherst.idm.oclc.org/10.1515/9780691247816.

84. Mark Owen Lee, "A Comparative Case Study of Four Partnership Campuses: Origin, Administration, Academics, and Student Services" (PhD diss., University of South Dakota, 2007) provides a discussion of four additional consortia-like partnerships that formed in this era, each with a focus on shared academic programs.

85. "ACS History: Associated Colleges of the South," Associated Colleges of the South, accessed July 8, 2024, https://www.acsouth.edu/about-acs/acs-history/; Wayne Anderson, *Creative Collaboration: The Associated Colleges of the South*, n.d., https://www.acsouth.edu/wp-content/uploads/2020/09/acs-creative-collaboration.pdf, 2.

86. Baus and Ramsbottom, "Starting and Sustaining a Consortium," 5.

87. Naida C. Tushnet, *A Guide to Developing Educational Partnerships* (Office of Educational Research and Improvement, 1993), 13.

88. Peter M. Senge, *The Fifth Discipline: The Art and Practice of the Learning Organization*, rev. and updated (Doubleday/Currency, 2006).

89. O'Sullivan, *Dynamics, Role, and Function*, 11.

90. Ralph L. Corrigan, *Answering the Call: The Story of Community Service and Volunteerism at Sacred Heart University* (Sacred Heart University Press Books, 2001), 4–5, https://digitalcommons.sacredheart.edu/shupress_bks/6.

91. Offerman, "Factors Leading to the Termination of Three Consortia," 133.

92. Tushnet, *Guide to Developing Educational Partnerships*, 17.

93. Churchill and Chard, *When Colleges Close*, 17.

94. Elkin, *Great Lakes Colleges Association*, 124.

Chapter Two. "Things Can Be Done" (Optimism)

1. Bethan O'Neil, "Understanding Collaborative Management in Higher Education, the Possibilities and Parameters of Partnership: A Case Study of CADISE" (PhD diss., University of Surrey, 2007), 104; Walter Lippmann, *Drift and Mastery: An Attempt to Diagnose the Current Unrest* (Mitchell Kennerley, 1914).

2. Donald A. Johnson, "The Limits of Cooperation," in Donn C. Neal, *Consortia and Interinstitutional Cooperation*, American Council on Education/Macmillan Series on Higher Education (Macmillan, 1988), 193.

3. Lorna M. Peterson, *Glancing Backward: Twenty-Five Years of Cooperation: A Retrospective Report on Five Colleges, Incorporated* (Five Colleges, Incorporated, 1984). The Four (and then Five) College Coordinator was the early version of what is now the Five College Executive Director role.

4. O'Neil, "Understanding Collaborative Management in Higher Education," 76.

5. James A. Yankech, "Trust Within Higher Education Consortia—a Phenomenological Study of the Experiences of Directors and Leaders" (PhD diss., University of Nebraska, 2015), 112.

6. Judith Laikin Elkin, *The Great Lakes Colleges Association: Twenty-One Years of Cooperation in Higher Education* (Great Lakes Colleges Association, 1982), 17.

7. O'Neil, "Understanding Collaborative Management in Higher Education," 145.

8. Mary Frances Forcier, "Innovation Through Collaboration: New Pathways to Success," *AGB Trusteeship Magazine* 19, no. 5 (2011): 8–12; Julie Goldman et al., *ACL Activities/Programs List 2010 Overview* (Association for Collaborative Leadership, 2010); compare the ACL list to one created 40 years earlier in Stanley F. Salwak, "New Patterns of Institutional Cooperation: Compacts and Consortia," *Journal of Higher Education* 39, no. 9 (1968): 492.

9. James Martin and James E. Samels, *Consolidating Colleges and Merging Universities: New Strategies for Higher Education Leaders* (Johns Hopkins University Press, 2017), 164–65.

10. Frederick Baus and Claire A. Ramsbottom, "Starting and Sustaining a Consortium: New Directions for Higher Education," *New Directions for Higher Education* 1999, no. 106 (1999): 13, https://doi.org/10.1002/he.10601.

11. Peter D. Eckel, Britany Affolter-Caine, and Matthew Hartley, *Cooperating to Compete: A Campus Leaders' Guide to Developing Curricular Partnerships and Joint Programs* (American Council on Education, 2004), 13.

12. Naida C. Tushnet, *A Guide to Developing Educational Partnerships* (Office of Educational Research and Improvement, 1993), 19.

13. O'Neil, "Understanding Collaborative Management in Higher Education," 89.

14. Cole Woodcox, COPLAC, to author, June 19, 2024, personal communication.

15. Robyn Dinicola, "Strength in Numbers: An Exploratory Case Study on the Impact of Conflict in Multi-Institutional Higher Education Collaborations" (PhD diss., Nova Southeastern University, 2023), 83, 84.

16. Baus and Ramsbottom, "Starting and Sustaining a Consortium," 13.

17. Johnson, "Limits of Cooperation," in Neal, *Consortia and Interinstitutional Cooperation*, 193.

18. Johnson, "Limits of Cooperation," in Neal, 194, 199; Deb Mashek, *Collabor(h)Ate: How to Build Incredible Collaborative Relationships at Work (Even If You'd Rather Work Alone)* (Practical Inspiration, 2023), 19, 26.

19. George C. S. Benson et al., *A Brief History of The Group Plan of the Claremont Colleges* (Claremont University Center, 1993), 13 (italics in the original).

20. Nicola V. Beltz and Lawrence George Dotolo, eds., *Pushing the Boundaries of Collaboration: What Consortia Can Accomplish*, vol. 5 (Association for Collaborative Leadership, 2016); Lawrence George Dotolo and John B. Noftsinger, *Leveraging Resources Through Partnerships*, New Directions for Higher Education No. 120 (Jossey-Bass, 2002).

21. O'Neil, "Understanding Collaborative Management in Higher Education," 379.

22. Peter Elbow, "The Believing Game or Methodological Believing," *Journal of the Assembly for Expanded Perspectives on Learning: JAEPL* 14, no. 1 (2008): 1.

23. Elbow, "Believing Game," 1–2.

24. For additional examples in this vein, see "What Is Appreciative Inquiry (AI)?," Center for Appreciative Inquiry, accessed July 23, 2024, https://centerforappreciativeinquiry.net/resources/what-is-appreciative-inquiry-ai/; Rosamund Stone Zander and Benjamin Zander, *The Art of Possibility*, rev. ed. (Penguin Books, 2002).

25. "99% Invisible," 99% Invisible, accessed May 17, 2024, https://99percentinvisible.org/.

26. "Roman Mars: How Great Design Can Be 99% Invisible." *Why Am I Telling You This? With Bill Clinton*, accessed May 17, 2024, https://omny.fm/shows/why-am-i-telling-you-this-with-bill-clinton/roman-mars-how-the-design-of-cities-reflects-our-v.

27. Carol S. Dweck, *Mindset: The New Psychology of Success* (Ballantine Books, 2008).

28. Robert A. Caro, *The Power Broker: Robert Moses and the Fall of New York*, 1st ed. (Knopf, 1974); Langdon Winner, *The Whale and the Reactor: A Search for Limits in an Age of High Technology* (University of Chicago Press, 1986).

29. O'Neil, "Understanding Collaborative Management in Higher Education," 124–25.

30. Martin and Samels, *Consolidating Colleges*, 163.

31. Yankech, "Trust Within Higher Education Consortia," 121.

32. North Burn, "How Five Colleges Cooperate: Liberal Education," *Liberal Education* 59, no. 3 (1973): 307–8.

33. Michael Vertovec, "ACM to Discontinue Off-Campus Study Programming," *Associated Colleges of the Midwest* (blog), December 5, 2022, https://acm.edu/features/feature/acm-to-discontinue-off-campus-study-programming/; "FAQ: ACM to Discontinue Off-Campus Study Programming," *Associated Colleges of the Midwest* (blog), February 15, 2024, https://acm.edu/faq-acm-to-discontinue-off-campus-study-programming/; "History," Associated Colleges of the Midwest, February 15, 2024, https://acm.edu/about/history/. Brian Williams, Associated Colleges of the Midwest, personal communication with the author, July 10, 2024, with additional information provided by Lisa Jasinski and Betsy Hutula at Associated Colleges of the Midwest on July 15, 2024.

34. "Harvard Explained," *Harvard Crimson*, October 24, 2002, https://www.thecrimson.com/article/2002/10/24/harvard-explained-where-does-the-phrase/.

35. Martin and Samels, *Consolidating Colleges*, 166.

36. Jon Marcus, "At the Edge of a Cliff, Some Colleges Are Teaming Up to Survive," *New York Times*, Education, October 6, 2022, https://www.nytimes.com/2022/10/06/education/learning/college-course-sharing.html.

37. O'Neil, "Understanding Collaborative Management in Higher Education," 19.

38. Yankech, "Trust Within Higher Education Consortia," 117.

39. "Sherman Anti-Trust Act (1890)," National Archives, September 9, 2021, https://www.archives.gov/milestone-documents/sherman-anti-trust-act.

40. Phillip Z. Yao, "Mergers Between Higher Education Institutions: Regulatory Considerations, Antitrust Concerns, and Best Practices," *Journal of Law and Education* 49, no. 4 (2020): 553, 555; Kellie Woodhouse, "Mergers on the Rise?," *Inside Higher Ed*, July 6, 2015, https://www.insidehighered.com/news/2015/07/07/colleges-struggle-some-look-partnerships-and-mergers-relief.

41. "Antitrust Issues Affecting Colleges and Universities," National Association of College and University Attorneys, February 11, 2015, https://www.smu.edu/-/media/Site/LegalAffairs/NACUANOTES/antitrust-issues.pdf.

42. Debra L. Zumwalt, Jennifer A. Zimbroff, and Thomas W. Fenner, "Stanford University Legal Office Memorandum: Antitrust Guidelines," June 22, 2023, 4, https://ogc.stanford.edu/sites/g/files/sbiybj22406/files/media/file/stanford_antitrust_guidelines_memo_2023.pdf (emphasis in original); Greg Hartman, *Antitrust and the Control of Higher Education* (Western Interstate Commission for Higher Education, 1972), https://eric.ed.gov/?id=ED092003; Donald B. Gould, "Antitrust and Higher Education: What Hath Justice Wrought?," *Journal of Student Financial Aid* 23, no. 1 (1993): 21–28, https://doi.org/10.55504/0884-9153.1115; Julia Porter Liebeskind and Amalya Lumerman Oliver, "From Handshake to Contract:

Intellectual Property, Trust, and the Social Structure of Academic Research," in Vol. 2, *Landmark Papers on Trust*, ed. Reinhard Bachmann and Akbar Zaheer, International Library of Critical Writings on Business and Management, vol. 10 (Elgar, 2008); Jeremiah Poff, "JD Vance Urges FTC Antitrust Investigation into Colleges Over Affirmative Action 'Collusion,'" *Washington Examiner*, August 10, 2023, https://www.washingtonexaminer.com/news/548618/jd-vance-urges-ftc-antitrust-investigation-into-colleges-over-affirmative-action-collusion/.

Chapter Three. Governing Together (Generosity)

1. Donn C. Neal, *Consortia and Interinstitutional Cooperation*, American Council on Education/Macmillan Series on Higher Education (Macmillan, 1988), 41; citing Frank E. Vandiver, "Universities: The Next Iteration?," *Science* 225, no. 4664 (1984): 791.

2. Michael Joseph Offerman, "Factors Leading to the Termination of Three Consortia of Higher Education Institutions: A Case Study" (EdD diss., Northern Illinois University, 1985), 160.

3. Peter D. Eckel, "The Shared Decision Making in Shared Programs: The Challenges of Interinstitutional Academic Programs," in *The Shifting Frontiers of Academic Decision Making: Responding to New Priorities, Following New Pathways*, ACE/Praeger Series on Higher Education (American Council on Education/Praeger, 2006), 58.

4. Franklin Patterson, *Colleges in Consort: Interinstitutional Cooperation Through Consortia*, 1st ed. Jossey-Bass Series in Higher Education (Jossey-Bass, 1974), 4.

5. Eckel, "Shared Decision Making," 61.

6. See, for instance, Richard T. Ingram, *Ten Basic Responsibilities of Nonprofit Boards*, 3rd ed., The Governance Series 1 (BoardSource, 2015); *Higher Education Governing Boards: An Introductory Guide for Members of College, University, and System Boards* (AGB, 2019), https://agb.org/product/higher-education-governing-boards-an-introductory-guide-for-members-of-college-university-and-system-boards/; Alice Lee Williams Brown and Elizabeth Richmond Hayford, *How Boards Lead Small Colleges* (Johns Hopkins University Press, 2019), https://doi.org/10.1353/book.66179; Robert A. Scott, *How University Boards Work* (Johns Hopkins University Press, 2018), https://doi.org/10.1353/book.57382; Josh Palmer, "What Is a Working Board? (Overview, Roles, and Responsibilities)," *OnBoard* (blog), September 19, 2022, https://www.onboardmeetings.com/blog/working-board/; Kathy Johnson Bowles, "Boards: Who's Really in Charge?," *Inside Higher Ed*, November 15, 2021, https://www.insidehighered.com/blogs/just-explain-it-me/boards-who%E2%80%99s-really-charge.

7. "Principles of Trusteeship," AGB, accessed July 3, 2024, https://agb.org/principles-of-trusteeship/.

8. Fritz H. Grupe, *Managing Institutional Change: Consortia in Higher Education* (Associated Colleges of the St. Lawrence Valley, 1975), 43–51, recognized a similar set of distinctions between consortial boards and traditional higher education trustees.

9. Offerman, "Factors Leading to the Termination of Three Consortia," 29, citing Richard Bailey Lancaster, "Interdependency and Conflict in a Consortium for Cooperation in Higher Education: Toward a Theory of Interorganizational Behavior" (PhD diss., University of Michigan, 1969).

10. Bethan O'Neil, "Understanding Collaborative Management in Higher Education, the Possibilities and Parameters of Partnership: A Case Study of CADISE" (PhD diss., University of Surrey, 2007), 5–7.

11. See, for instance, Cathy A. Trower, *Govern More, Manage Less: Harnessing the Power of Your Nonprofit Board*, 2nd ed. (BoardSource, 2010).

12. O'Neil, "Understanding Collaborative Management," 391; Herman B. Wells, "A Case Study on Interinstitutional Cooperation," *Educational Record*, Fall 1967, https://btaa.org/docs/default-source/news-pub/historyofcic3abf.pdf?sfvrsn=f0e4c898_2; a similar story is told by the historian of the Great Lakes Colleges Association of the importance of continuing self-sufficiency alongside creative collaboration. See Judith Laikin Elkin, *The Great Lakes Colleges Association: Twenty-One Years of Cooperation in Higher Education* (Great Lakes Colleges Association), 1982, 123 and elsewhere.

13. See, for instance, the guidance in Trower, *Govern More, Manage Less*, 14.

14. Grupe, *Managing Institutional Change*, 1.

15. Eric Klinenberg, *Heat Wave: A Social Autopsy of Disaster in Chicago* (University of Chicago Press, 2002), 23.

16. For an excellent discussion of the importance of such planning and practice, see Juliette Kayyem, *The Devil Never Sleeps: Learning to Live in an Age of Disasters* (Public Affairs/Hachette Book Group, 2022).

17. North Burn, "How Five Colleges Cooperate: Liberal Education," *Liberal Education* 59, no. 3 (1973): 310.

18. Mark E. Shelton, "Leadership Style and Outcome Behaviors of Higher Education Consortium Directors in the United States" (EdD diss., Johnson & Wales University, 2008), 5–6.

19. Shelton, 15; citing Fritz H. Grupe, "The Management of Consortium Priorities," *Journal of Higher Education* 45, no. 2 (1974): 141, https://doi.org/10.2307/1980558.

20. Grupe, *Managing Institutional Change*, 52.

21. Shelton, "Leadership Style," 21. See also Neal, *Consortia and Interinstitutional Cooperation*; Patterson, *Colleges in Consort*.

22. Neal, *Consortia and Interinstitutional Cooperation*, 31.

23. "What Is Transformational Leadership and Why Is It Effective?," University of Massachusetts Global (blog), accessed June 26, 2024, https://www.umassglobal.edu/news-and-events/blog/what-is-transformational-leadership.

24. Shelton, "Leadership Style," 8, 26–27.

25. Shelton, 32.

26. Offerman, "Factors Leading to the Termination of Three Consortia," 145.

27. Shelton, "Leadership Style," 17, 65.

28. Frederick Baus and Claire A. Ramsbottom, "Starting and Sustaining a Consortium: New Directions for Higher Education," *New Directions for Higher Education* 1999, no. 106 (1999): 8, https://doi.org/10.1002/he.10601.

29. Paul Schmitz, "10 Dangers to Collective Impact," *Stanford Social Innovation Review*, December 6, 2021, https://ssir.org/articles/entry/10_dangers_to_collective_impact.

30. See, for instance, Shelton, "Leadership Style," 19.

31. Baus and Ramsbottom, "Starting and Sustaining a Consortium," 13.

32. The term "logical incrementalism" originated with James Brian Quinn, *Strategies for Change: Logical Incrementalism*, Irwin Series in Management and the Behavioral Sciences (R. D. Irwin, 1980); "Logical Incrementalism Definition and Meaning," *The Law Dictionary*, October 19, 2012, https://thelawdictionary.org/logical-incrementalism/.

33. Kenneth R. Andrews, "Replaying the Board's Role in Formulating Strategy: Harvard Business Review," *Harvard Business Review* 59, no. 3 (1981): 18–26, on 19, 15.

34. For examples, see Debra Mashek and Michael Nanfito, "People, Tools, and Processes That Build Collaborative Capacity," Teagle Foundation, November 2015, https://www.teaglefoundation.org/Teagle/media/GlobalMediaLibrary/documents/resources/People_Tools_and_Processes.pdf; Daniel Coyle, *The Culture Code: The Secrets of Highly Successful Groups*, international ed. (Bantam Books, 2018); James W. Tamm and Ron Luyet, *Radical Collaboration: Five Essential Skills to Overcome Defensiveness and Build Successful Relationships*, 2nd ed. (HarperBusiness, 2019); and Max Weber's concept of "social relations," as in Max Weber and Keith Tribe, *Economy and Society: A New Translation* (Harvard University Press, 2019).

35. On psychological safety, a study by Fiona Lee and colleagues "examines how the inconsistency of organizational conditions affects people's willingness to engage in experimentation, a behavior integral to innovation." See Fiona Lee et al., "The Mixed Effects of Inconsistency on Experimentation in Organizations," *Organization Science* 15, no. 3 (2004): 310–26, https://doi.org/10.1287/orsc.1040.0076.

36. Stanley F. Salwak, "The Need for Cooperation and the CIC Response," *Educational Record* 45, no. 3 (1964): 313.

37. "New Model of Evolution Finally Reveals How Cooperation Evolves," *MIT Technology Review*, June 21, 2017, https://www.technologyreview.com/2017/06/21/151106/new-model-of-evolution-finally-reveals-how-cooperation-evolves/.

Chapter Four. Building a Backbone (Commitment)

1. Donn C. Neal, *Consortia and Interinstitutional Cooperation*, American Council on Education/Macmillan Series on Higher Education (Macmillan, 1988), 1–2.

2. John Kania and Mark Kramer, "Collective Impact," *Stanford Social Innovation Review*, Winter 2011, https://ssir.org/articles/entry/collective_impact.

3. Frederick Baus and Claire A. Ramsbottom, "Starting and Sustaining a Consortium: New Directions for Higher Education," *New Directions for Higher Education* 1999, no. 106 (1999): 13, https://doi.org/10.1002/he.10601.

4. "Minnesota Bridge Collapse: Lessons Learned, Training Synopsis," Memorial Institute for the Prevention of Terrorism, November 30, 2007, 3, http://www.abetteremergency.com/blog/?attachment_id=736.

5. Hollis Stambaugh and Harold Cohen, *I-35W Bridge Collapse and Response*, US Fire Administration/Technical Report Series (FEMA, August 2027), 44–45.

6. Adam Stone, "FEMA Course Lays Framework for Minneapolis Bridge Collapse Response," *Government Technology Magazine*, August 3, 2010, https://www.govtech.com/dc/articles/FEMA-Course-Lays-Framework-for-Minneapolis.html.

7. "Minnesota Bridge Collapse," 5 (emphasis removed from original).

8. *Collapse of I-35W Highway Bridge, Minneapolis, Minnesota, August 1, 2007*, Accident Report (National Transportation Safety Board, November 14, 2008), 118; Stambaugh and Cohen, *I-35W Bridge Collapse and Response*.

9. Stone, "FEMA Course Lays Framework."

10. Stambaugh and Cohen, *I-35W Bridge Collapse and Response*, 44.

11. Positivity in the face of crisis undergirds emergency preparedness as well. For an overview of emergency preparedness and crisis management, see, for example, Juliette Kayyem, *The Devil Never Sleeps: Learning to Live in an Age of Disasters* (Public Affairs/Hachette Book Group, 2022); David A. McEntire, *Disaster Response and Recovery: Strategies and Tactics for Resilience*, 3rd ed. (Wiley, 2022).

12. Peter D. Eckel, "The Shared Decision Making in Shared Programs: The Challenges of Interinstitutional Academic Programs," in *The Shifting Frontiers of Academic Decision Making: Responding to New Priorities, Following New Pathways*, ACE/Praeger Series on Higher Education (American Council on Education/Praeger, 2006), 72.

13. James A. Yankech, "Trust Within Higher Education Consortia—a Phenomenological Study of the Experiences of Directors and Leaders" (PhD diss., University of Nebraska, 2015), 106 (emphasis added). Pages 108–9 include quotations from consortial leaders on the importance of building relationships and trust, which increase the capacity to envision and engage in collaboration.

14. Deb Mashek, *Collabor(h)Ate: How to Build Incredible Collaborative Relationships at Work (Even If You'd Rather Work Alone)* (Practical Inspiration, 2023).

15. Baus and Ramsbottom, "Starting and Sustaining a Consortium," 15–16.

16. "About the New York Six Liberal Arts Consortium," September 28, 2021, https://newyork6.org/about.

17. "Fresh Combinations—Faculty," Mellon Foundation, accessed July 16, 2024, https://www.mellon.org/grant-details/fresh-combinations-faculty-5720.

18. "Mellon Foundation Grants Database Search for 'Consortium,'" Mellon Foundation, accessed July 16, 2024, https://www.mellon.org/grant-database/consortium.

19. Nina Berler, "College Consortia: A Cooperative Model That Offers Students Greater Value," *Forbes*, February 3, 2017, https://www.forbes.com/sites/noodleeducation/2017/02/01/college-consortia-a-cooperative-model-that-offers-students-greater-value/.

20. Charlotte Cox, "Academic Consortia as Strategic Alliances," *AGB Reports* 33, no. 1 (1991): 21.

21. "About Us: Baltimore Collegetown Network," Baltimore Collegetown Network, accessed June 21, 2024, https://baltimorecollegetown.org/home/about-us.

22. James Martin and James E. Samels, *Consolidating Colleges and Merging Universities: New Strategies for Higher Education Leaders* (Johns Hopkins University Press, 2017), 168–69.

23. Baus and Ramsbottom, "Starting and Sustaining a Consortium," 10.

24. Eckel, "Shared Decision Making."

25. Eckel, 61.

26. Maurice J. O'Sullivan, *Dynamics, Role, and Function in Inter-University Collaboration* (Higher Education Center for Urban Studies, July 1972), https://files.eric.ed.gov/fulltext/ED068044.pdf, 10.

27. Diane Dimitroff, now retired executive director of the Lehigh Valley Association of Independent Colleges used this term often in ACL meetings and with her staff and colleagues.

28. A. M. Brandenburger and B. J. Nalebuff, *Co-Opetition* (Doubleday, 1996).

29. Michael Joseph Offerman, "Factors Leading to the Termination of Three Consortia of Higher Education Institutions: A Case Study" (EdD diss., Northern Illinois University, 1985), 153; citing Richard Bailey Lancaster, "Interdependency and Conflict in a Consortium for Cooperation in Higher Education: Toward a Theory of Interorganizational Behavior" (PhD diss., University of Michigan, 1969).

30. Stanley F. Salwak, "The Need for Cooperation and the CIC Response," *Educational Record* 45, no. 3 (1964): 312.

31. Fritz H. Grupe, *Managing Institutional Change: Consortia in Higher Education* (Associated Colleges of the St. Lawrence Valley, 1975), 1.

32. Offerman, "Factors Leading to the Termination of Three Consortia," 154.

33. Jeff Weiss and Jonathan Hughes, "Want Collaboration?," in *HBR's 10 Must Reads on Collaboration* (Harvard Business Review Press, 2013), 92.

34. Eckel, "Shared Decision Making," 68.

35. Eckel, 67.

36. Eckel, 67.

37. Eckel, 63–65.

Chapter Five. Cautionary Tales from the Consortial Front Lines (Attention)

1. Rick Seltzer, "A New Direction in Appalachia," *Inside Higher Ed*, June 22, 2017, https://www.insidehighered.com/news/2017/06/23/appalachian-college-association-charts-new-course.

2. Seltzer, "New Direction in Appalachia."

3. Eric Casey, "Central Mass. Colleges Downsize Consortium, Appoint New Board Chair," *Worcester Business Journal*, June 21, 2024, https://www.wbjournal.com/article/central-mass-colleges-downsize-consortium-appoint-new-board-chair.

4. "Atlanta University Center," Wikipedia, June 17, 2024, https://en.wikipedia.org/w/index.php?title=Atlanta_University_Center&oldid=1229620036.

5. Judith Laikin Elkin, *The Great Lakes Colleges Association: Twenty-One Years of Cooperation in Higher Education* (Great Lakes Colleges Association, 1982), 127.

6. Deb Mashek, *Collabor(h)Ate: How to Build Incredible Collaborative Relationships at Work (Even If You'd Rather Work Alone)* (Practical Inspiration, 2023).

7. Joel Cutcher-Gershenfeld, et al, *The Consortia Century: Aligning for Impact* (Oxford University Press, 2025), 50.

8. Harry V. Scott, "Consortia in Higher Education: A Sober Reflection," *Educational Record* 58, no. 4 (1977): 433.

9. Michael Joseph Offerman, "Factors Leading to the Termination of Three Consortia of Higher Education Institutions: A Case Study" (EdD diss., Northern Illinois University, 1985), abstract, n.p., also in comparable wording on p. 4.

10. Bethan O'Neil, "Understanding Collaborative Management in Higher Education, the Possibilities and Parameters of Partnership: A Case Study of CADISE" (PhD diss., University of Surrey, 2007), 2; Peter D. Eckel, "The Shared Decision Making in Shared Programs: The Challenges of Interinstitutional Academic Programs," in *The Shifting Frontiers of Academic Decision Making: Responding to New Priorities, Following New Pathways*, ACE/Praeger Series on Higher Education (American Council on Education/Praeger, 2006), 57.

11. "Small Business Statistics—Chamber of Commerce," Chamber of Commerce, November 5, 2023, https://www.chamberofcommerce.org/small-business-statistics/.

12. Chuck McLean, "Vital Records: Births and Deaths in the Nonprofit Sector," *Nonprofit Quarterly*, Winter 2024, https://nonprofitquarterly.org/vital-records-births-and-deaths-in-the-nonprofit-sector/.

13. Stephanie Burns, "Longevity in Business: Why It Matters and How to Improve It," *Forbes*, April 21, 2022, https://www.forbes.com/sites/stephanieburns/2021/11/01/longevity-in-business-why-it-matters-and-how-to-improve-it/.

14. Tracy S. Ebarb, "Nonprofits Fail—Here's Seven Reasons Why," *NANOE* (blog), September 7, 2019, https://nanoe.org/nonprofits-fail/.

15. Robyn Dinicola, "Strength in Numbers: An Exploratory Case Study on the Impact of Conflict in Multi-Institutional Higher Education Collaborations" (PhD diss., Nova Southeastern University, 2023), 77.

16. O'Neil, "Understanding Collaborative Management," 2.

17. Cole Woodcox, COPLAC, to author, June 19, 2024, personal communication. See also Richard Bailey Lancaster, "Interdependency and Conflict in a Consortium for Cooperation in Higher Education: Toward a Theory of Interorganizational Behavior" (PhD diss., University of Michigan, 1969), 17.

18. Offerman, "Factors Leading to the Termination of Three Consortia," 4, 47.

19. Offerman, 49–51.

20. Offerman, 82, 83, 85–88.

21. Offerman, 93–94.

22. Offerman, 21, 97–98.

23. Offerman, 99, 101–2.

24. Offerman, 109, 132.

25. Offerman, 110–11, 113.

26. Offerman, 113–14, 119.

27. Offerman, 136.

28. Offerman, 138, 140.

29. Offerman, 141–42.

30. Offerman, 143.

31. O'Neil, "Understanding Collaborative Management," 102.

32. Oliver Morrison, "Amid Enrollment Decline, Pittsburgh-Area Colleges Ponder Combined Operations as Way to Save," 90.5 WESA: Pittsburgh's NPR News Station, September 28, 2023, https://www.wesa.fm/education/2023-09-28/college-enrollment-decline-pittsburgh-robert-morris-carlow-chatham-point-park-washington-jefferson; Josh Moody, "Proposed Pennsylvania Consortium Off to Rocky Start," *Inside Higher Ed*, October 23, 2023, https://www.insidehighered.com/news/business/mergers-collaboration/2023/10/23/proposed-pennsylvania-consortium-gets-rocky-start; Oliver Morrison, "Some Pittsburgh-Area Universities Back Away from Shared-Services Consortium," 90.5 WESA: Pittsburgh's NPR News Station, October 23, 2023, https://www.wesa.fm/education/2023-10-23/pittsburgh-colleges-consortium-layoffs.

33. See various lists and lessons in James Martin and James E. Samels, *Consolidating Colleges and Merging Universities: New Strategies for Higher Education Leaders* (Johns Hopkins University Press, 2017), 84–85, 101–2.

34. Mark La Branche, *Inside College Mergers: Stories from the Front Lines* (Johns Hopkins University Press, 2024), 12.

35. Martin and Samels, *Consolidating Colleges*, 163.

36. Offerman, "Factors Leading to the Termination of Three Consortia," 129–30.

37. Offerman, 157–58.

38. A. Paul Bradley, "The Five E's of Consortium Effectiveness" (Consortium Directors Seminar, 1971).

39. Offerman, "Factors Leading to the Termination of Three Consortia," 30–31.

40. Donn C. Neal, *Consortia and Interinstitutional Cooperation*, American Council on Education/Macmillan Series on Higher Education (Macmillan, 1988), 43; Naida C. Tushnet, *A Guide to Developing Educational Partnerships* (Office of Educational Research and Improvement, 1993), 9, provides similar advice.

41. Neal, *Consortia and Interinstitutional Cooperation*, 42–45.

42. See, for instance, James A. Yankech, "Trust Within Higher Education Consortia—a Phenomenological Study of the Experiences of Directors and Leaders" (PhD diss., University of Nebraska, 2015), 44.

Conclusion. People, People, People, and Resources

1. Frederick Baus and Claire A. Ramsbottom, "Starting and Sustaining a Consortium: New Directions for Higher Education," *New Directions for Higher Education* 1999, no. 106 (1999), 17, https://doi.org/10.1002/he.10601.

2. For additional tips and worksheets, see Michael Nanfito, "Collaboration: A Primer," *Michael Nanfito* (blog), January 17, 2015, https://mnanfito.wordpress.com

/2015/01/17/collaboration-a-primer/; and Morten T. Hansen, *The Collaboration Toolkit: Tools Adapted from the Book "Collaboration: How Leaders Avoid the Traps, Create Unity, and Reap Big Results"* (Harvard Business Review Press, 2009).

3. For more on the history of ACL, see "ACL History," Association for Collaborative Leadership, accessed February 9, 2025, https://www.national-acl.org/history, as well as James A. Yankech, "Trust Within Higher Education Consortia—a Phenomenological Study of the Experiences of Directors and Leaders" (PhD diss., University of Nebraska, 2015), 21; Baus and Ramsbottom, "Starting and Sustaining a Consortium."

4. Donn C. Neal, *Consortia and Interinstitutional Cooperation*, American Council on Education/Macmillan Series on Higher Education (Macmillan, 1988), 46.

BIBLIOGRAPHY

The literature on consortia, collaboration, and partnerships—both within and outside higher education—is robust, though varied in quality and comprehensiveness. The list here attempts to capture a few of the most accessible, useful, and timely resources that may be of interest to practitioners as well as scholars.

Abegglen, Sandra, Tom Burns, and Sandra Sinfield, eds. *Collaboration in Higher Education*. 1st ed. Bloomsbury Academic, 2023.

Affolter-Caine, Britany L. "Going Beyond Traditional Consortia: Exploring the Collaborative Process Among Traditional Private Liberal Arts Colleges and Universities Engaged in Interinstitutional Consortia That Promote Curricular Joint Ventures." PhD diss., University of Michigan, 2008.

Allen, Danielle S. *Talking to Strangers: Anxieties of Citizenship Since Brown v. Board of Education*. University of Chicago Press, 2004.

Barber, C. L. *The New College Plan: A Proposal for a Major Departure in Higher Education*. n.p., 1958.

Beltz, Nicola V., and Lawrence George Dotolo, eds. *Pushing the Boundaries of Collaboration: What Consortia Can Accomplish*. Vol. 5. Association for Collaborative Leadership, 2016.

Benson, George C. S., et al. *A Brief History of the Group Plan of the Claremont Colleges*. Claremont University Center, 1993.

Coyle, Daniel. *The Culture Code: The Secrets of Highly Successful Groups*. Int. ed. Bantam Books, 2018.

Daniels, Ronald J. *What Universities Owe Democracy*. Johns Hopkins University Press, 2021.

Davidson, Cathy N. *The New Education: How to Revolutionize the University to Prepare Students for a World in Flux*. 1st ed. Basic Books, 2017.

Dinicola, Robyn. "Strength in Numbers: An Exploratory Case Study on the Impact of Conflict in Multi-Institutional Higher Education Collaborations." PhD diss., Nova Southeastern University, 2023.

Dotolo, Lawrence George, and Jean Strandness, eds. "Best Practices in Higher Education Consortia: How Institutions Can Work Together." *New Directions for Higher Education* 1999, no. 106 (1999): 1–120.

Dweck, Carol S. *Mindset: The New Psychology of Success*. Ballantine Books, 2008.

Eckel, Peter D. "The Shared Decision Making in Shared Programs: The Challenges of Interinstitutional Academic Programs." In *The Shifting Frontiers of Academic Decision Making: Responding to New Priorities, Following New Pathways*. ACE/ Praeger Series on Higher Education. American Council on Education/Praeger, 2006.

Eckel, Peter D., Britany Affolter-Caine, and Matthew Hartley. *Cooperating to Compete: A Campus Leaders' Guide to Developing Curricular Partnerships and Joint Programs*. American Council on Education, 2004.

Elbow, Peter. "The Believing Game or Methodological Believing." *Journal of the Assembly for Expanded Perspectives on Learning* 14, no. 1 (2008–2009): 1–11.

Elkin, Judith Laikin. *The Great Lakes Colleges Association: Twenty-One Years of Cooperation in Higher Education*. Great Lakes Colleges Association, 1982.

Forcier, Mary Frances. "Innovation Through Collaboration: New Pathways to Success." *AGB Trusteeship Magazine* 19, no. 5 (2011): 8–12.

Grawe, Nathan D. *The Agile College: How Institutions Successfully Navigate Demographic Changes*. Johns Hopkins University Press, 2021.

Grupe, Fritz H. "The Management of Consortium Priorities." *Journal of Higher Education* 45, no. 2 (1974): 135–44.

Grupe, Fritz H. *Managing Institutional Change: Consortia in Higher Education*. Associated Colleges of the St. Lawrence Valley, 1975.

Hansen, Morten T. *The Collaboration Toolkit: Tools Adapted from the Book "Collaboration: How Leaders Avoid the Traps, Create Unity, and Reap Big Results."* Harvard Business Review Press, 2009.

Howard, Lawrence C., ed. *Interinstitutional Cooperation in Higher Education: Proceedings*. Conference on Interinstitutional Cooperation in Higher Education. Johnson Foundation Center at Wingspread, 1967.

Keim, Marybelle C. "Educational Consortia—a Longitudinal Study." *College and University* 74, no. 3 (1999): 30–36.

Lancaster, Richard Bailey. "Interdependency and Conflict in a Consortium for Cooperation in Higher Education: Toward a Theory of Interorganizational Behavior." PhD diss., University of Michigan, 1969.

Lee, Mark Owen. "A Comparative Case Study of Four Partnership Campuses: Origin, Administration, Academics, and Student Services." PhD diss., University of South Dakota, 2007.

Levine, Arthur. *The Great Upheaval: Higher Education's Past, Present, and Uncertain Future*. Johns Hopkins University Press, 2021.

Mashek, Deb. *Collabor(h)Ate: How to Build Incredible Collaborative Relationships at Work (Even If You'd Rather Work Alone)*. Practical Inspiration, 2023.

Neal, Donn C. *Consortia and Interinstitutional Cooperation*. American Council on Education/Macmillan Series on Higher Education. Macmillan, 1988.

Offerman, Michael Joseph. "Factors Leading to the Termination of Three Consortia of Higher Education Institutions: A Case Study." EdD diss., Northern Illinois University, 1985.

Patterson, Franklin. *Colleges in Consort: Interinstitutional Cooperation Through Consortia*. 1st ed. Jossey-Bass Series in Higher Education. Jossey-Bass, 1974.

Patterson, Franklin, and Charles R. Longsworth. *The Making of a College: A New Departure in Higher Education*. New ed. MIT Press, 1975.

Peterson, Lorna M. *Glancing Backward: Twenty-Five Years of Cooperation: A Retrospective Report on Five Colleges, Incorporated*. Five Colleges, Incorporated, 1984.

Quinn, James Brian. *Strategies for Change: Logical Incrementalism*. Irwin Series in Management and the Behavioral Sciences. R. D. Irwin, 1980.

Salwak, Stanley F. "New Patterns of Institutional Cooperation: Compacts and Consortia." *Journal of Higher Education* 39, no. 9 (1968): 490–96.

Senge, Peter M. *The Fifth Discipline: The Art and Practice of the Learning Organization*. Rev. and updated. Doubleday/Currency, 2006.

Shelton, Mark E. "Leadership Style and Outcome Behaviors of Higher Education Consortium Directors in the United States." EdD diss., Johnson & Wales University, 2008.

Tamm, James W., and Ron Luyet. *Radical Collaboration: Five Essential Skills to Overcome Defensiveness and Build Successful Relationships*. 2nd ed. HarperBusiness, 2019.

Wylie, Neil R., and Jon W. Fuller. "Enhancing Faculty Vitality Through Collaboration Among Colleagues." *New Directions for Higher Education* 1985, no. 51 (1985): 99–108.

Yankech, James A. "Trust Within Higher Education Consortia—a Phenomenological Study of the Experiences of Directors and Leaders." PhD diss., University of Nebraska, 2015.

Zander, Rosamund Stone, and Benjamin Zander. *The Art of Possibility*. Rev. ed. Penguin Books, 2002.

INDEX

Page numbers in *italics* refer to figures and tables. End note information is indicated by n and note number following the page number.